ROMAN BRITAIN AND THE
ROMAN NAVY

'. . . they cleft Hyperborean waves with
courageous oars.'

Panegyric on the Third Consulship of Honorius 51-6

ROMAN BRITAIN AND THE
ROMAN NAVY

DAVID J.P. MASON

TEMPUS

First published 2003
Cover picture: *detail of fourth-century mosaic floor in Low Ham villa, Somerset*

PUBLISHED IN THE UNITED KINGDOM BY:
Tempus Publishing Ltd
The Mill, Brimscombe Port
Stroud, Gloucestershire GL5 2QG

PUBLISHED IN THE UNITED STATES OF AMERICA BY:
Tempus Publishing Inc.
2 Cumberland Street
Charleston, SC 29401

British Library Cataloguing in Publication Data.
A catalogue record for this book is available from the British Library.

ISBN 0 7524 2541 2

Typesetting and origination by Tempus Publishing.
Printed in Great Britain by Midway Colour Print, Wiltshire.

CONTENTS

For Anne-Marie, brave in adversity,
and a constant source of support and encouragement

ACKNOWLEDGEMENTS

The author is extremely grateful to the institutions and individuals listed below who have given their permission for the reproduction of illustrations in their ownership.

Chester Archaeological Society: **36 & 54**
Chester City Council: **colour plate 12**
Colchester Archaeological Trust Ltd: **colour plate 5**
English Heritage: **colour plates 13 & 14**
Museum of London: **16, 17 & 20**, also **colour plates 6 & 11**
The British Museum: **71, 72, 73 & 74**, also **colour plate 7**
Museum of Antiquities, University and Society of Antiquaries of Newcastle upon Tyne: **colour plate 3**
Somerset County Council Museums Service: **colour plate 8**
Tim Pestell/Norfolk Museums and Archaeology Service: **colour plate 4**

Helen Anderson: **colour plates 1 & 2**
Peter Crew: **colour plate 18**
Sheppard Frere and Frank Lepper: **1, 2, 3, 4, 5, 6 & 7**
Andrew Pearson: **94**, also **colour plates 15 & 16**

All other illustrations were originated by the author.

I should like to extend particular thanks to Helen Anderson for preparing the originals of the illustrations which appear here as **colour plates 1 & 2**. I am indebted to my wife Anne-Marie for her patience and forbearance while I have been engrossed in researching and writing this book and to Peter Kemmis Betty for commissioning it. Finally, I would also like to thank Emma Parkin of Tempus without whose editorial skills this book would have been much the poorer.

1

INTRODUCTION

In the popular imagination it was Rome's legions that enabled her to win and hold an empire. The truth of that cannot be denied but what is not so widely known or appreciated is the equally important part played by the Roman navy in the acquisition, maintenance and protection of that empire. Rome's dominions encircled the Mediterranean, or *mare nostrum* ('our sea') as its citizens came to call it, and it was the facility for rapid and cheap communication and transport that it provided which bound together her provinces. That the Roman navy attracts less attention than the Roman army is understandable as the very nature of their respective operations inevitably means that we have plenty of evidence for the army's activities but precious little for those of the navy. The constructions of the first, being fixed, terrestrial and for the most part permanent, survive aplenty to remind us of its abilities and achievements. Those of the navy, by contrast, being largely mobile, seaborne, built of perishable materials, and designed to have a limited working life, generally do not.

Wrecks of Roman warships are very few and far between and are overwhelmingly of riverine as opposed to seagoing vessels. By way of compensation, detailed information concerning ship design and the tactics of naval warfare occurs frequently in the ancient literature, and in addition there are depictions of various types of ships in relief sculpture, mosaics, murals and on coins. While these contemporary representations give a useful impression of the general appearance of ships they cannot be relied upon for accuracy of detail. In some cases, as with coins, the size and nature of the space available simply did not give the artist sufficient room to show all the details. In others, elements were often omitted because of the artist's desire to give prominence to one particular aspect or feature. Thus, in the naval scenes on Trajan's Column, for example, giving emphasis to the figures in the ships resulted not only in them being completely out of scale and oversized but also caused the omission or distortion of certain elements of the ship's superstructure. In yet other cases, problems of interpretation can arise from the artist's desire to portray too much detail of the ships involved. For example, warships were often shown riding much higher in the water than they ever would have in reality so that their main armament – the projecting bronze-sheathed ram at the foot of the prow – could be highlighted.

The acquisition of information about the shore-based component of the Roman naval infrastructure – fleet bases, harbours, shipyards etc. – is beset with its own particular problems. Erosion, siltation, fluctuations in sea-level and changing currents have all either individually or collectively had an effect on ancient coastal and riverine sites. Some are buried beneath many feet of silt while others conversely have been partly, or in some cases totally, destroyed by the sea. Also, because they have retained their capability as a port, more than a few are overlain by modern settlement and harbour works which render them inaccessible.

This disparity in the evidence available for the two branches of the Roman military is reflected in the modern literature. Whereas there are scores of books on the Roman army there are but a handful devoted to the Roman navy. In many ways the standard work in English on the Roman fleets is still Chester G. Starr's *The Roman Imperial Navy 31 BC-AD 324*, first published in 1941. A second edition, incorporating the correction of minor misprints, appeared in 1960 which was itself reprinted in 1993 with the addition of plates illustrating images of Roman vessels and an updated bibliography. Another major work of the same vintage, though covering a much longer time period, is *Greek and Roman Naval Warfare* by William Ledyard Rogers, a retired Vice Admiral in the US Navy. Published in 1937, this was reissued in 1964. Although both were written more than 60 years ago, they are still useful reference works for the student of naval warfare in Classical Antiquity.

In more recent times Lionel Casson has been at the forefront of research into maritime aspects of the ancient world, his better known works including *The Ancient Mariners* (1959; 2nd edition, 1991), *Ships and Seamanship in the Ancient World* (1971), and *Ships and Seafaring in Ancient Times* (1991). The area of ancient ship design that has given rise to more discussion than any other must surely be the arrangement of oars and oarsmen in warships with more than one level of rowers. The late Professor John Morrison's researches in this field eliminated many uncertainties in this area while his collaboration with John Coates, amongst others, culminated in the magnificent achievement of a full-scale, working reconstruction of an Athenian trireme, the *Olympias*. The sea trials of this vessel and the lessons learnt from them are most recently reported in *The Athenian Trireme* (2nd edition, 2000), co-written with John Coates and Boris Rankov, while of his other works the most pertinent to the subject of this book is *Greek and Roman Oared Warships 399-30 BC* (1996). Returning to the narrower theme of the Roman Imperial Navy, mention must be made of Kienast's scholarly study of the subject, *Untersuchungen zu den Kriegsflotten der römischen Kaiserzeit* (1966), and the magisterial survey of the evidence by Michel Reddé, *Mare Nostrum: les Infrastructures, le Dispositif et l'Histoire de la Marine Militaire sous l'Empire Romain* (1986).

It must be said that the dearth of physical evidence is not the only reason for the modest amount of literature on the subject of the Roman navy. The subject has been a surprisingly neglected one until quite recently. Interest has been rekindled by a combination of factors. The archaeological potential of inter-tidal zones and riverine waterfront areas has at last been widely recognised and accorded greater importance both in terms of historic resource protection and the formulation of academic research agendas. At the same time important new evidence has come to light both as the result of accidental discoveries, such as the astounding collection of Roman vessels in the harbour at Pisa, and as the outcome of carefully planned excavations or research at major ports such as Caesarea, Alexandria and London which have greatly enhanced the corpus of available information.

For Rome, a serious involvement in naval warfare began in the third century BC. Once supremacy throughout the Italian peninsula had been achieved, the natural geographic unit of the Mediterranean Basin and the concentration of developed, wealthy nations lining its shores directed the focus of her future conquests. Conflict with existing naval powers was inevitable and, although not a seafaring people by nature, the Romans soon appreciated that the possession of a powerful navy was necessary not only to eliminate their chief rivals, but also to protect the burgeoning maritime commerce which followed and the revenues which it generated both for individuals and the state treasury. As Roman armies operated at ever greater distances from the Italian homeland, the matter of supply and provisioning became critical. In addition to confronting enemy naval forces and assisting in the besieging of coastal cities, the fleets assembled by Rome increasingly took on the support functions of transporting campaign armies and maintaining them in the field by the bringing in of supplies, extra equipment and reinforcements as required.

The expertise in 'combined operations' thus acquired was in fact to prove of great benefit at the beginning of the Imperial era when Roman forces began to conquer lands beyond the Mediterranean Basin. The campaigns which resulted in the acquisition of what were to become the northern frontier provinces owed much of their success to the close support given the legions by fleets operating along major rivers such as the Rhine and the Danube. Nor was the positioning of so many army bases along these and other major rivers due solely to their providing a convenient and formidable physical barrier which could serve as a frontier line. They also afforded the fastest and cheapest method of importing the enormous quantities of supplies required. It is easy to lose sight of the fact now but prior to the invention of mechanically powered vehicles, water transport was generally the cheapest, speediest and most reliable means of moving goods in bulk; indeed, it has been estimated that in the ancient world the cost of sending goods overland was fifty times greater than using water transport.[1]

The Roman navy's role in the acquisition and holding of the island province of *Britannia* was, of course, fundamental. Without a powerful navy Britain could neither have been invaded nor held. For the fleet and the army alike, the symbolic significance of the invasion of Britain was as great as the logistical effort involved. Along with neighbouring Ireland (*Hivernia*) it had long been used by writers and poets as a literary construct to represent remote and barbarous lands, separated from the known world by the stream of the great Ocean. This tradition continued right up to the time of Claudius despite the more informed picture built up as a result of increasing trade contacts since Caesar's expeditions nearly a century earlier. As far as many men in the invasion force of 43 were concerned, they were being transported to an island at the edge of the inhabited world surrounded by the unconquered and unconquerable Ocean. It was the army's task to subdue the Britons and it was the navy's task to master these unfamiliar and unfriendly northern waters. Transporting the massive invasion force across the Channel was a major achievement, but it would have counted for nought if the fleet had not been up to the job of keeping it supplied and reinforced, not merely for the initial conquest phase but throughout the entire history of the British province. The Roman navy's activities in British waters were more varied than in other parts of the Empire and changed significantly during the province's long history, facts which mean that the story of the British Fleet – the *Classis Britannica* – has a special contribution to make to the study of Roman naval history in general. The importance of the *Classis Britannica* is reflected in the fact that its commander was ranked higher and received a salary somewhat greater than his counterparts in most other provincial fleets.

While something of Roman naval operations off the British coast was known from the literary sources, principally Tacitus' *Life of Agricola*, study of the subject based on archaeological material found in Britain commenced in 1850 when Charles Roach Smith identified the letters 'CL.BR' stamped on tiles recovered from his excavations at Lympne as an abbreviation for *Classis Britannica*. Further examples of bricks and tiles bearing this stamp were found subsequently at a number of other sites along the south-east coast and some distance inland, while significant numbers were already known from a few places on the other side of the Channel, principally Boulogne, indicating that the British fleet operated from bases on both coasts. The additional discovery at Boulogne of inscriptions recording the captains of no fewer than four ships of the *Classis Britannica* confirmed its status as a major fleet base, hardly surprising given that this was the port from which the invasion of 43 had been launched. In 1923 a fine second-century villa was discovered near Folkestone, occupying a magnificent elevated site overlooking the Channel. The presence of 'CL.BR'-stamped tiles led its excavator – S.E. Winbolt – to put forward the attractive hypothesis that this was the residence of the Prefect of the British fleet. His report on the excavations, published only two years later, included a chapter that was the first attempt in print at a general history of the *Classis Britannica*.[2] It was accompanied by another that presented one of the earliest accounts of the Saxon Shore Forts (so named in the late Roman document known as the *Notitia Dignitatum*) with which the later history of the British fleet is inextricably linked.[3] Another review of the *Classis Britannica*, this one by Donald Atkinson, appeared in 1933. This drew heavily on Roach Smith's work both at Lympne and at certain other of the so-called Saxon Shore Forts along the south-east coast. It also set out the by the then generally accepted interpretation of these massively walled enceintes as elements of a late Roman coastal defence system each serving as the base for a small flotilla of warships charged with the protection of a specific stretch of coastline.[4]

New information was scarce for the next 30 years. Then, in the 1960s, there was a flurry of investigations at a number of the Saxon Shore Forts including Reculver, Richborough, and Portchester while Barry Cunliffe's final report on the work at Richborough included an interesting discussion of the British fleet.[5] At the same time the investigation of inland sites which had produced 'CL.BR'-stamped tiles began which was to demonstrate the *Classis Britannica*'s deep involvement in the development of the Weald iron industry as well as, presumably, the exploitation of its woodland for shipbuilding timber.[6] The beginning of the next decade saw a step-change in *Classis Britannica* studies with the discovery of the first positively identified fleet base on this side of the Channel. Excavations in advance of redevelopment at the heart of Dover not only finally located the Saxon Shore Fort listed in the *Notitia Dignitatum* but they also exposed lying partly beneath it the remains of an early second-century fort associated with hundreds of 'CL.BR'-stamped tiles. Brian Philp's report included a timely reappraisal of our understanding of the organisation, history and development of the British fleet in the light of these discoveries.[7] Two new works on the Saxon Shore appeared at the time the Dover excavations were taking place: Stephen Johnson's *The Roman Forts of the Saxon Shore* (1976), and *The Saxon Shore* edited by D.E. Johnston (1977). The second of these was a collection of papers presented at a research symposium in 1975 and included a further essay on the *Classis Britannica*, this time by Henry Cleere.

A new phase of research was also begun on the Continental in the late 1960s both on the distribution of 'CL.BR'-stamped tiles and on sites with *Classis Britannica* associations.[8] Another significant publication to appear in this period was *Roman Shipping and Trade: Britain and the Rhine Provinces* edited by Jean du Plat Taylor and Henry Cleere (1978). The 1980s brought a major advance with the discovery that the fleet base at Boulogne lay directly beneath the later walled town.[9] With a size of some 30 acres (12ha) this had clearly been the headquarters of the *Classis Britannica*; a discovery some on this side of the Channel may have found hard to accept. The origins of both the British and the German fleets were explored again in an article by Derek Saddington a few years later while John Casey included a useful essay on Roman naval warfare in his book dealing with the usurpers Carausius and Allectus.[10] The role of the British fleet in keeping the army supplied with its necessities was a theme explored by Middleton and Fulford among others.[11]

Naval activity and coastal defence installations along the western seaboard of Britain had received scant attention before the 1970s, an omission due in no small part perhaps to the absence of any useful indicator of the fleet's presence like the 'CL.BR' tiles found in the south-east. The notion of a continuous integrated defence system here in the later Roman period was first mooted by Anne Dornier in 1967 and was taken up again a few years later by Robin Livens but has still to be proved.[12] The Saxon Shore style fort at Cardiff had long been known because of its excellent state of preservation, while work at Lancaster in the 1960s and 1970s confirmed the existence of a similar installation there.[13] Numerous seasons of work by R.L. Bellhouse and later Professor Barri Jones demonstrated the existence of an extension of the Hadrianic frontier system down the Cumbrian coast, while in another essay Livens postulated the existence of a chain of lookout-posts and signal-stations along the north Welsh coast.[14]

The natural processes which have affected the British coastline and thus our understanding of the setting of Roman sites and their capacity to function as ports has rightly received increasing attention over the last two decades. The collection of essays edited by Hugh Thompson published in a volume in 1980 entitled *Archaeology and Coastal Change* was one of the earliest studies in this field, appearing a year after Devoy's classic study of periods of sea-level fall (regression) and rise (transgression) in the Thames estuary. The theme is one that has been taken up in many subsequent papers, the majority concentrating on specific geographical areas.[15] Pearson's recent study of the Saxon Shore Forts included a useful survey of just how much the setting of these forts has been affected by coastal change over the last two thousand years. All originally located in sheltered tidal environments, these changes have left some forts, such as Burgh Castle and Pevensey, landlocked as a consequence of silting while others, such as Walton Castle, have been completely destroyed by erosion.[16]

While it is very plain from the research undertaken so far that there is still much to learn about the detail of fluctuations in sea-level during and since the Roman period, there have been a few instances where excavations have provided sound information on this point. The investigation of London's waterfront over the last 20 years or so is the prime example. Here the remains of successive timber quays reveal a gradual reclamation of land from the river prompted by a 5ft (1.5m) fall in its general level between *c*.AD 50 and 250.[17] This situation was presumably mirrored at other sites along the south coast. However it is clear that both regressions and transgressions affected different parts of the British coastline at differing rates and to varying degrees, owing to the interaction of a variety of factors. For example, the regression that affected London in the first century AD had begun around 200 BC on the west coast, with the subsequent transgression commencing around AD 100 compared to AD 250-300 on the south coast.[18] Whether this rise in sea-level began sufficiently early to make it easier for sea-raiders to gain access to the country's major river systems, and the rich pickings which lay along them, is a question only future research can answer. In the centuries since the end of Roman Britain, however, it is thought that the sea-level around our coasts has risen by a minimum of six feet (2m), and is still rising. If so, then this has profound implications not only for the interpretation of Roman harbour structures but also for the future management, protection and investigation of their remains.

From the foregoing it will have become evident to the reader that there has never been a book devoted exclusively to the *Classis Britannica*; that omission has now been rectified.

2

THE ORIGINS OF THE ROMAN IMPERIAL NAVY

In her earliest days Rome maintained only a modest naval force. As she subjugated other cities and peoples of the Italian peninsula the treaty conditions imposed on her allies regularly included the obligation to supply men for military service on request. In the case of the Greek seaboard towns the requirement was for the supply of warships and transports. With the incorporation of maritime communities into the Roman State and the foundation of coastal colonies such as Ostia, Terracino and Brindisi merchant ships 'flying the flag of Rome' soon became engaged in long-distance trade. Agreements with other states dependent on maritime commerce for their wealth and power were necessary in order to avoid conflicts and, according to the Roman historian Polybius, the first such treaty signed by Rome was with Carthage in 509 BC. This guaranteed Romans and Carthaginians the right to enter each other's ports and to trade in areas coming under their respective influence. Further such treaties with states in the eastern Mediterranean followed and many of these continued to be renewed for generation after generation. Rome had no need of a permanent naval force and it was not until the Second Samnite War of 328–304 BC that she acquired such – a squadron of 20 triremes.

Rome's need for military might at sea as well as on land first materialised as a consequence of her rivalry with Carthage in the third century BC. At that time Carthage was the premier maritime power in the western Mediterranean. She had established fortified trading-posts along a great stretch of the North African coast as well as the shores of southern Spain, on Sardinia, and also the western half of Sicily. This vast commercial empire was run by the Carthaginian nobility and was protected by armies and fleets manned by conscripts and mercenaries. Carthage's main maritime rivals in the eastern Mediterranean were the various Hellenistic states established by Alexander's successors. Sicily, the eastern half of which was under Greek control, became the principal point of friction between all three powers and it was against this background that the importance of possessing a fleet was first taken seriously by Rome. She gradually became embroiled in the complex alliances and rivalries of the Sicilian city-states in such a way that brought her on a collision course with the Carthaginians on the island.

A consular army was despatched across the Straits of Messina in 264 BC, marking the beginning of the First Punic War. Polybius tells us that at this time the Romans 'had no warships at all, not even light craft'.[1] To transport the army across the Straits they borrowed *penteres* (ships with 50 oars) and some triremes (ships with rowers arranged in three levels) from the Greek maritime cities in southern Italy, places such as Lokroi, Neapolis, Tarentum and Velia. The Carthaginians attacked the convoy but most of it survived. The Roman army enjoyed considerable success but the conflict dragged on and the Carthaginian fleet began to pillage the coasts of Italy. This decided the Senate to begin the construction of Rome's first proper fleet, consisting of 100 *penteres* (quinqueremes) and 20 *trieres* (triremes), the latter used for fast reconnaissance.[2] Warships depicted on coins of the period – known as the 'Prow Series' – may represent these vessels which are characterised by a deep projection or oarbox along their sides.[3] Like the threes, the rowers in the fives were arranged in three tiers or banks, although in their case the oars in two of the banks were manned by pairs of oarsmen. In addition to a crew numbering around 300 the *penteres* could each carry a complement of 120 soldiers.

Being novices in naval warfare, and recognising the inferior quality of both their seamanship and their ships, the Romans strove to overcome these disadvantages by turning each engagement in effect into a land battle in which the superiority of their soldiers in hand-to-hand fighting would prevail. To this end, they fitted many of their ships with a device known by the ordinary sailors as the *corvus* or raven.[4] This was a boarding bridge 36ft long and 4ft wide, equipped with a large iron spike on the underside at the outer end. At the inner end was a long slot which fitted around a mast in the forepart of the ship. When not in use the bridge was stacked upright against the mast. In battle, ropes allowed it to be both lowered and swung around. On closing with an enemy vessel the bridge would be manoeuvred so as to fall and penetrate the enemy's deck thus locking the two vessels together and allowing the legionaries to storm across. Highly effective in their early engagements with the Carthaginians, including the important Battle of Mylae in 260 BC, the latter soon dropped the tactic of ramming bow to bow and instead used their greater speed and manoeuvrability to attack from astern.

By 256 BC both sides had increased the size of their fleet to something in excess of 300 vessels. The Romans were determined to carry the war to the enemy and set about launching an expedition to mainland Africa with an army of some 50,000 men. A Carthaginian fleet sent to intercept the Roman force before it left Sicily was defeated by skilful seamanship which prevented the enemy warships from closing on the vulnerable transports. The crossing to Africa was made without loss shortly thereafter and although defeat for the Roman forces was to follow, through a combination of over-confidence and bad luck, this was an important moment in the development of Rome's military strategy as it was the first time she used the combined might of land and naval forces to project her power overseas – indeed to another continent. Many lessons will have been learned about naval tactics, the design of transports, and the organisation and management of supply lines across water as well as land. The First Punic War finally came to an end in 240 BC when Rome achieved complete mastery of the sea around Sicily. The Carthaginians, no longer able to supply their army, were forced to discuss terms. Polybius tells us that by the end of the war each side had lost more than 500 quinqueremes through enemy action and shipwreck.[5]

Naval warfare was renewed with the Second Punic War of 219-203 BC. Further raids on the African coastline culminated with Scipio's landings in 205 BC for which an expeditionary force, including cavalry, siege engines and supplies, was conveyed by a fleet of nearly 400 transports accompanied by 40 quinqueremes and ten quadriremes.[6] Although the decisive engagements were fought on land, Roman naval supremacy was of paramount importance to her ultimate victory. Hannibal could lead a Carthaginian army into Italy, but apart from the short crossing of the Straits of Gibraltar he had to take an overland route to the enemy's capital. Rome's generals by contrast could have their forces transported directly to the place of operations, be it Sardinia, Spain or Africa. Henceforth, men and supplies were moved routinely by sea and whenever possible, military advance was achieved by the army moving along the coast accompanied by a fleet carrying its supplies.[7] In the Republican period, military officers or junior magistrates were placed in command of fleets and naval supply and were responsible to the campaign commanders; frequently a *praetor* would be put in charge of a fleet under the overall authority of a *consul*.[8]

While it can be said that it was the geography of their empire which enabled the Romans to move the bulk of their military supplies by water, it is equally if not more valid to say that it was the facility to move military supplies by ship that dictated the shape of their empire. Conquering states nearer to hand rather than those ranged around the entire rim of the Mediterranean basin might seem more sensible, but the sea gave Rome an enormous advantage in being able to move men and supplies from one end of its Empire to the other far easier and faster than overland. The military advantages of speedy transport are obvious. The financial aspects, however, were equally important for in this period most of the troop carriers and supply ships were merchant vessels under contract.[9] The cost of sea transport was thus a major factor.[10] The logistics involved in transporting and supplying a campaign army were considerable. For example, the transportation of Pompey's force of seven legions and its supplies from Sicily to Africa in 81 BC needed a fleet of 800 transports.[11] Two years earlier an even larger fleet – 1,200 ships – had carried Sulla's army across the Adriatic from Greece to Italy.[12] A few decades later, a fleet of more than 600 transports was assembled to carry Caesar's second expedition across the Channel to Britain.[13] Provisions had to be replenished of course and if they were not available from local allies or confiscation, then these too were brought in by ship along the supply-line or *commeatus*.

Roman forces further developed their skills in maritime warfare during the subsequent conflicts with Philip V of Macedon, Antiochus III of Syria, and the third and final conflict with Carthage (149-146 BC). The first century BC saw Rome dealing with the last two obstacles to her attainment of naval supremacy throughout the Mediterranean. The first of these was King Mithridates VI of Pontus who was determined to thwart Rome's ambition to control the Hellespont and Bosporus, and equipped himself with an army and fleet, both of considerable size. Hostilities commenced in 88 BC and continued until his death in 63. The second opponent with whom Rome had to contend was the pirates who had originally been hired by Mithridates and who subsequently increased in number and power until they became a real threat to Rome's maritime trade and power. In the years 70-68 they pillaged settlements on the Italian coast, abducted travellers using the Appian way including two *praetors* with their *lictors*, and even attacked a consular fleet as it lay at anchor in the port of Ostia.[14] The fleets that the Romans mustered to counter these threats were, however, very different from those which it had raised earlier to defeat Carthage. With the relative calm in naval affairs during the second half of the second century, Rome increasingly relied on her Greek allies and levies on the maritime cities of the East for naval support when it was required and this in part explains the initial successes of both Mithridates and the Cilician pirates. Not only Rome's corn supply but also her dignity and prestige were under threat and the Senate responded by putting Pompey in command of the campaign against them. In a very swift campaign he swept them from the seas. The scale of his operations and victory is indicated by an inscribed tablet set up in 62 BC to commemorate his triumph which recorded the capture of over 600 ships with bronze rams.[15] Romans could now truthfully boast that the Mediterranean was '*mare nostrum*'.

The ravaging of the Italian coast by pirates, along with the war against Mithridates, highlighted the importance of sea-power, something gradually forgotten after the end of the Third Punic War. The civil wars which rent the Roman world from 50 BC until Octavian's final victory 19 years later were to demonstrate this truth forcibly and repeatedly. The conflict, or rather series of conflicts, involved the full range of naval operations. Armies were transported to various provinces and supply lines maintained. Reinforcement by sea was attempted by one side while the other tried to intercept them and prevent them from reaching shore. Amphibious landings were undertaken to outflank and/or surprise the enemy. Blockades of coastal cities were enforced and the tactic of cutting off Rome's grain supply was successfully employed by Sextus Pompey.[16] There were also sea-battles some of which, such as Cumae, Mylai and Naulochus, were very substantial engagements. The battle which brought the civil wars to an end was also itself a naval encounter when Octavian's fleet defeated that of Antony and Cleopatra at Actium in 31 BC. After this battle

Octavian, or Augustus to use the name he adopted from 27 BC, was left in possession of a fleet of 700 ships. Well aware of the crucial importance of naval power he set about organising a permanent navy, paralleling his arrangements for a standing army, both being elements of his formula for eliminating further internal conflict and re-establishing peace throughout the Roman world.

Part of the naval force at his disposal was formed into a fleet and stationed at Forum Iulii where it could guard the Mediterranean coast of Gaul and Spain. If required it could also land forces far up the Rhône should trouble break out in the newly conquered areas of the Gallic interior. This was merely an interim measure, however, and new bases were soon built at Misenum on the Bay of Naples and Ravenna at the head of the Adriatic to protect Italy and Rome's corn supply. Detachments of the Misenum Fleet served at ports such as Puteoli, Centumcellae, Ostia and the new harbour of Portus constructed near the latter during the reign of Claudius. Small flotillas were out-stationed to deal with outbreaks of piracy or other local emergencies but some bases probably functioned more as stores depots and refitting yards rather than having ships permanently attached. Ostia was of course the main port for Rome's grain supply and it was from here also that senators and knights set sail for their provincial commands and appointments. Misenum and Puteoli were also the main ports for imperial couriers carrying despatches and messages to and from the provinces. Going by the evidence of their tombstones the largest detachment from the Misene Fleet was stationed at Rome itself. Originally quartered in the camp of the Praetorian Guard, they were given new quarters in the Flavian period close to the newly erected Colosseum. Part of their duties appears to have been connected with enforcing law and order in the capital, but their duties also included, at least for a time, responsibility for operating the large awnings in the Colosseum which provided shade for the audience, and perhaps organising the occasional mock naval battles or *naumachia* staged there. They would not of course have participated in the actual fighting; that was the fate of the condemned criminals who made up the doomed crews.

As at Misenum the establishment of a naval base at Ravenna entailed major engineering works which included the construction of moles, a lighthouse or *pharos*, and a large fort. The base here not only enabled control of the Adriatic but also allowed a close watch to be maintained on the Dalmatian coast, an historic centre of piracy. It was also well placed as a base from which the conquest of Illyricum could be supplied and reinforced. A detachment of the Ravennate Fleet was stationed at Salona, the capital of Dalmatia, and another may have been based at Aquileia. The largest detachment of men was at Rome, where their *castra* was situated in *Regio XIV* west of the Tiber. Their duties were presumably similar to those of the men from the Misenum Fleet. Given the importance of protecting the grain supply, the *Classis Alexandrina* based at Alexandria was also probably founded during the reign of Augustus. With all rival maritime powers eliminated there was no longer any real need for ships larger than quinqueremes. Henceforth, as the evidence of inscriptions from Misenum, Ravenna and other bases reveals, fleets were largely composed of triremes and biremes with one or two larger vessels used as flagships.[17]

Although Roman merchant ships, and presumably some warships too, must have been operating along the Atlantic coast of the Iberian Peninsula from at least the end of the third century BC, it is not until Caesar's day that we first hear of the Roman fleet operating in the Atlantic. This was also the first occasion in northern waters when Roman naval power was challenged and in fact very nearly defeated. Their opponents were the Veneti, a tribe residing on the Armorican coast of Brittany who feared the Roman advance into Gaul would end their monopoly of cross-Channel trade. The episode is fully described in chapter 5 and so need not be recounted in detail here. Suffice to say that it quickly became apparent to Caesar and his naval commanders that in these waters vessels sturdier than those to which they were accustomed were a necessity. This and the need to gather more detailed information about the tides, currents and winds in the Channel would have been made even clearer by events during Caesar's expeditions to Britain in 55 and 54 BC, also described in chapter 5.

By the time of Augustus the Roman navy was operating even further north, supporting the campaigns of the Elder Drusus in Germany. Flotillas were active on the lower Rhine in 12 BC.[18] Its naval commanders still had much to learn about the tides, however, for their ships were left high and dry in the Zuyder Zee and had to be rescued by Frisian allies. In his memoirs Augustus refers to his fleet operating in the North Sea which went on a voyage of exploration as far as Jutland.[19] Drusus also had a canal built, known as the *Fossa Drusiana*, from the Rhine to the Ijsselmeer to improve navigation to the North Sea. This was used by his son Germanicus whose campaigns made great use of naval support, building on the achievements and tactics used by the future emperor Tiberius in AD 5.[20] A significant number of the major campaign bases of this period were positioned on low-lying ground beside rivers even when a higher and more easily defended site was available. The tactical advantage of a more elevated site was apparently outweighed by the facility for easy and swift re-supply by water. The scale of the provisions required is indicated by the recent discovery at Oberaden of around 40 superbly preserved wooden casks, each of which was capable of holding up to 1,200 litres.[21]

Combined land and sea operations took place in AD 14 and the following year a force of four legions was transported by the fleet to the mouth of the Ems.[22] Marching back along the bank, however, they were overtaken by autumn gales and a rising tide and were rescued just in time. The following year Germanicus ordered the construction of 1,000 ships and we are fortunate in having a description of the type of craft built and their special features:

> Some were short and broad – with little prow or stern – to withstand
> a rough sea. Some were flat-bottomed, so that they could be run

aground undamaged. Others, more numerous, had rudders at each end so that the oarsmen could suddenly reverse direction and land them on either side of a river. Many had decks for catapults and also served to carry horses and supplies. The fleet was well adapted for sailing or rowing.

Tacitus Annals 2, 6–8

These craft were clearly transports not warships and would have been assembled by legionaries and auxiliaries most probably working under the direction of experts from one or more of the imperial *classes*. Fleets used on the great rivers for campaign purposes were usually built by the army. Shipwrights (*naupegi*), along with pilots (*gubernatores*), are listed among the category of men known as *immunes* in the legions who were excused normal duties.[23] Germanicus' fleet transported eight legions and a number of auxiliary units along with their supplies up the Ems. For the return journey some of the force marched back on land while the majority embarked on the ships once more. This time a storm struck the fleet as it moved along the shore of the North Sea. Some ships were driven out to sea, others onto rocks, and yet others onto shoals. A number sank and others were cast up on remote islands where the men were forced to eat the horses washed up with them or starve to death. Germanicus' flagship – a trireme – was separated from the rest of the fleet and landed in the territory of the Chauci where he spent days and nights wandering along the rocky headlands cursing himself for the catastrophe.[24] When the storm abated, ships began to make their way back and were rapidly repaired to be sent out to search and rescue stranded survivors, many of whom had to be ransomed. Some ships had even been driven as far as Britain, their crews being returned unharmed.[25] These losses, coming on top of the destruction of three legions in the Varian disaster only seven years earlier, persuaded Tiberius to order Germanicus to return to Rome: 'You have won great victories' wrote Tiberius, 'but you must also remember the terrible, crippling losses inflicted by wind and wave.'[26] The Roman offensive in Germany was brought to a close and a permanent fleet – the *Classis Germanica* – established with a main base at Alteburg, near the double legionary fortress and later *colonia* at Cologne. Henceforth its duties, except in times of emergency, consisted of keeping the army supplied and patrolling the Rhine. In time, preventing crossings by those trying to evade customs duties probably became far more important than keeping a watch for infiltrators.

The other great fleets of the northern frontier, the *Classis Pannonica* and the *Classis Moesica*, developed around the same time and in much the same way as the *Classis Germanica*. Under Augustus, the Danube became the frontier of the central and eastern sectors of the northern *limes* from its headwaters all the way to the Kingdom of Thrace, the latter itself becoming a Roman province in AD 46. The conquest of this vast region was achieved by armies moving north from Macedonia, and north and north-eastwards from Dalmatia. Initially administered as a single province known as Illyricum, this was soon divided into Pannonia and Moesia. By the end of the first century BC a chain of forts had been established along the south bank of the Danube. As one would expect, and as Strabo confirms, the Romans moved the bulk of their war supplies in this theatre by ship, the majority built on the spot under the guidance of sailors and shipwrights drafted in from the Mediterranean fleets. Military transports moved the supplies while warships kept the rivers free of enemy vessels and entrapments. During the reign of Claudius, the Moesian Fleet on the lower Danube extended its operations to the northern coasts of the Black Sea where it was used to support rulers of the Bosporus appointed by Rome. The exploits of the *Classis Moesica* are graphically depicted in the spiral band of reliefs on Trajan's Column in Rome which, although specifically illustrating the conquest of Dacia in AD 101-6, also provide a general impression of the navy's role in any major campaign.

After scenes depicting watch-towers and signal-stations along the south bank of the Danube, the location changes to a legionary fortress with a harbour and stores-base where ships in the foreground are being loaded with barrels and what appear to be tent packs (**1** & **2**).[27] Preparations for the campaign are clearly underway with supplies being loaded onto transport vessels, a scene which recurs at intervals throughout the early section of the reliefs. Next the army is shown emerging from a gate and crossing two parallel pontoon bridges, illustrating a less regular but nonetheless important use for boats (**3**).[28] In another scene, Trajan is shown embarking on an imperial galley at a major harbour town or fortress. The ship appears to be a bireme with the lower level of oars rowed through ports and the upper through a latticework screen (**4**).[29] Of the ships depicted in the subsequent disembarkation scene, two are rowed military transports. The lower ship is a horse transport while the upper is a decked cargo vessel; both have a single level of oars rowed over the top wale. Two other vessels are clearly warships, both biremes, and the one in the lower register may well be the flagship as it has an elaborately decorated bow, a stern shelter, and apparently two helmsmen (**5**).[30] Later scenes show Trajan setting out from a seaport (usually taken to be Ancona) at the beginning of the Second Dacian War in June 105. Three warships are shown, one of which, presumably Trajan's flagship, is a trireme (**6**).[31] A little later, in yet another harbour scene, the only large merchant vessel shown on the Column can be seen, its furled main sail and rigging rising above the figures in the foreground (**7**).[32]

Other fleets existed. The *Classis Pontica*, founded under Nero, was responsible for the southern and eastern sectors of the Black Sea while the *Classis Syriaca* patrolled the east end of the Mediterranean.[33] Detachments from both the latter and the *Classis Alexandrina* also maintained a naval presence in the western Mediterranean, operating out of a base at Caesarea Mauretania. By AD 180, a new African fleet had been formed the *Classis Nova Libica*.[34]

1 *Trajan's Column. Boats on the Danube being loaded with supplies ready for Dacian campaign*

2 *Trajan's Column. Movement of supplies by boat along the Danube*

3 *Trajan's Column. Campaign begins with the army crossing Danube on pontoon bridges of boats*

4 *Trajan's Column. Trajan's embarkation at a riverside harbour*

5 *Trajan's Column. Trajan's river voyage and disembarkation*

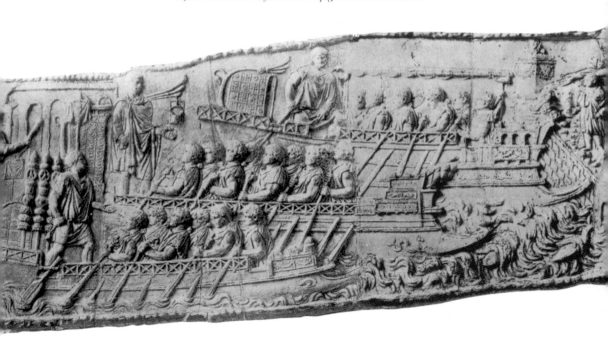

6 *Trajan's Column. Trajan setting forth from a seaport at the beginning of the Second Dacian War in AD 105*

7 *Trajan's Column. Trajan disembarking at a harbour town*

3

ORGANISATION AND SIZE OF THE IMPERIAL FLEETS

Organisation

As organised by Augustus, each fleet of the Imperial Navy was commanded by an equestrian *praefectus* transferred from the army, often a former legionary tribune or senior centurion. Claudius began the process of integrating military and civil branches of the imperial administration, placing naval prefects on the same footing as senior financial officers known as procurators.[1] As a consequence, freedmen from the Imperial household began to be appointed to fleet commands under Nero. Sea power played an important part in Vespasian's ultimate victory in the civil war of 68-9 and it is notable that in the commemorative coinage issued in AD 71 and later years, the only type which refers specifically to the civil war carries the legend *Victoria Navalis*, 'Our Lady Victory of the Fleet'. The rewards given to the fleets were greater than those bestowed upon any other force, and a number of changes to the hierarchy of the navy were also introduced. In future, freedmen were barred from holding naval prefectures which now became some of the most elevated posts in the equestrian career structure. Henceforth the prefectures of the home fleets at Misenum and Ravenna, now given the honorific title *praetoria*, ranked next in seniority to the great prefectures of state such as those of the *vigiles* (Rome's fire brigade), the *annona* (corn supply), Egypt and the Praetorian Guard. Commensurate with their elevation in status, the annual salary of the *Praefectus Classis Praetorii Ravennas* was increased from 60,000 to 200,000 *sesterces* and that of the *Praefectus Classis Praetorii Misenensis*, the more senior of the two, to 300,000 *sesterces*.[2] The Elder Pliny, natural historian and writer as well as career administrator, was Prefect of the *Classis Misenensis* when he took his ships across the Bay of Naples to get a closer look at the eruption of Vesuvius in AD 79 and paid for his curiosity with his life. The prefects of the provincial fleets received a salary of 60,000 *sesterces* except for those of the important British and German Fleets who ranked as *centenarii* and were thus paid 100,000 *sesterces* per year. The German and Alexandrian fleets received the title *Augusta* while the Pannonian and Moesian fleets were even more highly honoured by the title *Flavia*.

Command of a fleet was a rung on the ladder of the equestrian career path and the men who held these positions were professional administrators, not specialists in naval warfare. At earlier stages in their career they would have commanded an auxiliary cohort, then been a legionary tribune, followed by a spell as prefect of an auxiliary cavalry *ala*. The command of a provincial fleet was a very senior position in the military command structure, second only to the provincial governor. He was assisted by a *subpraefectus* while the mundane duties of administration were attended to by his staff or *officium* of sailors seconded to naval headquarters as *librarii* and *beneficiarii*.[3] Here records were kept of crews, pay, bases, stores and supplies, harbours, navigations, the ships themselves and the myriad other administrative aspects of managing a permanent fleet, its infrastructure and its personnel. The organisation of the fleet below the rank of *subpraefectus* was based largely on that of the earlier Greek navy. Indeed, in many cases the Greek terms for the various crew positions persisted, hardly surprising given that the design of the ships was based on Greek predecessors and many of the recruits were themselves drawn from the eastern Mediterranean. The commander or admiral of a squadron was called a *navarchus*. Originally this term had been applied to the commander of a ship, but during the Hellenistic period it came to denote the superior rank. Although the size of squadrons probably varied according to circumstances there is some evidence that ten was the usual number of ships.[4] There were various grades within the navarchy, the most senior being the *navarchus princeps* or *navarchus archigubernes*.[5] In the same way that the legionary legate received professional military advice from the *primus pilus*, so the naval prefect was advised by the *navarchus princeps*. Below the *navarchus* was the *trierarchus*, ship's captain. Again, this had originally referred to the captain of a trireme but in later times was used to designate the master of any class of warship.[6]

Although the Romans carried on with the Greek organisation of a warship's crew, they imposed upon it some of their own military posts. The result was an organisational structure which appears rather complex to our eyes but which undoubtedly functioned very straightforwardly in practice. It reflected the fact that the basic strategy of the Roman navy, in contrast to its Greek precursor, was to close on enemy ships so that the superior fighting skills of the Roman soldier could prevail, in effect turning the naval encounter into a land battle. Thus the crew of every warship, irrespective of its size, constituted a century and was commanded by a centurion in the same way as a legionary *centuria*. This included not only the strictly military personnel – such as the small complement of archers (*sagitarii*), artillerymen (*ballistarii*), and decksoldiers (*propugnatores*) – but also all of the oarsmen (*remiges*) and even the steersman and clerks as is evident from the fact that on inscriptions they are all referred to, and refer to themselves as, *milites* – 'soldiers', not *nautae* – 'sailors', and are assigned to a ship's century. As Ulpian put it, 'in the fleets all rowers and sailors are soldiers'.[7] The centurion was assisted by an *optio* and *suboptio*, the *armorum custos* or armourersergeant, and the bugler *bucinator*. The trierarch also had a small staff who looked after the overall running and administration of the ship. This was headed by a *beneficiarius* below whom was the *secutor*, who implemented the trierarch's orders and maintained discipline, along with several clerks. The *scriba* was responsible for preparing and forwarding the trierarch's routine reports to headquarters. Other clerks mentioned in inscriptions include the *adiutor* or higher clerk, the *librarius*, whose duties appear to have been largely concerned with financial reports, and the *exceptor* or stenographer.

The most senior member of the purely naval personnel, apart from the *trierarch* himself, was the *gubernator* who supervised the operation of the steering-oars, directly controlled the ratings in the aft part of the ship, and was also responsible for navigational matters. The steersman's chief assistant was the *proreta*. He was stationed in the forward part of the ship and an important element of his duties was giving information to the steersman about shoals, rocks and other hazards in the ship's path. *Gubernatores* are also attested in the ranks of the legions, an example close to home being Marcus Minucius Audens of the Sixth Legion who set up an altar to the African, Italian and Gallic Mother-Goddesses at York.[8] One assumes his expertise lay in a detailed knowledge of the Ouse and it was presumably his responsibility to ensure that vessels bringing in supplies for the legion avoided its particular hazards and docked safely. Legionary *gubernatores* presumably existed in the legions based at Caerleon (*II Augusta*) and Chester (*II Adiutrix* followed by *XX Valeria Victrix*). Their skills would have been especially valuable at the latter because of the vagaries and complexities of the Dee estuary with its shifting sands and shallows.

The chief rowing officer was the *celeusta* whose main responsibility was ensuring the rowers worked rhythmically and in unison to allow the ship to make smooth and efficient progress. He may also have been known as the *pausarius* although this person could have been his junior. Seneca writes of the *pausarius* giving the time for the oarsmen with his very penetrating voice.[9] Sometimes a regular beat was maintained with the aid of a flute-player or *symphoniacus*, at other times by the pounding of a mallet (*portisculus*) wielded by the *pitulus*. The crew also included a few *velarii* who looked after the sails, the *medicus* or doctor, the *fabri* or ship's carpenters, and the *nauphylax* who probably acted as quartermaster. The duties associated with the posts of *coronarius*, who garlanded the ship on religious festivals, and the *victimarius*, who sacrificed offerings on behalf of the crew, were presumably undertaken by existing crew members rather than full-time positions. For their various specialist skills many of the crew received double pay and as a consequence styled themselves as *duplicarii*. There would have been some on higher pay amongst the oarsmen, most obviously the stroke-oars.

Onshore, the military element of the fleet would have taken care of the maintenance of the base and its accommodation, barrack routines and combat training. Beside the harbour at each fleet base would have stood the shipyards easily recognisable from their long, narrow shipsheds or *navalia*. In addition to the construction of new ships, this is where the vessels were stored under cover during the winter for repair and maintenance. In these, or store buildings alongside, were kept replacement sails, rigging and other gear. At the larger establishments, there was probably an officer in overall charge of the shipyard and shipbuilding although no record of such a post has survived.

The precise size of any of the fleets is unknown. However, some indication of the manpower of the two Italian fleets is provided by the fact that each furnished enough men to put together a legion during the Year of the Four Emperors, the Misene *Legio I Adiutrix* and the Ravennate *Legio II Adiutrix*. In addition, Otho took well in excess of another 1,000 sailors from Misenum to fight against Vitellius – the fleet still having sufficient manpower for an expeditionary force – and soon afterwards Vitellius himself was considering raising or actually raised yet another legion at Misenum.[10] The *Classis Misenatium* would seem therefore to have had a complement in excess of 10,000 men and the *Classis Ravennatium* one of at least 6,000. What then of the *Classis Britannica's* establishment? The fort at the fleet headquarters at Boulogne enclosed an area of *c*.31 acres which is about 60 per cent of the area of the standard legionary fortress of about 50 acres which accommodated around 5,500 men. One might deduce from this that the Boulogne fort housed in the region of 3,500 men. If Philp's analysis of the barrack accommodation in the fort at Dover is correct then it could have held around 640 men.[11] The as yet unlocated base at Lympne may well have housed a detachment of similar strength and there may have been another at Pevensey. From these bases, warships would have voyaged regularly to and from the many other military ports around the coast transporting despatches, important personages, and perhaps pay-chests for the army. There was also the British Fleet's involvement in the iron industry of the Weald. From time to time part of a squadron may have been out-stationed at some of these other ports and of course when the occasion demanded, such as the staging of a major campaign, much of the fleet would have been based away from its home port.

Yet given the length of the British coastline, the number and distribution of coastal military bases, and the need for naval support of one form or another in the north and west, one is drawn to conclude that – despite the lack of stamped tiles or similar evidence – there must have been additional squadrons. These may have been part of the *Classis Britannica* or, as is suggested in chapter 7, they could have been attached to and operated by the three legions in the province. Whatever the case, a minimum of three other squadrons seems necessary; one each for the east and west coasts – the former with a base on the Humber estuary and the latter on the Dee estuary, most probably Chester – with the third controlling the Bristol Channel and the waters off the south-west peninsula. On this reckoning the total complement of the naval forces attached to Britain would have been somewhere in the region of 7,000 men.

Recruitment and status

The manpower for the Roman Imperial Navy was recruited overwhelmingly from freeborn but non-citizen provincials (*peregrini*) just like the auxiliary forces. The Romans were not natural sailors and relied upon the expertise of those who were, recruiting heavily from the seafaring peoples of the Mediterranean. Thus, much of the strength of the *Classis Ravennas* was recruited from the tribes of the Dalmatian coast on the opposite side of the Adriatic while the *Classis Misenensis* drew men preponderantly from Sardinia, Corsica, Africa and Egypt.[12] Proven ability in seamanship was not though a prerequisite for eligibility, as Starr's analysis of the evidence has shown. Many came from inland rural communities and small towns and presumably viewed the navy as an attractive alternative to service in the *auxilia*. Although of vital importance in the process of acquiring and holding an empire, the navy was never accorded a status anywhere near that of the legions, and so it held little attraction for those with Roman citizenship. Slaves were definitely not used except in dire emergencies. The modern cinematic image of war galleys rowed by slaves chained to their oars is a gross misrepresentation of the normal state of affairs. The crews were highly trained, professional soldiers proud of their abilities and with a strong esprit de corps; prisoners were forced into service as rowers only as a last resort.

Evidence for the general recruiting profile of the provincial fleets is scanty. However, the little information that we do possess concerning the German and British Fleets suggests, as one might expect, that Rome made full use of the seafaring abilities of the indigenous peoples. At the time of the conquest and pacification of the north-western provinces, the composition of the naval forces that were to evolve into the *Classis Germanica* and the *Classis Britannica* would have been much the same as the rest of the navy, with a high proportion of men from the eastern Mediterranean.[13] Fairly soon, however, the Roman military began to look for naval recruits from amongst the very experienced seafaring tribes of the Channel and North Sea coasts, tribes such as the Batavii, Chauci, Frisii, Menapii, Morini and Veneti. By the time of the Civilis Revolt in AD 69, for example, there was already a considerable number of Batavian rowers in the *Classis Germanica*.[14] Indeed, even its commanding officer, Julius Burdo, was a Batavian.[15] Whether the recruitment of Britons into the navy proceeded at a similar pace is unknown. A man who was a *miles* in the *Classis Germanica* and described as '*civis Dumnonius*' may have been a Briton if he really did hail from British Dumnonia rather than a similarly-named region of some other province.[16]

Information about individual members of the *Classis Britannica* derives largely from inscriptions found at the fleet headquarters at Boulogne. Two marines are recorded, one whose name is lost, hailed from Syria, and the other, named Didius, was a Thracian.[17] As to trierarchs, the earliest known is Titus Claudius Aug. l. Seleucus, a freedman of the Emperor Claudius from the eastern Mediterranean.[18] The others are Quintus Arrenius Verecundus and P. Graecius

Tertinus, the latter also an Easterner.[19] The latest known is Saturninus, named on an inscription from Arles, who was ship's captain during the reign of Philip in the mid-240s.[20] Several commanders of the British Fleet are known from inscriptions elsewhere in the Empire which record their careers. The earliest is Quintus Baienus Blassianus who was successively procurator of Armenia and then Cappadocia before becoming prefect of the *Classis Britannica* under Trajan. He was then appointed to the prestigious post of prefect of the praetorian fleet based at Ravenna.[21] Sextus Flavius Quietus went from being senior centurion (*primus pilus*) with the Twentieth Legion to commander of the British Fleet in the reign of either Antoninus Pius or Caracalla.[22] A man who definitely did hold this post under Antoninus Pius was Marcus Maenius Agrippa L. Tusidius. In fact he combined it with the office of *procurator provinciae Britanniae*, an indication of the importance in the fleet's duties of the transport of supplies for the army.[23] Finally, from this side of the Channel is the altar dedicated at Lympne by Lucius Aufidius Pantera, another prefect of the mid-second century.[24]

Conditions of service

Under the early Empire the normal length of service for sailors was 26 years, with Roman citizenship as the reward on discharge like men retiring from the *auxilia*. This term applied to all ranks up to and including the rank of *trierarch* and it was only *navarchs* who could be enfranchised before discharge. This period was probably fixed by Augustus when he put both army and navy on a permanent footing and set the terms for legionary and auxiliary service at 20 and 25 years respectively. The implication seems to be that service in the navy was regarded as being inferior to auxiliary service, although not markedly so. Discharge diplomas of the later second century show that the term for naval service was increased to 28 years at some time after c.AD 160, possibly reflecting difficulty in obtaining sufficient recruits.[25] Individuals were sometimes rewarded for outstanding service by immediate discharge and occasionally this happened with entire crews; for example, the complement of the ship who apparently saved the Emperor Trajan in a storm.[26] In a few instances, either when there was a pressing need for additional soldiers or as a means of expressing imperial gratitude, whole sections of a fleet were enrolled in the Roman legions, a move which immediately bestowed Roman citizenship on the sailors involved. This happened very rarely, the best known example being the creation during the civil war of AD 68-9 of *Legiones I* and *II Adiutrix* from the Misene and Ravennate fleets respectively, the first by Nero and the second by Vespasian.

It has been calculated that the basic annual pay of the ordinary infantryman in the *auxilia* from the late first to the late second century was around 100 *denarii* and it seems very likely that this was also the amount received by the lowest ranking sailor.[27] Like the legionary and the auxiliary soldier a sailor received a payment on enlistment, the equivalent of the 'Queen's shilling'. Perhaps surprisingly, the amount – three gold pieces or 75 *denarii* – was the same for all three services. That increases in pay were available for taking on extra responsibilities, as in the *auxilia*, is clear from reference in inscriptions of men on 1½ and 2 times normal pay (*sesquiplicarii* and *duplicarii*).[28] Income could also be supplemented by war booty, although such opportunities for the fleets must have been fairly limited for much of our period. These were, however, increased for the British Fleet under the later Empire as the accounts of the Carausian episode demonstrate (chapter 9). Gifts of money or donatives were frequently distributed to the military by emperors on their accession and other special occasions but these were not generally distributed to units other than the praetorians and the legions until the bestowal of Roman citizenship on all free-born men and women by Caracalla in AD 211. There would have been stoppages from the sailor's pay, just like his counterparts on dry land, to cover the costs of food, arms and equipment. A sum would also have been deducted for deposit in the fleet's or squadron's savings bank to build up his retirement fund. The wording on discharge diplomas changes around AD 166 in such a way as to imply that sailors in the praetorian fleets of Ravenna and Misenum were now allowed to contract legal marriages while on active service, a privilege not bestowed on the rest of the armed services for another 30 years.[29] It may be, as Starr suggested, that this concession was easier to make in the navy's case because a sailor's military duties were always undertaken in circumstances where his family would not be an impediment.

As with all other aspects of the lives of the ordinary sailor serving with the *Classis Britannica*, we have no evidence as to their activities on retirement. If they were anything like their counterparts in other fleets, many will have returned to their place of origin on retirement. A high proportion, however, probably settled down with their families in the civil settlement which had developed around the naval base. Some may have set themselves up in land-based businesses with others putting their seamanship to good use by serving on merchant ships, working as shipwrights, or becoming fishermen. A proportion continued in service far beyond the normal term. Those with technical skills were much valued and the navy was keen to retain them. Examples of 37, 45 and 48 years are known and all were still on active duties when they died.[30]

Training

The warships of the Roman navy relied principally upon oar power and to function efficiently their crews needed to be highly trained and well drilled so that they could respond to orders quickly and in unison. Even though for most of the period under discussion these skills were not put to the ultimate test of the set-piece naval battle so typical of earlier times, they were nonetheless essential and training would have been just as rigorous in Hadrian's or Severus' day as it had in the time of Augustus. Then, as now, it was only by repetitive practice that rowing crews attained the ability to pull together as one. This was of course especially true of raw recruits and newly-formed crews. Sometimes the first step in training new recruits was done not at sea but on land as they were taught to row seated in mock-ups of the oar system known as *icria*.[31] At this stage they would learn all the basics of rowing; rowing in unison to the rhythm of the time-beater, dipping and holding the oars, shipping oars, backing water, and rapid changes in stroke speed.[32] Following extensive practice both at sea and in harbour, the new crew would then join with other ships to gain experience in operating as part of a flotilla or larger squadron including the rehearsal of battle manoeuvres. The proficiency of experienced crews also had to be maintained. Again this was achieved not only by frequent exercises but also by racing competitions. This mirrored the manoeuvres and training exercises undertaken by the army which have left traces in the landscape such as practice camps and siege-works. Given their expertise in such matters, mock amphibious operations would undoubtedly have featured in the training programme.

Clothing and equipment

Preserved papyri bearing correspondence between a marine serving in the Alexandrian fleet and his family gives some information about the sailor's uniform. In one letter he requests *byrrum castalinum et tunicam bracilem cum bracis* ('a cloak with belted tunic and trousers') and in another *caligas cori subtalares ed udones, par* ('low-cut leather boots and a pair of felt stockings').[33] Sailors' tomb-stones at Athens depict them wearing a short armless tunic as well as the military cloak or *sagum*.[34] In general, the uniform worn by men serving in the navy seems to have been little different from that of the army.[35] Variations in climate would obviously have led to some differences in clothing between the provincial fleets. Again using the evidence provided by funerary reliefs and papyri, the marine's weaponry appears to have been similar to that of the auxiliary consisting of a sword, a spear and a shield. The last may have been round like that of the auxiliaries or hexagonal as depicted in scenes on Trajan's Column which shows *classiarii* engaged in road-building, a task often set them on land according to Hyginus.[36] Two other specialised items were the grapnel and the axe, the latter wielded by the *dolatores* and used for cutting enemy grapnels. Equipment was issued by the authorities and deductions made from the men's pay. Some preferred to purchase their weapons from other sources or have them sent by their families like the Alexandrian recruit mentioned above who wrote to his father asking for *gladium pugnatorium et . . . dolabrum et copulam et longas duas quam optimas* ('a battle sword . . . and an axe and grapnel and two spears of the best quality').[37] In a subsequent letter he asks for another axe because the one sent previously had been appropriated by his *optio*.[38]

4

SHIPBUILDING, SHIP-TYPES AND NAVAL BASES

Shipbuilding

There are basically two ways of constructing a vessel of timber. In one a skeleton consisting of keel and frames is constructed to which the planks of the hull are then fastened. In the other the process is reversed; a shell of planks is built up from the keel, each line or strake of planks locked to that above and below, into which frames are then introduced to add rigidity. Vessels of the Roman period were, apart from small regional craft, usually constructed using the second method. Unlike the Viking Age and later 'clinker-built' ships of northern Europe, which used overlapping planks pegged or nailed together (**8**), the Roman shipwright (*faber navalis*) arranged the planks to form a smooth skin by setting them edge to edge and locking them together by the employ-ment of numerous, close-set mortise-and-tenon joints (**9**). All major vessels discovered so far were constructed using this technique, often described as 'carvel' construction. As far as warships were concerned, the advantages of this method were that it resulted in a hull that was not only robust and rigid but also lightweight, which in turn meant that the length of the ship, the number of oars per side and thus the speed of vessels could be increased. To be successful, however, it required great skill. Ships built entirely of timber and, in the case of the low, sleek warships with a typical ratio of length on the waterline to structural depth of hull of between 12 and 14 to 1 had to be constructed to a very high standard to give any useful length of service.

The first step in the process was the arranging of stocks and the laying of the keel. Stempost and sternpost were then jointed to the keel and the lowest (garboard) strakes slotted into a rebate or rabett in the latter. The hull, whose base was not flat but rose sharply on each side of the keel, was then built up by adding further strakes of planks joined together using mortise-and-tenon joints. The tenons were sometimes slightly wedge-shaped towards the tip to achieve a stronger joint. Indeed Ovid uses the word *cunei*, 'wedges', when describing the tenons of a ship's planking.[1] The transverse frames joining the strakes were then added. Judging from the examples recovered from wrecks,

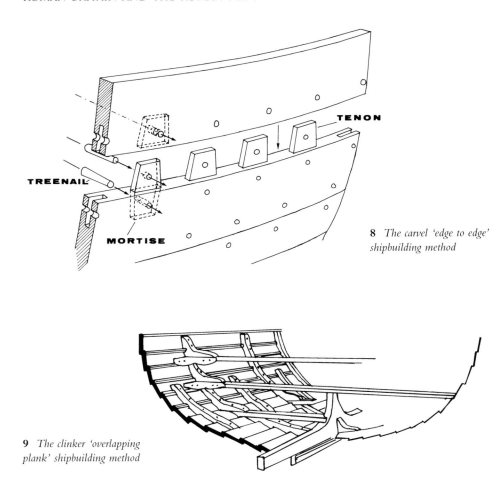

TENON

TREENAIL

MORTISE

8 *The carvel 'edge to edge' shipbuilding method*

9 *The clinker 'overlapping plank' shipbuilding method*

the planks varied from 1½ to 4in (5-10cm) in thickness. The thickest planks were used at certain points on the hull where added strength was required, such as the strakes beside the keel known as the garboard strakes. Sometimes two layers of planking were used. The tenons were generally 2-3in (5-7.5cm) wide, spaced at intervals of 10in (25cm) apart and penetrated some 50 per cent into the receiving plank. Once slotted together, the tenons were pinned with wooden pegs to ensure they did not pull out of their mortises when stressed. The planking may seem surprisingly flimsy and indeed ancient writers liked to highlight the fact that all that separated a sailor from a watery grave was three fingers thickness of wood.[2] However, the quality of the carpentry more than compensated for the thinness of the shell. While this was obviously a labour intensive and highly skilled method of construction, it produced a hull that was not only lightweight yet sturdy but also, because of the close jointing, one that was less prone to leaks. It was thus faster and required less maintenance than a vessel of the same size built using cruder methods employing thicker planks and generous caulking to seal the joints. This method also allowed the construction of long hulls capable of withstanding the twisting and shearing forces to which they were inevitably subjected.

The selection of timber was of course critical: too green and the joints would be too loose on drying out; too dry and the wood would split when the planks were united. The period from the beginning of July until 1 January was considered the best period for felling timber, and winter was the usual shipbuilding period. As the late Roman writer Vegetius put it:

> For in these months the moisture evaporates and the wood is drier and therefore stronger. Avoid sawing timbers immediately after felling, or putting them into the ship as soon as they have been sawn, because both trees that are still whole and those divided into 'double' planks deserve a period for further drying. Those fitted when still green exude their natural moisture and contract, forming wide cracks; nothing is more dangerous for sailors than for the planking to split.
>
> *Epitoma rei Militaris* 36

Naval operations normally ceased at the onset of autumn and so more men were available to work as or assist the shipwrights.

Once the shell was substantially complete the shipwright would insert the frames. The tombstone of the shipwright P. Longidienus, who died at Ravenna *c*.AD 200, bears a relief showing him in the process of shaping a frame.[3] Timbers were placed in tiers which overlapped but were not joined, while the spacing between timbers in each tier generally did not exceed 18in (0.45m). The frames were joined to the planking by copper spikes, having tapered square shanks and large, dome-shaped heads. The spikes themselves were usually driven up pine dowels inserted into holes bored through frame and plank and then clenched over and driven back into the face of the framing. An inner lining of planks was then laid down and fastened to the frames. A keelson rested on the keel, notched to take account of the floor timbers. To give the mast a sound bedding a large block of wood was attached to the keel with a socket hollowed out of its top to accommodate the heel of the mast. Attached to the exterior of the keel was what is known as a false keel. Made of a resistant wood such as beech or oak, this was added to protect the keel proper from damage when the ship was hauled out of the water for maintenance or repair. Lines of thick broad planks known as wales were attached to the ship's sides. These reinforced the hull and on a merchant vessel protected it from damage when the ship was moored alongside solid structures such as a stone quayside. On warships of any size there was usually a wale at the waterline as protection against ramming and another – the gunwale – at the top of the hull. The wales were affixed to the hull using long spikes or bolts that went right through to the inner lining and were paralleled on the interior by heavy horizontal timbers known as stringers.

The details of the rest of the structure varied according to the type and specification of the vessel. In warships with more than one bank of oars, the system of frames carrying the fixed seats for the oarsmen and the supports for whatever form of decking lay above could be quite complex. As they were propelled by a 'human engine' of *c*.200 manpower, good ventilation in fully decked vessels was essential to expel excess heat, moisture and carbon dioxide and draw in cooling, oxygen-laden fresh air. To this end, louvres were incorporated in the hull wherever possible. Where oar ports pierced the hull near the waterline, they were fitted with leather sleeves (Greek=*askomata*; Latin=?*ascoperae*) to prevent the ingress of water. These can be seen on a number of sculptural representations.[4] Long shallow hulls like those of ancient warships were subject to extreme longitudinal stresses which, without countermeasures, could result in the ship either sagging down in the middle or at both ends ('hogging'), leading to joints springing apart and the ship's destruction. To prevent this, each ship was fitted with *hypozomata* – literally 'undergirdings' – which were powerful ropes stretched in a straight line close under the deck beams and connected to strong points in the bow and stern where the tension could be adjusted.[5]

Ships were normally allowed to stand for a while after completion so that they could 'dry out'. This meant that when they were launched the wood absorbed a certain amount of moisture and so the joints became tighter, thus eliminating leaks. For good measure, the seams or even the whole hull was also given a protective coating of pitch or pitch and wax. As well as ensuring watertightness, a coating of wax also enhanced the performance of the vessel by reducing frictional resistance. It was also commonplace for merchant vessels to have the underwater section of the hull protected from marine-boring creatures by encasing it in a sheath of lead sheets placed on an underlay of tarred fabric and held in place by large-headed copper tacks. Needless to say, this approach was not adopted for warships as the additional weight would have drastically reduced their speed. Also they were hauled out of the water and laid up during the winter months in order both to complete repairs and to allow the hull to 'dry out'. A variety of timber was employed in shipbuilding, usually influenced by what was available locally. Some woods, however, were preferred for particular purposes. Fir, cedar and pine were preferred for planking, frames and keel, while oak was used widely for frames and especially tenons and treenails because of its high crushing-strength across the grain. Oak was not recommended for planking, however, because it was thought to rot too easily in salt water, although it could be used for frame-first clinker-built ships because their planks were much thicker.

Maintenance was normally carried out during the winter months when, because of the likelihood of storms and reduced visibility, seaborne activity was restricted to essential voyages such as the carriage of important despatches and the transport of urgently needed supplies and equipment. Given its generally high level of efficiency and discipline there is every reason to believe that the regime of maintenance imposed on naval personnel 'out of season' was no less strict than in the army. The removal of marine growths, the repair and/or replacement of damaged or rotten woodwork, and finally the recoating of the hull with pitch and wax would all have been included in the 'annual service' schedule. To carry out these operations the ship obviously had to be hauled out of the water (*subducere*) and then supported on props. This was done under cover in shipsheds (*navalia*). This not only protected the shipwrights from the worst of the winter weather but was also necessary to allow the hull to dry out as otherwise the new coating of pitch or wax would not adhere properly. The ship was then re-launched (*deducere*) in the spring and no doubt subjected to various sea-trials before being pronounced fit for operational service.

Ship-types and their uses

The nature of the evidence
WARSHIPS — *NAVES LONGAE*

When Octavian (later Augustus) established the Imperial Navy as part of his regularisation of Rome's military forces after the civil war with Antony, there was no longer a naval power in the Mediterranean to oppose her. The naval arms race of the Hellenistic period was well and truly over and so practicality and efficiency could be applied in shaping the Roman navy for its future duties which consisted essentially of protecting maritime trade, maintaining imperial communications, and, most important of all, transporting, supplying and supporting the army. With regard to its ships, speed and manoeuvrability rather than size and weight were now paramount, as was standardisation, for effi-ciency in design and construction. Large fleets of great battleships featuring 'sixes', 'sevens', 'tens', and even larger vessels were redundant. Henceforth the Roman navy boasted but a single 'six' and that was the flagship of the senior fleet at Misenum. There were a handful of 'fives', perhaps a few dozen 'fours', scores of triremes and, particularly in the northern provincial fleets, large numbers of the type of vessel with two banks of oars known as the *liburna* named after and an adaptation of the fast light ships used for piratical pursuits by the Illyrian tribe called the Liburni.[6]

There was a notional grouping of warships into two broad categories: the larger type (probably comprising 'fives' and above) *'naves maioris formae'* and the smaller ('fours' and below) *'naves minoris formae'*.[7] There were various types of smaller ships, some with a specialised function, along with the oared troop transports (*naves actuariae*) which were usually built in large numbers for specific campaigns and which featured in Caesar's second expedition to

Britain and undoubtedly in the Claudian invasion a century later.[8] We know from an inscription found at Boulogne that the *Classis Britannica* had at least one trireme on its establishment while Tacitus' account of Agricola's campaigns in the north shows, as one would expect, that it also featured Liburnians.[9] The list which follows describes the range of vessels of the Imperial Roman Navy which are known or are very likely to have operated in British waters.

TRIREME, QUADRIREME AND QUINQUEREME –
TRIREMIS, QUADRIREMIS, QUINQUEREMIS

The design of ancient oared ships, particularly that of the type of warship known as the trireme which gave Athens control of the eastern Mediterranean, has been one of the major subjects for debate among naval historians since the early sixteenth century. Discussion centred on how the comments of ancient authors (who frequently lacked naval experience and used terms casually and/or inaccurately) about the arrangement of oars should be interpreted; some believing they indicated one level or bank of oars per side each pulled by three men, others that they implied oars arranged in three banks per side with one man per oar. Renewed interest and research over the last 60 years by a number of scholars, but most particularly by John Morrison, whose work culminated in the building and trialling of a full-size reconstruction of a trireme named the *Olympias*, put the matter beyond any doubt; the oar-system of the trireme consisted of three superimposed and staggered banks of seated rowers.[10] It became clear that misunderstandings had arisen because ancient writers frequently failed to indicate whether they were referring to the number of banks/levels or files/ranks; the latter denoting the lines of rowers from stem to stern. Solving the 'trireme question' also clarified the arrangements in some of the larger vessels.

The general appearance of the trireme, like many other types of vessel, is depicted variously on coins, vases, mosaics, frescoes and relief sculpture.[11] Physical evidence of the ships themselves is absent as triremes were endowed with positive buoyancy and did not sink, thus explaining why no wrecks have been found on the sea bed; neither have any remains been found on shore. However, the ship-sheds at Zea, one of Piraeus' three naval harbours, provide information about the overall size of the standard trireme.[12] These afforded a covered area 121ft 5in (37m) long with a clear width of 19ft 6in (5.92m) between the columns which separated neighbouring sheds. The width of the ship would have been slightly smaller to allow space for manoeuvring. More detailed information is contained in a collection of fourth-century BC inscriptions from Piraeus – known as the Naval Inventories – which record the activities of the Boards of Dockyard Overseers.[13] Amongst the most important items are the entries concerning oars which reveal that there were 62 rowers in the top level and 54 in each of the middle and lower levels (31, 27 and 27 each side). This was because the curvature of the hull meant there was less room at the lower levels. The lowest level of rowers were known as the thalamites because their oars were worked through ports in the hull known as *thalamiai*. Above them were the zygites and above them again were the thranites. Along with the total of 170 oarsmen there were around 14 sailing crew and a small number of deck soldiers to give a full complement of some 200 men. The number of non-rowing crew may have increased by the time of the Roman Imperial Navy and under campaign conditions the number of marines carried could be considerable (**colour plate 1**).

Sculptural depictions indicate that the Roman navy used both decked (cataphract) and open (aphract) types of trireme. For a while the Greek model, characterised by the upper level of oarsmen accommodated in an outrigger, and the Phoenician type, minus an outrigger and with the topmost bank of oars placed in ports which pierced the hull, existed side by side. Under the Empire, the Phoenician type gradually came to predominate which, because all the oars were placed within the span of the hull, was somewhat wider than the Greek trireme. On many ships, a long box-like projection running from bow to just short of the steering-oars was still provided even though they no longer accommodated oarsmen (**10** & **11**). This not only afforded some protection to the oars and oarsmen in the event of an enemy vessel trying to come alongside and break off the blades, but it also sheltered the rowers from missiles. In addition it could function as a platform from which marines could more easily leap aboard an enemy vessel when alongside.[14] Representations show that in the typical cataphract galley the upper bank of rowers were now completely enclosed by the walls of the hull which rose either to the projection or, where none existed, to the gunwhale. Louvres were incorporated in order to provide ventilation. The deck above (the *katastroma*) is edged by a low bulwark to which shields could be attached for increased protection. There was usually a gap in this towards the bow to allow for the placing of a gangplank when tied up at the quayside.

The Roman naval architects of the early Empire introduced a number of other significant changes to the trireme design. During the first century AD the three-pronged ram of the Hellenistic period was dispensed with, in favour of a single ram (the *rostrum*) like those on Phoenician galleys. This consisted of a robust timber construction attached to the cutwater at the foot of the bow and forming a projection which ended in a point on the waterline 6-7ft in front of the stem. The main component was a massive horizontal timber which was braced in the horizontal plane by diagonals running back to the bow and vertically by a brace sloping up to the stem and, from below, by the keel piece. Other timbers filled in the gaps and the entire construction sheathed with a tightly-fitted bronze casting, the whole estimated as weighing around 484lb (200kg). This was relatively thin but was equipped with three horizontal cutting blades at the fore-end (**10** & **12**). Rather than perforating

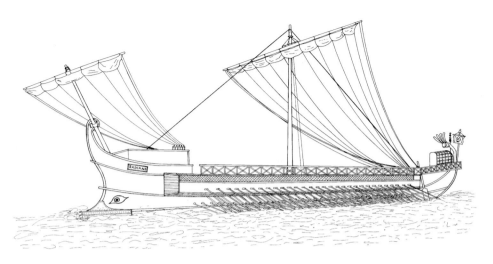

10 *Reconstruction of a flagship trireme – the 'Radians' or 'Resplendent'*

11 *Cross-section of a trireme with* parados *illustrating the arrangement of oarsmen.* After Coates & Morrison

11 *Cross-section of a trireme with* parados *illustrating the arrangement of oarsmen.* After Coates & Morrison

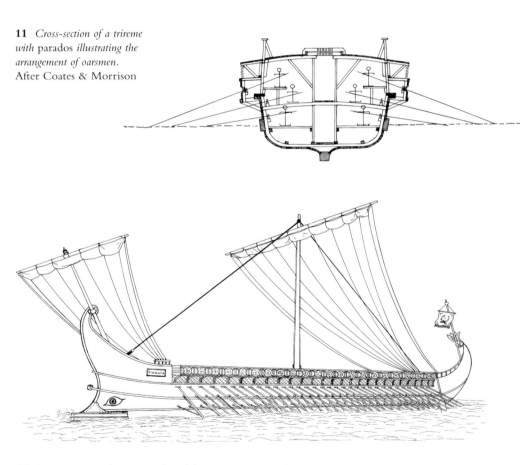

12 *Reconstruction of a trireme adapted for troop transport with projecting deck = the 'Pinnata' or 'Winged'*

the timbers of an enemy ship, which would bring with it the risk of entanglement and possible sinking, the ram may have been intended to spring them apart. A rare preserved example is the Athlit ram dating to the early second century BC found about 12 miles south of Haifa in 1980.[15] The stempost usually had a prominent outward curve as in earlier times but instead of terminating in a simple volute it was often the subject of more elaborate carving; for example in the shape of a sea-serpent's head on one of the ships depicted on the triumphal arch at Orange,[16] or as a helmeted head on that shown on the funeral monument of C. Cartilius Poplicola at Ostia.[17] The point approximately halfway up the stempost where the central wale timbers met was usually elaborated into a secondary ram or *proembolium* terminating in an animal head such as a lion or crocodile. A more obvious innovation was the addition just behind the stempost of a forecastle of considerable size. At the stern, the high, up-curving and fan-shaped *aplustrum* of earlier times was also retained, and in the space beneath it there was a small cabin for the captain and centurion. Nearby were the ship's standards along with a carved image of the *tutela* or patron deity of the ship. As before, a mast carrying a single square sail was positioned amidships, but was now supplemented by an *artemon*, an ancient version of the bowspritsail adopted from the merchant rig of the period and perhaps used chiefly to assist in the steering of the vessel. When not in use the mast was taken down with the mainsail furled around it and stowed on 'crutches' a few feet off the deck as depicted on Trajan's Column.[18] Experience with the *Olympias* suggests that a trireme would have a total weight when fully equipped and crewed of around 50 tons and could reach a maximum speed approaching 8 knots although only for short stints.[19] The height of the deck above the waterline would have been about 9ft (2.75m) and the ship's draught around 4ft (1.2m).[20]

Quadriremes or 'fours' generally had two banks of oars per side with two men per oar and it has been calculated that the total number of oars was around 88. Thus the total number of oarsmen was *c*.176. The four was about the same size as a three although its deck level was a little lower as it had only two banks of oars to accommodate. With a displacement of around 60 tons, its advantages were speed and the ability to carry in the region of 75 troops. The five or quinquireme was a Syracusan development of the three intended principally to replace the great naval skills needed to operate a three successfully in battle with sheer bulk and the number of troops carried. It had three banks of oars per side but with two men per oar in the two upper banks and one per oar in the lowest. Polybius gives a figure of 300 for the total number of oarsmen which would mean 30 oars in each bank per side – 60 oarsmen in the upper and middle banks and 30 in the lower (Polybius, 1.26.7). Its deck was some 10ft (3m) above the waterline and its overall length has been estimated as *c*.145ft (44m). Weighing somewhere in the region of 90 tons it was capable of carrying upwards of 120 troops.[21]

BIREME — *LIBURNA/LIBURNICA*

The *liburna,* the principal warship of the provincial fleets, was based on the light, fast vessel used for piracy in the Adriatic by the Dalmatian tribe known as the Liburni.[22] The distinguishing characteristic of the *liburna* was its two banks of oars with one man per oar, classifying it as a bireme. They were used initially by Roman naval forces in the Republican period chiefly as scouting ships, undertaking reconnaissance in advance of the main fleet and also for maintaining communications. As Appian puts it, 'reconnaissance was carried out on land by cavalry and at sea by liburnians' (*Roman History* 5.103). They came to be used in increasing numbers from the first century BC and they became the main vessel of the provincial fleets where the absence of any major rival sea power obviated the need for larger ships. Liburnians are for example the most common type of warship in the scenes on Trajan's Column which depict the transportation of his campaign army along the Danube by the Pannonian Fleet. In these reliefs the liburnian is shown as a modestly sized aphract galley with no outrigger (**4-7 & 13**). As depicted, the upper bank of oars are worked through a latticework screen, but this is due to the artist sacrificing accuracy in order to give prominence to the figures of the rowers. In fact the oars protruded through slits below the latticework screen which functioned as a ventilation course.[23] The size and form of the *liburna* could vary, however, and those shown operating on the Danube may well have been among the smallest and simplest manifestations. Decked or cataphract liburnians also existed like the example shown on a tomb relief of around AD 100 in the British Museum.[24] A comment by Propertius confirms that *liburnae* were equipped with rams (*rostrata*) while both Appian and Aristotle refer to the sharply pointed form of their prows; these vessels were clearly built for speed, as befitted their early employment for piracy and reconnaissance.[25] Although chiefly oar-powered, like the trireme and most other warships the liburnian was also equipped with a square main sail and a much smaller foresail.

The seagoing biremes used by the British and German Fleets were almost certainly among the largest and most robust examples of *liburnae* (**14**). The majority were probably decked to protect the rowers (perhaps more from the weather and swell than the enemy), having a length approaching 100ft (30.5m) and a beam of around 18ft (5.5m). They had a complement of around 100 oarsmen accompanied by a force of marines which varied in strength according to the circumstances. Such a vessel would have had a displacement of around 35 tons. Such was the predominance of the liburnian that by the fourth century the term *liburna* came to be used to refer to any sizeable warship.

MONOREMES — *MYOPARO* AND *SCAPHA*

The *myoparo* was another type of light but swift vessel favoured by pirates which was adapted by the Roman navy. In Appian's account of the wars with Mithidates we hear of Cilician pirates hired by the Pontic king who, as they

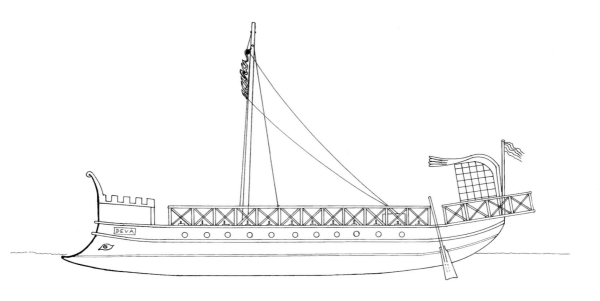

13 *Reconstruction of a river bireme – the 'Deva' or 'Dee'*

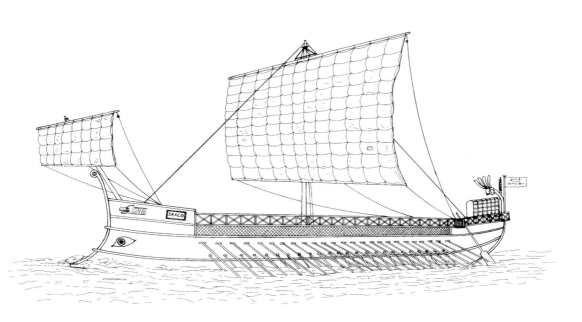

14 *Reconstruction of a seagoing bireme – the Liburnian 'Draco' or 'Dragon'*

became more successful, graduated from small boats (*scaphae*) to *myoparones* and then to biremes and triremes.[26] Thus they were clearly larger than *scaphae* but smaller than standard warships. The only representation of one, considered to be unreliable, occurs on the Althiburus mosaic.[27]

Scaphae (also *picta*) were longboats which accompanied and/or were towed behind the larger warships. Caesar refers to them in the context of the first landing in Britain when he ordered them to be manned in order to assist with the disembarkation of troops from the much larger and taller *onerariae* which, because of their considerable draught, had to stand some distance off shore.[28] The presence of *scaphae* implies in turn that quadriremes or quinquiremes were also among the vessels of Caesar's fleet. While scouting and reconnaissance were obviously among their functions, another would have been the carrying of personnel and supplies to and from land on those occasions when the mother ship had to anchor some distance off shore. Fully manned, they may also have assisted the manoeuvring of larger vessels in harbours and other confined spaces by towing. Another term used to describe a scouting vessel was *speculatoria*. This seems to have indicated the function of the ship rather than a special type. Commenting on the Roman navy in the early fifth century AD the writer Vegetius says:

> As for size, the smallest warships have a single bank of oars . . . . Associated with the larger warships are scouting skiffs, which have around twenty oarsmen per side, and which the Britons call *Pictae* (painted ships). These are intended to locate and at times intercept the passage of enemy ships and to discover by observation their approach or intentions. To prevent these scout vessels being detected through the brightness of their appearance, their sails and rigging are dyed Venetian Blue, which resembles the ocean waves, and even the wax used to pay the ship's sides is made that colour. The sailors and marines wear Venetian Blue uniforms also, so as to escape detection more easily not only by day but also by night.
>
> *Epitoma Rei Militaris* 4.37

Some of a group of partially preserved vessels found on the ancient foreshore at Mainz in 1981 illustrate a variant of the smallest class of warship used for patrol duties on major rivers and coastal waters.[29] Classified as Mainz Type A, this was a long, narrow open boat propelled by both oars and sail (**90**). Approximately 69ft (21m) long by 9ft (2.7m) wide, it had a mast set well forward in a heavy frame and could accommodate 15 pairs of oarsmen. It was constructed to a typically sturdy Romano-Celtic specification in which large, close-set frames were assembled to which the planks were then attached. Although the planks were joined edge-to-edge, they were not carefully shaped to fit snugly together nor were mortice-and-tenon joints employed as in the

Mediterranean tradition. Instead, caulking with Stockholm tar was employed to render the hull watertight. With a shallow draught of about 18in (45cm) these vessels were lightweight, fast and highly manoeuvrable. They would also have been cheap, easy and quick to build and would therefore have been ideally suited to the scouting, patrol and occasional interception role described by Vegetius. The construction of two of the vessels was dated by dendrochronology to AD 375/6, one later having been repaired in AD 385 and again in 394.[30] Thought to have been abandoned when Mainz was evacuated in 406, they had presumably been operated by the legionary garrison as the *Classis Germanica* was based at Cologne.

Tactics, weapons and protection

Direct ramming of an enemy vessel or running alongside in an attempt to snap off its oars and disable some of the rowers were the two basic forms of attack, which had been used for centuries. The use of missiles to inflict casualties at a distance, usually before closing for boarding, was equally ancient. Hand-thrown javelins, sling-shot and arrows were among the first employed but could be countered relatively easily by erecting light wooden screens and covers. By the third century BC collapsible wooden towers, which could be quickly erected or dismantled fore and aft, began to be used to give the archers and missile-throwers a clearer field of fire down onto the enemy's deck.[31] In expert hands, even simple missiles could prove quite effective, as the captains of the Roman ships ranged against the Cathaginians discovered when their crewmen were picked off in increasing numbers by the enemy's Balearic slingers. This was one of the reasons for the Romans' invention of the so-called *corvus* or 'raven'. Essentially this was a deck-mounted boarding bridge 4ft (1.2m) wide and at least 18ft (5.5m) long with a sharp iron spike at the end (the 'raven's' beak). When dropped onto the deck of an enemy ship it stuck fast in the deck timbers and prevented it from breaking away. The Roman legionaries were thus able to rush onto the enemy vessel where their superior fighting skills would usually prevail.[32] The device, however, did not stay in use very long; possibly it made the ships top-heavy and liable to capsize in rough weather. Grappling hooks were a more conventional way of ensnaring the enemy and later these were fired by catapult.[33]

Cutting the rigging by use of a sharp, curved blade attached to the end of a long pole and known as the *falx* was another useful device for disabling, or at least slowing down, the opponent's ships. This proved very effective in Caesar's encounter with the high, sail-powered ships of the Veneti in 56 BC and was still in use four centuries later.[34] Another device – known as the *asser* according to Vegetius – consisted of a long pole with an iron point at both ends which was hung by ropes from the rigging. Once alongside an enemy this could be swung around to cause mayhem and injury amongst his crew. The double-ended axe was a weapon favoured by marines both for its effectiveness in close quarter fighting in confined spaces and for cutting rigging, steering-gear ropes and grapnel-lines.

The invention of catapult-based artillery had – as one might say – a considerable impact upon ship design. Artillery-propelled bolts, javelins and rocks could penetrate the thin hulls of warships and this was a contributory factor in the development of heavier ships with greater protection for the rowers, usually achieved by the boxing-in of the outriggers. They could also tip the balance of power in favour of smaller vessels in an engagement if they were sufficiently well armed. Thus, during the sea battle off Massilia in 49 BC, a warship in the fleet of the Caesarian commander Decimus Brutus came alongside a Massiliot vessel whereupon it was assailed by fishing boats which had been fitted out with catapults; it suffered severe losses.[35] The general run of such machines probably had an effective range of 600–1,000ft (200–300m) and regular practice would have been necessary to achieve and maintain proficiency. They would also have required frequent maintenance because of the adverse effects of the maritime environment on the mechanisms. One no doubt much feared projectile occasionally fired by catapults was the container filled with either hot coals and/or flaming pitch.[36] Sometimes iron pots of blazing material were slung from the ends of long poles projecting out over the bows which could be dropped on the deck of an enemy vessel.[37] Artillery could also be very useful for providing covering fire when attempting to disembark troops on a hostile shore, Caesar's first landing in Britain being a good example.[38] During the Hellenistic period, heavier artillery pieces were frequently deployed in laying siege to coastal cities, for example Alexander at Tyre.[39]

Transports

While some of the larger warships in the Roman navy could carry significant numbers of troops, the transport of large numbers of soldiers required special arrangements. It was common practice, at least in earlier periods, for triremes to be converted to transports for both infantry and cavalry by reducing the number of rowers.[40] For his hastily mounted first expedition to Britain in 55 BC, Caesar commandeered nearly 100 ships from the territory of the Morini and neighbouring coastal districts to act as transports (*onerariae*), 18 of which carried the cavalry force about 500 strong.[41] These were accompanied by his fleet of warships. Some of these transports were driven back by unfavourable winds, while those that made it across the Channel had to anchor some distance from the shore because of their considerable draught. These were clearly sailing ships and their unsuitability for mounting a cross-Channel landing nearly brought Caesar's adventure to disaster. The modified form of

Venetic vessel which he personally designed for the following year proved far more suitable as a troop transport. This was broader, had a lower freeboard, and was powered by both oars and sail.[42]

The remains of seagoing vessels and boats used for riverine traffic found throughout north-west European waters, examples of which are cited later on in this chapter, conform in terms of their general characteristics to the vessels of the Veneti described by Caesar. They have a hull built of stout planks laid edge-to-edge but, in contradistinction to the Mediterranean tradition, the planks were not edge-jointed but secured by large iron nails to massive and closely-spaced framing timbers.[43] The nails typically were bent back on themselves and the point hammered into the frame. The hulls were either flat-bottomed with no keel or built with the central plank slightly thicker than the rest. This enabled them to move easily through shallow water. It also meant that, compared with a deeply-keeled vessel, not only could they be drawn up onto a beach with ease, but also because they sat upright on the shore, they were less susceptible to rapid inundation if a storm should break. Vessels such as these have been seen as representing a distinctive and long-lived tradition of shipbuilding which has been designated as 'Romano-Celtic'.[44] The advantages of such vessels as military transports, especially in campaign conditions where landings were made on an open shore, would have been obvious.

Caesar's experiences and the advantages of the native ship types would not have been lost on those responsible for organising the invasion force of AD 43. We do not have any direct information about the type of transports employed but they would undoubtedly have been based on the Caesarean derivative of Venetic ships. This conclusion is supported indirectly by Tacitus' description of the fleet constructed for Germanicus' naval expedition from the Rhine to the Ems in AD 15:

> A thousand ships were considered sufficient. They were constructed quickly. Some were short and broad with little poop or prow capable of withstanding a rough sea. Some were flat-bottomed, allowing them to be run aground undamaged. Many others were equipped with a rudder each side so that the oarsmen could suddenly reverse direction and land them on either side of a river. Many had decks to support catapults which could also serve to carry horses and supplies.

Annals 2.5

Vessels similar to these would have transported the invasion force across the Channel in 43 and then *inter alia* supported Vespasian's 'combined ops' campaign across the south of England and into the south-west peninsula. Later still they would have been an essential element in the fleet used by Agricola in the conquest of northern Britain.

Merchant galleys/naval auxiliaries

For some commodities transported by sea – perishable foodstuffs for instance – a swift journey was essential and so merchant ships equipped with oars instead of sails alone were developed (**colour plate 5**). Speed and the ability to reach their destination even if the wind dissipated or became adverse also made them well suited for the carriage of passengers and urgent messages. In addition, their design meant they were easily adaptable for military use and they often served as naval auxiliaries. Merchant galleys were broader than the thoroughbred warships having a length to width ratio in the region of 6:1 instead of 10:1. Various types are known, the larger having a concave prow with a projecting forefoot or cutwater and the smaller having a rounded or straight prow.

ACTUARIA

Naves actuariae, literally 'driven' (as opposed to sail) ships, was a term (derived from the Greek *akatos*) applied by the Romans to all forms of merchant galley.[45] However, it was also used to refer to a particular type of large galley powered by up to 50 oarsmen (25 per side in a single bank) and distinguished by its possession of a projecting forefoot and a curved prow.[46] Due to its size and characteristics, this specific type of *actuaria* was often adapted for military use. Livy refers to *actuariae* used as landing-craft at the siege of Syracuse in 212 BC while Caesar designed a variation of this vessel type for his second assault on Britain in 54 BC.[47] These *vectoria navigia* 'transport ships' were broader and lower than usual to ease loading and hauling ashore and were equipped with both sail and oars. A few years later Caesar's general Vatinius had to assemble a scratch fleet at Brindisi to go to the aid of his master on the other side of the Adriatic. Lacking conventional warships he fitted out a number of *actuariae* with rams.[48]

LEMBUS

Lembus, from the Greek *lembos*, was used in the same way as *actuaria*, having both a wide and a narrow sense. Originally it was applied more or less indiscriminately to harbour boats, fishing smacks, ship's boats and rivercraft. By the third century BC it had also come to be used of a particular type of vessel similar to the *actuaria* in that it was the largest in this general grouping, had a projecting forefoot and a concave prow, and was frequently used as a naval auxiliary.[49] Some had as many as 50 oarsmen, sometimes disposed in two banks.[50] Like *actuariae* their chief advantage was speed.

CERCERUS AND CYBAEA

These two craft were similar types of cargo galley. They could apparently vary considerably in size although the seagoing versions of both exceeded *c.*65ft (20m) in length. The *cybaea* was broader than the *cercerus* with a blunter bow as its name 'box-like' implies.[51]

PHASELUS

The *phaselus* was a long, narrow vessel as its name, meaning 'bean-pod', indicates. Like many other craft it could vary in size, some being little more than skiffs and others capable of voyaging around the Mediterranean like that on which Catullus travelled from the Black Sea to Italy.[52] Transporting people rather than cargo, Sallust refers to one example carrying a complete cohort of men.[53] Like *actuariae* and *lembi* they were powered by both oars and sail and could be adapted for military use.[54]

CELOX

As its name implies (*celox* meaning 'fast'), the *celox* was renowned for its speed. Its original Greek name *keles* meant 'racehorse'. Among the vessels represented on the Althiburus mosaic it was smaller than a *lembus* and had a straight prow. Particularly useful for carrying despatches and passengers it probably had a rowing crew of 20 or fewer.

Sailing ships/freighters

The general Latin term for a seagoing cargo or passenger ship was, appropriately, *navis oneraria*, meaning 'ship of burden' which, because all true cargo vessels were sail driven, also indicated a sailing ship.[55] The only named type known to have been in general use was the *corbita*, meaning 'basket', a name derived from the large, rounded shape of its hull. Like warships, sailing vessels are depicted in reliefs, mosaics and wall-paintings, but in addition there is also the evidence from a number of excavated wrecks (**15**).[56] Information on cargoes has also survived in the form of inscriptions and written references from which the tonnage of ancient freighters can, within broad margins, be determined.[57] Although, strictly speaking, they were not part of the Roman navy, merchant ships and shippers were contracted, or in certain circumstances compelled, to transport military supplies and equipment. Consequently, because of the important role they played in military logistics – especially as regards an island province like Britain – a brief description of the vessels seems appropriate.

Some sailing ships had a concave prow with a jutting cutwater while others had a very rounded bow of traditional form (**colour plate 4**).[58] Ancient images of freighters in general indicate that they were broad vessels with large hulls as befitted their function. As to size, the majority were between 50 and 120ft long (15 x 37m) and had a carrying capacity of 60 to 150 tons.[59] Ships of 300 to 500 tons were not unusual, at least in the Mediterranean, and a few even exceeded 1,000 tons. These were for the most part engaged in the grain supply to Rome. Whatever their size, the length to width ratio was usually of the order of 6:1, instead of the 10:1 ratio typical of a warship. As can be seen in the reliefs of a sarcophagus found at Portus, and now in the Copenhagen Museum, the sides

15 *Image of a merchant ship reproduced from a sarcophagus relief in the National Museum, Beirut*

of sailing vessels were notable for the prominent wales which protected the hulls from damage inflicted by rubbing against quaysides.[60] Near the stern was a deckhouse which, according to the size of the vessel, accommodated the galley, quarters for the owner, his agent and/or the captain, and one or more cabins for passengers travelling 'first class' – the other passengers either camped out on deck or were given space in the dark and usually unpleasant areas below. The roof of this structure acted as a poop deck where the helmsman stood, who from his lofty position could see over the bow while operating the steering oar. The sternpost usually terminated in a high curving goose-head, the bird sacred to the Egyptian moon-goddess, Isis, patron deity of seafarers. Quite often a small gallery was built out around the sternpost to house a modest shrine to the goddess, and sometimes there was an equivalent structure in the bow to protect the hands working the sails. The normal seagoing rig consisted of a foresail or *artemon*, a single square mainsail, and a topsail or *siparum*.[61] The largest ships were equipped with additional masts and sails. During the Roman period the triangular 'lateen' sail, which allowed a ship to sail more directly into the wind, came into general use. This device could well have been of particular value to vessels operating in British waters and the North Sea. Most ships of any size usually had an oared longboat (*scapha*) towed astern.[62] Capable of serving as a lifeboat in emergencies, it was perhaps most frequently used to tow the mother ship when entering or leaving congested ports.

Due to the more violent tides and currents, fewer wrecks have been or are likely to be found in northern waters. Some are indicated only by the scattered cargo they were carrying. This applies to the Pudding Pan Rock wreck off the Kent coast near Whistable where a vessel carrying a considerable amount of samian pottery among its cargo came to grief at some time in the second half of the second century.[63] Pottery, coins and other artefacts found on the small island of Nornour in the Scillies may have originated from another shipwreck, or possibly two successive losses.[64] There are, however, two examples which give us some idea of the sort of modestly-sized sailing vessel which was probably typical of those that plied the seas around Britain. One of these was discovered in the Thames at London in 1910 on the site of the new County Hall (**16**). Known unsurprisingly as the County Hall ship, this was a seagoing merchantman of middling size dating to the end of the third century.[65] It was of carvel construction with oak planks set edge-to-edge but without the mortice-and-tenon joints common in Mediterranean ships. Upwards of 60ft (18.25m) long and about 16ft (5m) wide it had a rounded hull and a draught of around 6ft (1.8m). Its carrying capacity was probably between 50 and 100 tons depending on the nature of the cargo (**17**). The second example, a Gallo-Roman merchantman, was found in the approaches to the harbour at St Peter Port, Guernsey, and was excavated in the late 1980s. Typical of the sturdy vessels of the Romano-Celtic tradition of shipbuilding, this too was built of thick oak planks secured to strong frames. It was flat-bottomed, had a single mast positioned well forward of amidships, while pottery, tiles and a hearth at the rear of the ship are thought to derive from a deckhouse.[66]

Estimates of the speed of ancient vessels understandably vary. From the literary and other evidence he collected and analysed, Lionel Casson concluded that an average sailing speed in favourable conditions was probably around 5 knots (9kph). In a similar exercise, Sippel estimated the average speed at between 4.5 and 6 knots (8.3-11kph) in good conditions or 2 to 2.5 knots (3.7-4.6kph) in unfavourable circumstances. Others have estimated maximum speeds approaching 11 knots depending on conditions.[67] The overall length of voyages was of course very much affected by prevailing winds. Thus, while it took Rome's grain fleet nine days to sail from Puteoli to Alexandria (1,000 nautical miles), the return voyage against the northwesterlies dominant in the summer sailing season lasted one to two months.[68]

The range of cargoes carried was considerable: building materials, ingots of metal, wine, olive oil and a wide range of foodstuffs. For ease of handling, grain was transported in sacks while wine and olive oil were carried in long, narrow cylindrical *amphorae*. As evidenced by a number of wrecks the *amphorae* were stored in layers, often as many as four or five, with the points of those in one layer fitted in between the necks of those in the layer below.[69] Twigs and branches were commonly used as packing or dunnage between *amphorae* to prevent breakages. In the north-west provinces where there was a greater availability of timber, barrels were often used as containers for wine instead, as depicted in the famous relief of a river craft on a funerary monument at Neumagen.[70]

16 *The remains of the 'County Hall' ship as found.* Copyright MoL

17 *Reconstruction model of 'County Hall' ship with lighter alongside.*
Photograph, Jon Bailey, Museum of London Archaeology Service, Copyright MoL

Coastal and river craft

Coastal vessels (*oraria naves*) were understandably somewhat smaller than seagoing ships. A single-masted rig was the norm judging from the surviving depictions, while named types of craft restricted to coastal work alone are the *caudicaria* and *prosumia*. Modest-sized examples of ship-types already mentioned also undertook coastal work, including merchant galleys such as *actuariae*, *celoces*, *cercuri*, *cybaeae* and *lembi*.[71] Not having to rely on favourable winds, these were a natural choice for coastal trade. Vessels in this class exhibited far more regional variation in form and construction than their larger counterparts. This is demonstrated by the remains of three vessels found in the Thames. The County Hall ship, the largest of the three, has just been described.[72] If there was an insufficient depth of water to allow seagoing vessels like this to tie up at the quayside, or only so for short periods, then they would have anchored in mid-stream to have their cargo offloaded onto lighters – known variously as *levamenta*, *lenunculi* or *barcae*.[73] Another wreck discovered in London, at New Guys House, Bermondsey, in 1959, belongs to this type. Unlike the County Hall ship, this was clinker-built with planks nailed to a skeleton formed of keel and frames and with the joints carefully caulked with a mixture of hazel twigs and some type of root. Also approximately 60ft (18.25m) long and with a beam of around 14ft (4.25m) this was flat-bottomed and therefore could rest on the foreshore at low tide. It was about a century older than the County Hall vessel.[74]

Yet a third vessel found in the Thames at London, the so-called Blackfriars I ship discovered in 1962, was also flat-bottomed and of a similar length but was somewhat broader at around 22ft (6.7m) and with a draught of at least 7ft (2.1m). Its mast was located well forward of amidships as with many vessels in the Romano-Celtic tradition and it probably had a cargo capacity of around 50 tons (**18**). Like the County Hall ship this was of carvel construction. In use during the second century and ideal for river work, it had also voyaged around the coast, for the planks of its hull were riddled with holes made by the *teredo*, a saltwater wood-boring worm.[75] Oak appears to have been in widespread use for ships plying northern waters, presumably because it was so plentiful. As sea conditions were rougher than in the Mediterranean, it is also likely that the design of merchant vessels here continued to incorporate many of the features of the Venetic ships of Caesar's day; most particularly their very sturdy construction, high prows and sterns, sails of hide rather than linen, and anchor cables not of rope but of iron chain.[76]

The round-hulled *caudicaria* served on rivers as well as being used for coastal duties. Employed on the Tiber, they are among the best documented. They were equipped with a sprit-mast set forward of amidships which could double as a towing mast.[77] A line was run from the team on the riverbank over a block at the top of this mast and then down to the stern where it was secured, often to a capstan, which meant these craft could winch themselves upstream along

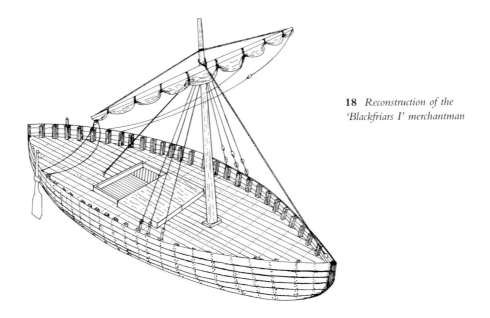

18 *Reconstruction of the 'Blackfriars I' merchantman*

sections where the going was particularly arduous for the teams. There were many different types of smaller craft in use on rivers such as the *linter*, the *stlatta* and the *lusoria*. As to the last of these, by the fourth century AD *lusoria* had come to denote the small, light galley which the Roman navy regularly used for the flotillas it maintained on rivers such as the Rhine and Danube.[78] These were of the Mainz Type A kind of vessel described above, the design of which may well have copied the ships used by Franks, Saxons and others. Barges were of course the most common type of working boat used for estuarine and riverine traffic. Quite a number of examples are known from excavations on the Continent, the most famous being the groups of such vessels found at Zwammerdam in the Netherlands and Pommeroeul in Belgium.[79] These ranged in size from 30ft long by 3ft wide (10 x 1m) to 110ft long by 13ft wide (34 x 4m) and were built of thick oak planks nailed to frames. The mast in the larger examples was capable of supporting a sail. A more recent discovery closer to home of a vessel in this general category is the Barland's Farm boat found near Magor, Monmouthshire, on the north side of the Severn estuary.[80] Measuring approximately 37 by 10ft overall (11.4 x 3.2m) it is dated by dendrochronology to the end of the third century and seems to have had a short life.

General sailing and operation, miscellaneous equipment

Under normal circumstances, both naval and mercantile operations were restricted to the period from late spring to early autumn. Vegetius states that the best period for sailing is from 27 May to 14 September and that the outside limits are 10 March to 10 November.[81] Ancient vessels were not well equipped to deal with winter storms and rough seas, while reduced visibility raised navigational problems in an age lacking the mariner's compass. Out of season traffic was restricted to the carrying of important despatches and the transport of vital military supplies. In emergencies, military campaigns involving the fleet were undertaken in winter, such as the crossing to Britain by Constans in the winter of 340. The restricted sailing season obviously had important ramifications for military supply logistics with the collection and transportation of goods having to be compressed into a period of a few months. In the case of the island province of Britain, the sudden installation of a massive military force probably created a situation where the importation of basic supplies such as grain continued to be of critical importance for a considerable period until such time as its agricultural system was capable of producing surpluses of the required quantity. Navigating the Channel successfully on a regular basis would of course have required a detailed knowledge of its tidal streams, prevailing winds, and localised hazards.[82]

Usually equipped with one main sail (*velum*), ancient vessels were designed for voyaging with the wind astern or on the quarters. When the occasion demanded however they could 'tack', which involved following a zigzag course by slanting the sail around to take the wind first on one bow and then on the other. The rigging was sufficiently sophisticated (including halyards, brails, sheets and lifts and both forestays and backstays) to allow the sail to be lowered and raised quickly and to enable different portions of it to be shortened when a strong wind blew from a particular quarter. Blocks or pulleys were very similar in size and shape to their modern equivalents. Some were entirely of wood while others had metal sheaves and axles. Lines were made fast using belaying pins. Esparto grass, especially that from Spain, was the favoured material for making cordage although hemp, papyrus and flax were also used.[83] Sails were usually made of rectangular lengths of linen sewn together and reinforced at the corners with leather.[84] Horizontal lines or strips of leather were spaced at regular intervals on the front of the sail which intersected at right-angles with the brails to form a chequerboard pattern (**15**). The sail, normally left white, could be dyed for specific purposes. Purple for example was used to distinguish a royal vessel or the flagship. The leading face of the sail could also be emblazoned with devices and/or inscriptions like that of Trajan's flagship on the Tigris which bore the imperial title and royal titles set out in gold letters.[85]

Oared warships and galleys also used their sails as much as possible to ease the burden on the *remiges*. In normal circumstances when rowing was necessary, only a proportion of the oars would be manned and the crew would be divided into squads to row in shifts. It was only in battle conditions or when urgent messages had to be conveyed that all the oars would be manned and even then, of course, maximum speed could only be maintained for short periods as the rowers needed frequent rest periods.[86]

There was a varied collection of gear that ships of all types had to carry. The Inventories of the Athenian dockyards provide useful information about the range of items regularly carried, and presumably ships in the Roman fleets would have been similarly equipped. This could include heavy coverings (probably hide) which could be hung on the sides as protection against missiles and grapnels, lighter covers to keep off spray and act as awnings, rigging and sail, landing ladders and gangways, poles, a spare set of the straining ropes or *hypozomata*, replacement blocks, mooring lines and anchor cables and, of course, the anchor of which there were usually at least two. By the Roman period anchors of the type we would recognise had emerged and were usually made of a combination of wood and iron with curved arms. Sometimes lead was added. Every ship also carried a sounding line to check depths. Its lead weight had a hollow underside which could be filled with wax or grease to bring up samples from the seabed.[87]

Identification, decoration and signalling

In the names and markings it applied to its warships, Rome largely continued the naval traditions of the Classical Greek and Hellenistic periods. No differentiation between types of ship or fleets was exercised, the same kinds of name were employed universally and the same name could be used for a vessel of any size. Also, unlike modern practice, names could be of either gender. Names that celebrated the appearance or reputed qualities of a ship were commonplace: *Pinnata* 'winged' (i.e. speedy), *Armata* 'armed', *Fortuna* 'lucky', *Triumphus* 'triumph' and *Victoria* 'victory'. Another was *Radians* 'gleaming' and this indeed was the name of one of the triremes attached to the *Classis Britannica*, recorded on a relief found in the fleet headquarters at Boulogne.[88] The benefits of Roman rule were also regularly employed: *Clementia*, *Concordia* 'harmony', *Constantia* 'constancy', *Fides*, *Justitia*, *Libertas*, *Pax*, *Pietas* 'dutiful conduct', *Providentia* 'foresight', *Salus* 'soundness', *Spes* 'hope' and *Virtus* 'courage'. The names of animals with appropriate characteristics were popular both real – *Aquila* 'eagle', *Crocodilus*, *Taurus* 'bull' – and mythological – *Draco* 'dragon', *Gryps* 'griffin'. Mythological figures and the lesser deities also featured: *Castor* and *Pollux*, *Diomedes*, *Perseus* and *Hercules* along with *Cupido* (Venus' son), *Nereis* (the sea-nymph) and *Triton* (the merman). Naming ships after the senior deities was very common: *Apollo*, *Aesculapius*, *Ceres*, *Diana*, *Juno*, *Jupiter*, *Liber Pater*, *Mars*, *Mercurius*, *Minerva*, *Neptunus*, *Sol*, *Venus*, and *Vesta* are all represented along with the Egyptian deities *Ammon* and *Isis*. *Augustus* is the only known example of naming after a ruler. Major rivers occur such as *Danuvius*, *Nilus*, *Tiberus*, *Tigris*, *Eufrates* along with *Padus* 'Po' and *Rhenus* 'Rhine' as well as *Oceanus*. *Dacicus* and *Parthicus* celebrate the campaigns against Dacia and Parthia respectively while *Athenonike* 'Athena's victory' commemorates Athens' earlier command of the Mediterranean. Instruments of war also make an appearance as witnessed by *Clipeus* 'shield' and *Quadriga* 'chariot'.[89]

The names given to merchantmen were similar in type. Deities predominate in the preserved examples and these mostly belong to the Greek pantheon as the majority of vessels known are Greek. *Apollo, Athena, Artemis, Aphrodite, Demeter, Dionysus, Hermes, Nik,* and *Poseidon* all occur while *Isis* – especially revered by seafarers – and *Dioscuri* were particularly popular. *Asklepius* (Roman *Aesculapius*), the god of healing, achieved great prominence under the Roman Empire and was perhaps chosen as a ship name because he could ensure the soundness of the vessel. *Heracles* and *Tyche* 'Lady Luck' also featured along with the Egyptian deities *Ammon* and *Serapis*. From the Roman pantheon we have *Jupiter* and *Juno*, and from mythology *Europa*. *Fortuna Redux* 'Good Luck that ensures a safe return home' may have been another. Some vessels were named after cities. One such is the enormous grain-transport *Alexandris*, previously the *Syracusia* built by Hiero II c.240 BC, renamed when he gave it to Ptolemy of Egypt. *Halion Griphos* 'sea-fishnet' and *Thalia* 'abundance' are examples of more prosaic names.

The ships plying British waters would have carried names similar to or identical with those listed above. There were probably local variants some perhaps named after British and Gallic ports or cities (the *Londinium*, the *Dubris*, the *Deva* and the *Gesoriacum* seem very plausible possibilities), others after major rivers (the *Tamesis* and the *Sabrina* meaning the Thames and the Severn), and yet others after Romano-British divinities (the *Brigantia*, the *Maponus* or the *Epona*?). Apart from the *Radians* mentioned above we know the name of only one other warship in the *Classis Britannica* – the *Ammilla Augusta* (**46**).

The identity of a warship was emblazoned on either side of its prow by means of an appropriate device or emblem known as the *parasemon* which could be carved, painted or in the form of a bronze plaque. This was distinct from the carved figure – usually an animal – on the prow. On merchantmen it was positioned on both sides of the stempost. It may also have been indicated in writing but this is uncertain. Also painted on the prow was a pair of mystic eyes to enable the ship to see its way safely and avoid hidden dangers. The sternpost or *aphlaston*, curving up above the poop and ending in four or five radiating fingers, afforded additional space for carvings, some of which might be related to the ship's identity. Warships displayed military insignia here while on both warships and merchant vessels alike a statue of the patron divinity or *tutela* was placed near the sternpost. Victory holding a wreath was a popular subject. On merchantmen of any size the sternpost usually terminated in a goose head, often gilded for added effect. Its popularity is explained by the fact that the goose was sacred to the Egyptian moon-goddess, Isis, and was regarded as the protecting deity of seafarers.

In addition to the protective exterior coating of pitch, or pitch and wax, many ships were painted above the waterline. The paint used was encaustic, that is wax melted to the point where it could be applied using a brush to which colouring had been added. Pliny mentions white, purple, blue, yellow, brown, green and red.[90] Brighter colours were employed for particular decorative effects. That brightly painted vessels were commonplace is also clear from their representation in mosaics and frescoes although the brightness of the decoration may be due more to the artist's imagination than reality. If left unpainted the hull remained black from its coating of pitch. The decorative schemes on warships were probably more restrained than those of merchant vessels. Sometimes it was used for camouflage, as revealed by Vegetius in his description of the scouting-vessels of the fourth century, used to detect sea-raiders whose rigging, sails and hull-wax were coloured Venetian Blue to blend in with the colour of the sea.[91]

The development of large fleets brought with it the need to devise systems for distinguishing friendly from hostile vessels at a distance, for ship to ship communication especially in combat, and for the sending of messages from ship to shore and vice versa. Flags, pennants and, at night, lights were used from the earliest days as a means of ship identification. It was already common practice in Classical Greek times for warships to fly a standard indicating the navy or fleet to which they belonged. Flagships flew a special pennant to indicate the admiral's presence. In the Roman navy this was known as the *vexillum* or *insigne* and was usually flown from either the mast, when cruising, or at the bow or stern, during action.[92] A special sign was used as the signal for going into action. This could be a flag of a particular colour, usually purple, or a gilded shield. Merchant vessels also flew identification pennants and flags, usually at the stern and the masthead. The single square sail of a warship could be different colours for particular purposes: purple to designate a royal vessel or a flagship,[93] black for mourning, sea green or blue for camouflage,[94] or a variety of colours for decorative effect.[95] Similarly, the leading face of the sail could be emblazoned with devices and/or inscriptions. For example, Trajan's flagship on the Tigris had the imperial name and titles picked out in gold lettering at the top of its sail.[96] Every ship carried lights at night, an absolute necessity when travelling in convoy to avoid both collision and dispersal. For his expedition against Carthage in 204 BC Scipio gave the instruction that 'warships were to carry one light each, transports two, and so as to be easily distinguishable the flagship would display three' (Livy 29.25.11). As the flagship usually took the lead at night its identification was especially important: 'Toward evening [Caesar] set sail, instructing the rest of his captains to follow the lantern of his ship' (Appian *Bell. Civ.* 2.89).

Ship to ship communication was achieved by the use of flags of various colours and sizes. These were flown from various positions on the ship while others could be used for signalling by semaphore. The Greek writer Leo gives a description of the ancient method of semaphore which is indistinguishable from that of the modern era: 'Signal with the flag by holding it upright, dipping it to right or left and then shifting it back again to right or left, waving it, raising it, lowering it, removing it from sight, changing it, switching it around by orienting the head now in one direction and now another, or using flags or different shapes and colours as was the practice among the ancients' (*peri thal.* 46 – Dain 30). There are a number of references in the sources to the use of shields for giving signals.[97] The contexts imply the short-range communication of simple signals by moving the shield to different positions on the mast, but it is also possible that burnished shields were used as heliographs. If so, the range could have been extended to many miles. The opportunities for signalling by heliograph in northern waters must obviously have been far more limited than in the Mediterranean. It may however have featured among the array of signalling devices available to the *Classis Britannica* both for communications between ships and between lookout stations on the coast and vessels at sea. By far the most common method of signal transmission ashore was of course the fire-beacon, frequently organised in chains. This was an uncomplicated, fast and reliable means of communicating a simple signal over long distances and as such was very useful for conveying an alert to danger. Producing both smoke and light beacons could be operational 24 hours a day. The operators needed no specialist skills, although for the system to work properly they had to be reliable and trustworthy. The fourth-century chain of signal-stations along the Yorkshire coast is a good example (**98-104**). Located on prominent headlands they were well placed to spot sea-raiders, signal their approach to sections of the fleet based further along the coast, and perhaps communicate with the latter once they had put to sea.[98]

Fleet bases and other shore installations

Like any permanent navy the Roman *classes* needed a considerable terrestrial infrastructure to support them in order to maintain their operational efficiency and effectiveness. Naval bases were established at carefully selected locations and, where necessary, major engineering works were undertaken to create a sheltered anchorage. For many towns and cities on the coast the possession of well organised harbour facilities was vital not only to facilitate and encourage maritime trade but also because a considerable proportion of their food supplies was brought in by ship. Rome and her corn supply is the prime example. With a restricted sailing season food had to arrive, be unloaded and placed in storage with maximum efficiency. The same was true, of course, for military bases, often sited in newly won territory where even basic supplies had to be imported. This explains the massive investment in harbour works by the Roman state, including such ambitious enterprises as the construction of enormous artificial harbour basins at Ostia, first by Claudius and then by Trajan.[99] Deploying their engineering, construction and organisational skills, the Romans were able to create harbours where none had existed before. New channels and basins were excavated and their sides revetted with masonry to form solid quaysides where ships could tie up easily and their cargoes could be unloaded quickly with the aid of simple cranes;[100] breakwaters were built to create sheltered anchorages protected from storms; and nearby the infrastructure of warehouses needed to store supplies. Masonry construction using large blocks of dressed stone was the traditional method employed for quaysides and similar structures at major sites, but the Romans could also deploy their mastery of concrete in this area, including the type made with volcanic sand known as pozzolana which would set under water and was thus ideally suited for use in the construction of harbour works and bridge piers.[101] The greater availability of timber in the northern provinces meant this was equally likely to be used in harbour works especially by the military as their facilities, at least to begin with, often had to be built in haste.

Each naval base or *navalia* contained accommodation for the crews as well as the essential shipyard where vessels were not only built but also repaired, maintained and replenished. Ancient warships in particular needed regular and intensive maintenance. Usually designed for speed above all else, the regular removal of marine growths to retain the smooth profile of the hull was essential, while the fact that they were less robust than merchant vessels meant they were more susceptible to damage. Sails and rigging would also have needed attention and possible renewal at the end of each tour of duty. The bulk of maintenance and minor repair work would have been carried out during the winter months when warships rarely put to sea. Some of this would have been done in the open air and some under covered shipsheds. Spare rigging, sails, oars and many other items of equipment might be stored in the latter or in separate arsenal structures within the naval base (*navalia*). Some, perhaps most, of these would also have been manufactured in the shipyard.

While much is known about some of the major commercial harbours of the Roman world such as Ostia/Portus, Caesarea, Lepcis Magna and more recently Alexandria, comparatively little is known about Roman naval bases. The situation has, however, improved a little in recent years, not least because of discoveries in the north-west provinces. A much smaller and of course more mobile branch of the armed forces than either the legions or the *auxilia*, the navy required far fewer major installations. As well as its home bases, facilities to support its purpose and activities were provided at the many army bases accessible by its ships and those of the merchant marine. For the most part these consisted of quays, jetties and moles which because of their very location have been destroyed either by erosion or by harbour works of later periods, or have been buried beneath thick deposits of silt. Information about such structures is thus hardly plentiful and in any case is always difficult to acquire.

An exception is the Tiberian site known as Velsen I situated on the Dutch coast at the mouth of the Oer-IJ, possibly the northernmost branch of the Rhine in the Roman period (**19**). Excavations here in the 1980s revealed the

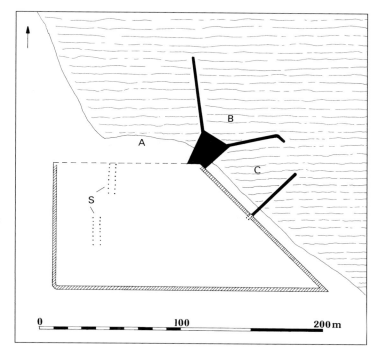

19 *Plan of the Julio-Claudian coastal fort and ship haven at Velsen I, Netherlands. KEY:*
A = beach suitable for hauling ships ashore,
B = outer harbour.
C = inner harbour,
S = ship-sheds.
After Morel

remains of a complex sequence of harbour works which entailed the construction of open jetties and solid breakwaters or moles to form an outer and inner basin.[102] The latter were about 7ft (2m) wide and consisted of two timber revetments linked by cross-members to form compartments which had then been filled with clay. Although occupied for a period of only 15 years (*c*.AD 15–30) the harbour structures had to be constantly repaired and modified to cope with the effects of currents and silting and there was also evidence that dredging had been necessary. Constructions of similar complexity undoubtedly existed at some of the early military harbours in Britain. Although discoveries of such structures are few and far between in the military sphere, the remains of the massive timber quays and jetties found at London provide a general indication of the type of robust and sophisticated carpentry involved (**20**).[103]

It has long been known that the men of the Roman navy were accommodated in forts very similar to those of the army. For example, although still unexplored, the base of the imperial fleet at Ravenna, situated at Classe, 2 miles south-east of the Roman and modern town, is known from its outline to have resembled a legionary fortress.[104] Similarly the headquarters of the *Classis Germanica* at Alteburg, near Cologne, excavated principally in the 1880s and the 1920s, consisted of a pentagonal-shaped fort about 8.9 acres (3.6ha) in size.[105] Although little is known about the shore installations of the *Classis Britannica* in the first century, excavations in recent decades at both Boulogne and Dover have confirmed that later its men too were accommodated in conventional forts. Details of these are given in chapter 7.

20 *Remains of timber quay at Fish Street Hill, London.* Photograph, Jon Bailey, Museum of London Archaeology Service, Copyright MoL

When it comes to the structures associated with building and maintaining naval vessels, we are dependent for much of our information on discoveries at the major maritime centres of the Greek and Hellenistic periods in the Mediterranean: sites such as the Piraeus near Athens, Apollonia, Kition on Cyprus, Thassos and Carthage.[106] Although these examples belong to a time well before Imperial Rome, warships did not change much over the intervening centuries nor did the maintenance facilities required. In a number of cases, including the sites just mentioned, we are fortunate in having inscriptions and accounts by ancient authors to supplement the results of modern excavations. The most obvious feature of military harbours was the shipsheds. If not to be used for any length of time, vessels were not simply left moored alongside a quay or jetty but hauled ashore on special covered slipways or 'shipsheds'. This prevented the timbers from becoming waterlogged, and ensured maintenance and repairs were carried out as soon as possible. Although differing in terms of overall layout, according to the shape of the harbour the shipsheds examined at the above sites conform to a standard type (**21**). They were linked by a solid back wall from which rows of columns ran down to the sea forming partitions between the actual 'slips' and supporting a roof, usually gabled, over each pair. Solid walls at intervals divided the shipsheds into groups. From the front therefore the shipsheds had the appearance of a colonnade. The average shipshed was 19–20ft wide and 120–130ft long, a size suitable for triremes, but more modest examples are also known. The actual 'slips' up which the ships

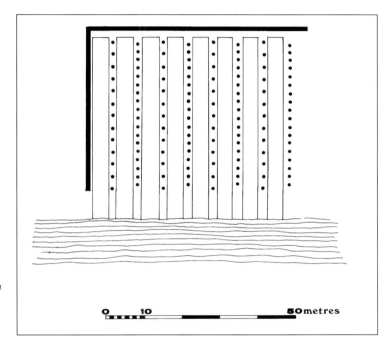

21 Right and below: *plan, elevation and cross-section of ship-sheds at Zea, Athens' naval-base*

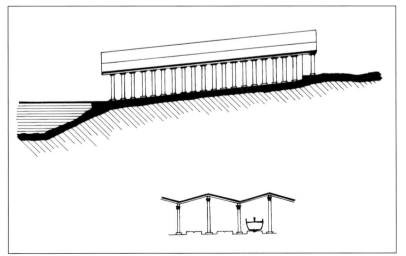

were hauled consisted of a low platform either cut in the rock or formed in the earth and sloping down into the water at a gradient usually varying from 1:10 to 1:14. Timber runners – likely to have been greased – were set crosswise in the base of the slips to aid the hauling-up process while, except for slips of the most gentle gradient, pulleys or winches must have been employed to haul the vessels up the ramps.[107] Once drawn inside, timber props would have been inserted to keep the vessel upright and secure.

Although we have literary, epigraphic and pictorial evidence of Roman shipsheds, excavated examples of such structures are extremely rare.[108] Several inscriptions mention a *navalia* at Mainz and it has been suggested that the group of fourth-century warships found there lay in a breaker's yard in view of the woodworking tools and masses of oak shavings discovered beside them.[109] Returning to the Tiberian site of Velsen I, two structures here have been tentatively interpreted as shipsheds.[110] Positioned within the defended area, each consisted of two parallel rows of posts set approximately 20ft (6m) apart and with an overall length of 65ft (20m). Thus, they would have been capable of accommodating a vessel of bireme size. If the interpretation is correct these are the first shipsheds to be identified in the northern provinces. Shipsheds would have been required at the bases of the British fleet and perhaps also at those major army bases with harbours.

Many major ports were equipped with one or more lighthouses to guide ships towards the harbour. The most famous of all of course was the *Pharos* at Alexandria built in the third century BC which was listed as one of the Seven Wonders of the Ancient World by the Roman geographer Strabo and after which all other lighthouses were named. The harbours at Lepcis Magna and Ostia both had lighthouses.[111] Little more than foundations are left of these but an unusual survival is the great lighthouse at La Coruña (*Flavium Brigantium*) situated at the north-west tip of Spain. Known as the Tower of Hercules this still stands to a height of 112ft (34m) and although the present facing is eighteenth-century, the core is Roman work.[112] Closer to home, Boulogne had a lighthouse which survived into modern times (**38**) while Dover had two, set on high ground to either side of the harbour (**41**, **45**, **colour plates 2** & **15**). There may well have been others. The range of installations also included chains of towers used for maintaining a watch on stretches of coastline vulnerable to seaborne attack or raiding. The system of towers, mile-fortlets and forts which formed an extension of Hadrian's Wall down the Cumberland coast is one example, while another is provided by the late fourth-century chain of signal-stations down the Yorkshire coast.[113]

5

CAESAR'S NAVAL CAMPAIGNS IN THE WEST, 56-54 BC

Caesar's expeditions across the Channel (the *Fretum Gallicum*) in 55 and 54 BC marked the Roman navy's first major experience of Britain's coastal waters and one as it turned out that was certainly not 'all plain sailing'. We are, of course, extremely fortunate in having Caesar's own account of this eventful and nearly catastrophic episode in his career. Together with the preceding description of his defeat of the powerful navy of the Veneti, which until then had controlled the Channel, it provides an all too rare and unusually detailed insight into the strategies and tactics employed by the Roman Fleet – especially the landing of troops on hostile shores – as well as those of the principal opposing maritime power. It also illustrates once again the organisational skills of the Roman military and their ability to overcome reverses, and so ultimately triumph.

In 57 BC, during the second year of his combined governorship of Illyricum with Cisalpine and Transalpine Gaul, Caesar led his forces against the confederation of tribes known as the Belgae in what is now Belgium. In the process of defeating them, and also receiving the submission of the maritime tribes of Brittany and Normandy, Caesar learned of the close ties between the tribes of south-eastern Britain and their Gallic neighbours. Those from areas of Gaul already conquered who were unwilling to submit to Roman authority had found refuge across the Channel and were followed in 57 by the surviving chieftains of the defeated Bellovaci. Commius, leader of the Gaulish Atrebates, claimed suzerainty over the British tribe of the same name, and some generations before, Diviciacus king of the Suessiones had also ruled in Britain. Caesar records that the Gauls were regularly supported by reinforcements from the island.[1]

The strong political and military links between the tribes on both sides of the Channel were sufficient reason for Caesar to plan an expedition to Britain. There was also an economic incentive. The mineral wealth of the island – specifically the tin deposits of Cornwall – had been well known for centuries and it was reputed to be rich in other metals as well as pearls (Caesar was later to dedicate a breastplate studded with British pearls in the temple of Venus

Genetrix). The Roman historian Strabo's oft-cited list of exports from Britain includes grain, cattle, gold, silver, iron, hides, slaves and hunting dogs.[2] Trade in the opposite direction is illustrated by the imports of raw glass, pottery and *amphorae* of Italian wine found on late Iron Age sites at or close to natural harbours such as Hengistbury Head on the Solent, Poole Harbour, and around the mouth of the River Arun in East Sussex.[3] There were four main embarkation points for making the crossing to Britain which were already ancient by the time that Strabo listed them at the end of the first century BC; from the mouths of the Garonne, the Loire, the Seine and the Rhine.[4] The scale of cross-Channel trade is indicated by the recent discovery of very substantial jetties and other harbour-works at Poole which date to *c*.250 BC.[5] These and even earlier trade routes can be traced through the spread of Roman goods. The presence of Roman forces and then settlements in Provence from around 125 BC accelerated the dissemination of Roman culture northwards into Gaul resulting from trade and exchange in a trail of Roman products across central France and on to the southern shores of Britain.

By the time that Caesar arrived on the scene there was already clearly a considerable volume of maritime traffic between Britain and the Continent. The Veneti, the chief tribe of southern Brittany, held the monopoly on cross-Channel trade and they were understandably alarmed by the rumours of Caesar's intentions. Appalled at the prospect of losing the basis of their livelihood and prosperity they rebelled. Caesar states that the Veneti were the most powerful tribe of the coastal region because of their large fleet of ships which they used to sail to and from Britain for the purposes of trade. They apparently exceeded the other maritime tribes in their knowledge of the sea and in their expertise in navigation and as they controlled the few harbours on this exposed coast they were in a position to exact tolls from all others who sailed these waters.[6] From Caesar's point of view no expedition across the Channel could even be contemplated while the Venetic fleet remained intact.

Caesar was wintering in Illyricum when news of the revolt reached him. He sent instructions to his subordinates to use the time until his return 'in building warships (*naves longae*) on the River Loire, which flows into the Atlantic, training oarsmen recruited in the province, and enlisting sailors and helmsmen' (Caesar, *Gallic War* 3.9). The Veneti were confident because they controlled the harbours and knew all the dangers of the coastal waters. They also secured support from the neighbouring maritime tribes of the Menapii and Morini and summoned reinforcements from Britain. On his return, Caesar put the young Decimus Brutus in charge of the fleet which was reinforced with ships and crews commandeered from the Pictones, Santoni and other conquered tribes nearby. Throughout the summer, the Veneti used their ships to transfer the population of any of their coastal strongholds threatened by Roman forces to neighbouring settlements, most of which were also promontory sites. They were helped in this by the fact that Caesar's fast ships on their way from the Mediterranean were delayed by storms. Once these did arrive the scene was set for the decisive confrontation off Morbihan but victory for the Romans was by no means certain (**22**). The Veneti had the twin advantages of local knowledge and ships that were more suited to northern waters. In the event, it was the reliance of the Venetic ships on sail alone that determined the outcome.

Caesar gives a detailed description of the ships of the Veneti:

> They were made with flat bottoms, to help them to move in shallow water caused by shoals or ebb-tides. Exceptionally high bows and sterns suited them for use in heavy seas and violent gales, and the hulls were built entirely of oak to withstand violent shocks. The cross-timbers, which consisted of beams a foot wide, were fastened with iron bolts as thick as a man's thumb. The anchors were secured with iron chains rather than ropes. They used sails made of raw hides or thin leather, either because they had no flax and were ignorant of its use, or more probably because they thought that ordinary sails could not stand the violent storms and squalls of the Ocean and were not suitable for such heavy vessels. In coming up against them the only advantage our ships possessed was that they were faster and could be propelled by oars; in other respects the enemy's were much better adapted for sailing such treacherous and stormy waters. We could not injure them by ramming because they were so solidly built, and their height made it difficult to reach them with missiles or board them with grappling-irons. Moreover, when it began to blow hard and they were running before the wind, they weathered the storm more easily; they could bring into shallow water with greater safety, and when left aground by the tide they had nothing to fear from reefs or pointed rocks – whereas to our ships all these risks were formidable.
>
> *Bell. Gall.* 3.13

The Roman fleet from the Mediterranean eventually arrived but the Veneti, far from being intimidated, set out to do battle with 220 ships of their own. The height disadvantage of the Roman ships meant that their missiles were largely ineffective and so towers were added to the larger ones – probably 'fours' or 'fives' – as a counter-measure. But they were still overtopped by the sterns of their opponent's vessels. A device that did prove very effective for the Romans consisted of a sharp hook or sickle attached to a long pole. They used this to grab hold of the ropes which held the yards to the masts on the enemy ships which were then cut through as the Roman ship increased its stroke-rate and speed. Any Venetic ship which had its rigging thus dismantled was rendered powerless and its destruction or capture was inevitable owing to the superior fighting skills of the Roman marines. Caesar tells us that once this fate

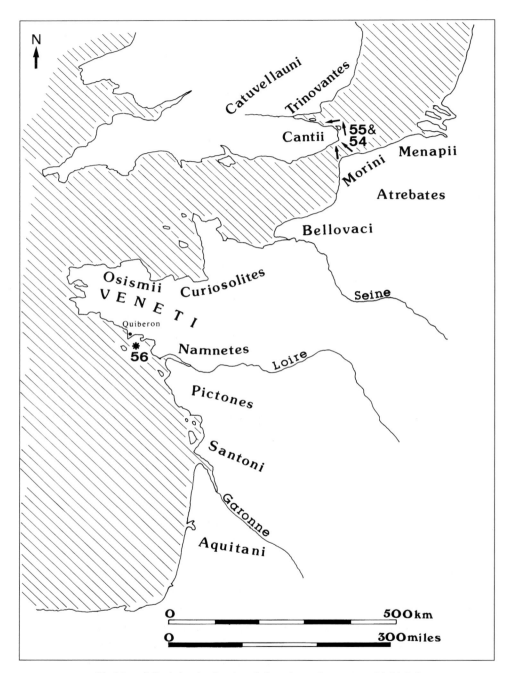

N

Catuvellauni
Trinovantes
Cantii
55&
54
Menapii
Morini
Atrebates
Bellovaci

Osismii   Curiosolites
V E N E T I
Quiberon
56
Namnetes
Seine
Loire
Pictones
Santoni
Garonne
Aquitani

O   500km
O   300miles

22 *Map of Gaul showing location of Caesar's naval campaigns 56-54 BC*

had befallen a number of their ships, the Veneti decided to flee. As they were moving away they became concentrated in one area and at that particular moment the wind dropped. Becalmed, the Venetic ships were at the complete mercy of the Roman fleet and were simply picked off one by one, the battle lasting until sunset.[7]

The destruction of the Veneti's navy removed any immediate threat to an expedition across the Channel, and the fleet Caesar had assembled to defeat them was available both to protect the crossing and to deal with any naval forces sent out by the British tribes. Strangely for an island nation involved in mercantile commerce there is no mention of British ships either now or at the time of the Claudian conquest. Presumably anything other than coastal trading was dominated by Mediterranean merchants and the seafaring peoples of the continental Atlantic and North Sea coasts who were more experienced in the transhipment of large cargoes over long distances. First, however, Caesar had to contend both with subduing the Menapii and Morini who controlled the Channel coast close to the Straits of Dover, and also with repelling a German incursion across the Rhine. Consequently it was not until the late summer of 55 BC that he could afford to turn his attention once more to Albion. Although the campaigning season was nearly at an end he decided that a reconnaissance in strength would yield information of great use in planning the main expedition the following year. Information which he had been unable to acquire by interviewing Gallic merchants such as the location of landing-places, the nature of the terrain immediately inland from the coast, and the military strength and capabilities of the British tribes.

Caesar had already marched his entire army into the territory of the Morini where he ordered ships from neighbouring regions to rendezvous with the fleet that had defeated the Veneti at *Portus Itius* (probably *Gesoriacum*, Boulogne), the starting-point for the easiest crossing to Britain. This is where he established his field headquarters so that he could oversee preparations personally. While these were taking place he despatched the tribune Caius Volusenus in a single warship (*navis longa*) to scout the British coastline and identify a safe landing place. He was away for five days, but although he clearly reconnoitred the coast from Hythe to Sandwich he failed to discover the harbour at Richborough, a failing that was to have unfortunate consequences. The expeditionary force was to consist of two legions – the Seventh and the Tenth – accompanied by about 500 cavalry, a total force of approximately 12,000 men. The fleet to convey them across the Channel included 80 transports (*naves onerariae*) for the two legions with a further 18 transports especially adapted for the cavalry assembled at Ambleteuse 8 miles to the north.[8] Protecting the transports were a number of warships. Most of these were probably triremes, but the reference to *maioris formae* suggests that a number of fours and fives were also present. To these can be added the scoutships or *speculatoria navigia* and the boats (*scaphae*) towed behind the larger warships.[9]

With preparations complete Caesar waited for favourable weather conditions and eventually set out on the evening of 24 August, instructing the cavalry to go to the distant harbour, board ship and follow the main part of the fleet. In the event, loading the transports at Ambleteuse took longer than expected and by the time they were ready they had missed the evening tide. Their commander sailed on the morning tide but contrary winds drove him back into harbour and they did not set sail again for four days. By mid-morning on the 25th, Caesar and the first ships lay off the British coast in the vicinity of Dover or Folkestone where he could see British forces massing on the cliff tops above a narrow beach. Attempting an opposed landing in such circumstances would clearly have been suicidal so he waited at anchor for the rest of the ships to arrive. After a meeting with his senior officers, and with the wind and tidal current in his favour, he gave the signal to weigh anchor. Proceeding about 7 miles he moored his ships on an open and evenly sloping shore, most probably somewhere in the vicinity of modern Walmer or Deal. The British had shadowed the Roman fleet along the coast and were ready to oppose the landing with cavalry and chariots. This presented the Romans with serious difficulties because the size of the transports made it impossible to run them aground except in fairly deep water, leaving the heavily laden soldiers no option but to jump down into deep water and wade ashore under a hail of enemy javelins and other missiles. Seeing his men understandably dismayed by this prospect Caesar

> . . . ordered the warships – which were lighter and more manoeuvrable than the transports, and likely to impress the Britons by their unfamiliar appearance – to pull back from the *onerariae*, and then to be rowed hard so as to run ashore on the enemy's right flank in an attempt to dislodge them by the use of slings, bows and artillery. This manoeuvre was highly successful. Scared by the strange shape of the warships, the motion of the oars, and the artillery barrage, the natives halted and then retreated a little.

This is an interesting demonstration of how warships could be deployed to provide covering fire for the infantry. The artillery pieces referred to were undoubtedly *catapultae* fixed securely to the decks of the larger naval vessels. They could hurl heavy javelin-shaped bolts upwards of 1,000 feet and a volley of these would certainly have had an effect on the Britons most of whom had never before seen such weapons. The legionaries however did not immediately seize the opportunity presented by this lull in the battle. But there then occurred one of those moments when the course of history turned on the actions of one man:

> But as the Romans still hesitated, chiefly on account of the depth of the water, the man who carried the eagle of the Tenth Legion, after

praying to the gods that his action might bring good luck to the legion, cried in a loud voice: 'Jump down, comrades, unless you wish to surrender our eagle to the enemy; I, at any rate, intend to do my duty to my country and my general.' With these words he leapt into the water and advanced toward the enemy with the eagle in his hands. At this the soldiers, exhorting each other not to allow such a disgrace, jumped down from the ship as one, and the men in the ships nearby, inspired by their example, followed them and made their way ashore to close with the enemy. The battle was keenly contested by both sides. The Roman soldiers were unable to maintain a firm foothold, keep rank, or follow the right standards and so men from different ships fell in under the first standard they saw resulting in great confusion. The British knew all the shallows, and when they saw small parties of soldiers disembarking from their vessels, they galloped up and attacked them from their chariots driven at full speed into the water, surrounding them with superior numbers, while others hurled javelins from the open flank. Caesar therefore ordered the warship's boats – *scaphae* – and the scouting vessels – *speculatoria navigia* – to be loaded with troops so that help could be sent to groups of his men outnumbered by the enemy.

After some time the Roman forces managed to group themselves into some form of effective formation and pushed the Britons back from the beach and eventually put them to flight. Soon afterwards the British leaders sent an embassy to sue for peace. Caesar must have been greatly relieved by a victory won in such difficult circumstances. However, he was soon to learn that the main threat to his enterprise was not the Britons but the Ocean, a force less easy to master.

On the fourth day after setting foot on British soil the 18 transports carrying the cavalry finally managed to set out from Ambleteuse. When they embarked there was a gentle breeze blowing but by the time they were in sight of the British shore this had deteriorated into a violent storm. None of the transports could hold its course. Some were blown back to port. Others were driven westwards, and despite the risks eventually decided to cast anchor in an attempt to ride out the storm, but they began to fill with water and were also forced to head back across the Channel. Worse was to follow. That night there was a full moon which as usual brought with it a particularly high tide, something of which the Romans were unaware. The beached warships became filled with water and the transports, riding at anchor offshore, received a severe battering. Many ships were badly damaged and even the remainder lost their cables, anchors and other gear.[10] There were no other ships they could use nor were there the materials required to effect repairs; and, since it had been assumed they would return to Gaul for the winter, they had not brought sufficient grain supplies to over-winter in Britain. Caesar was in effect marooned in a land which was not only wholly unfamiliar, but which also rapidly reverted to a very unfriendly one again when the Britons learned of his plight and decided to renege on their promises. A number of engagements were fought over the ensuing few days during which time the Romans managed to repair most of the transports by stripping the 12 worst damaged of the necessary gear. Caesar decided to return to the Continent as soon as possible and took advantage of the next favourable wind, setting sail shortly after midnight.[11]

Caesar was determined to return to Britain the following season and so, before setting out for Italy where he was to spend the winter, he gave his legates orders to have as many new ships as possible built and the old ones repaired. In typical fashion, he personally drew up the specifications for the new vessels. So that the transports could get closer inshore, he instructed that these should be built with a lower freeboard than usual. Also, so that they could carry a heavy cargo, including a large number of pack animals, they were to be made broader than was customary. Furthermore, they were to be suitable for both rowing and sailing and he refers to them as *vectoria navigia* – oared transports.[12]

Caesar arrived in Rome uncertain as to the impact on senatorial and public opinion of his foray across the Ocean. It was possible his expedition might be seen as exceeding the remit of the command voted to him by the Senate. He need not have worried. The invasion of Britain was well received and the Caesarean faction in the Senate ensured the passing of a proposal for an unprecedented 20 days of thanksgiving, five more than voted in 57 for the subjugation of Gaul itself. His political agents, the equivalent of today's spin-doctors, roused popular support by emphasising Caesar's achievement in vanquishing not just the wild Britons at the edge of the world but also the Ocean itself. This was a theme taken up again to even greater effect by Claudius nearly a century later and also by Vespasian. Indeed, victory over the barbarians in the remote islands at the ends of the earth was to become a recurrent theme – justified or not – in the panegyrics to later emperors.

When he returned from Italy in the spring of 54 BC he found 600 of the specially adapted transports and 28 warships had been built and fitted out. Along with the 80 or so surviving transports from the previous year and about 200 privately owned vessels he had gathered, this enabled him to take a much larger expeditionary force than in 55, amounting to five legions and 2,000 cavalry – a total of around 30,000 men – along with a considerable baggage train. Delayed by unfavourable winds for three to four weeks, Caesar finally set sail shortly before sunset on 6 July. Vagaries in wind and currents caused some deviation from their course but by determined rowing the transports managed to keep up with the warships and by midday the fleet reached the best landing place identified the previous year. This time the army disembarked unopposed. The British had been surprised by the appearance of a fleet the previous year but this time were completely astounded by the number of ships they saw. As

Caesar learned from prisoners captured shortly after landing, 'although a large force had gathered on the beach they withdrew when they saw the size of the fleet' (*Gallic War* 5.8). Leaving a force behind to build and guard their base camp and the ships, Caesar made a night advance, encountered the enemy and defeated them. He was pursuing the survivors the next day when messengers on horseback arrived with news that 'a great storm had arisen the previous night and that almost all the ships were damaged and cast up on the shore because neither the anchors nor the ropes had held, and the seamen and the helmsmen had been unable to control the ships with the result that they ran foul of one another'.

Cutting short the pursuit and returning to the beach Caesar saw that about 40 ships were total wrecks while the remainder looked as though they could be repaired, but only with a considerable amount of work. Accordingly he sent a message back to his second-in-command across the Channel, Titus Labienus, to despatch skilled workmen from the other legions and to commence the construction of more transports. In addition, although it was a task involving enormous labour, he decided that the best plan was to haul all of the ships out of the water and enclose them together with the camp by a single fortification. This was completed after ten days working night and day. The lesson had finally been learned that Mediterranean mooring practices were inappropriate in northern waters.

While the repair work was proceeding, he renewed the advance inland. He defeated the Britons in several engagements, forced a crossing of the Thames and then took the stronghold of Cassivellaunus, leader of the British forces. At this point Cassivellaunus sued for peace. In the interim a direct attack on the beach head encampment had been repulsed. Terms having been agreed, Caesar marched the army back to the coast. He found the ships repaired but as so many had been lost he decided to take the army, and the considerable number of prisoners and hostages he had acquired, back across the Channel in two trips. All went well with the first journey and no ships were lost. For the return trip to Britain they were joined by 60 extra transports which Labienus had had built. However, nearly all were blown off course and forced back to land. Caesar waited some time for them to return. In the end, to avoid being marooned in Britain by the autumn gales and fearing an uprising in Gaul, he decided to pack the remainder of his force into the ships available. The date of his evening sailing can be identified as 25 September from letters received by Cicero from his brother who was serving in the expedition and also from Caesar himself.[13] Boulogne was reached at dawn the following day without the loss of a single ship.

When in Rome the previous spring, Caesar had learned that his command in Gaul had been extended for a further period of five years and it was undoubtedly his intention to return to Britain in 53 BC to complete his work. In his description of the conditions of surrender Caesar uses legal and technical terms normally associated with the first steps in formally constituting a province out of conquered territory. It was not to be, however, for in the autumn of 54 a major rebellion erupted in Gaul that was to take four years to crush and which received some support from British tribes. Its consequences included heavy losses for three of Caesar's legions and the death of his trusted general Labienus. But by the end of this period Caesar was in a far stronger position than his rivals, Pompey and Crassus, the other two members of the First Triumvirate. He had a loyal and battle-hardened army behind him and plenty of war-booty to pay both them and his political supporters in Rome. By March 45 BC he had become the undisputed master of the entire Roman world but remained so for only 12 months. Had he not been assassinated perhaps he would have despatched Roman forces across the Channel again in due course. As it turned out Britain remained outside the Empire for almost another full century.

Even so, a new era had arrived for the island. Rome was now on the other side of the Channel and the existing cultural and economic patterns were broken. Henceforth trade was with the Roman Empire and the demise of the Veneti's sea-power may have stimulated British merchants to become more directly involved in maritime commerce. The geographer Strabo, writing several decades after Caesar's expeditions lists the chief exports of Britain as grain, cattle, gold, silver, iron, hides, hunting dogs and slaves.[14] He also says that 'the Britons submit so readily to heavy duties both on the exports from there to Gaul and on the imports from Gaul – these consist of ivory chains, necklaces, amber, glassware, and other such trinkets – that there is no need to garrison the island' (*Geographica*, 4.5.3). Archaeological evidence shows that the aristocracy of certain tribes in the southernmost parts of Britain, especially the Atrebates, the Trinovantes and, following their conquest of the latter, the Catuvellauni, were becoming very fond of wine, olive oil and fine pottery from the other side of the Channel.[15] For 20 years after Caesar's second expedition, Roman attention was focused elsewhere. Yet during the 9 years from 34 to 26 BC there were no fewer than three occasions when Octavian (the later Augustus) assembled forces in Gaul ready to cross the Channel and emulate the achievements of Caesar, his father by adoption.[16] On each occasion this would have involved considerable naval activity. Each time, however, trouble elsewhere on the frontier required his attention and Roman influence in Britain continued to be exercised instead by means of treaties with various tribes of the south-east. The only time prior to the Claudian invasion when the Roman navy ventured again to British shores, and then unintentionally, occurred in AD 16 when some of the transports conveying part of Germanicus' army along the North Sea coast were blown off course and ended up in Essex. They were returned safely to the Continent by the British chieftains.[17]

6
INVASION AND CONQUEST

From Boulogne to Colchester

A false start to the invasion of Britain took place in AD 40 when the Emperor Gaius ordered an expeditionary force to be assembled in readiness to cross the Channel. The army was less than enthusiastic about the enterprise and Gaius called off the invasion. Before doing so, however, he had the legions and their siege engines drawn up in battle array on the seashore and then, adding to his already long list of eccentric actions, ordered them to gather sea shells which he declared spoils of war from his victory over the Ocean. These were sent back to Rome as booty (overland) as were some of the triremes assembled to protect the invasion fleet.[1] Despite the farcical nature of this event it did have a positive outcome for his successor Claudius three years later. Much of the military and logistical planning for the enterprise had been done and merely remained to be implemented. In addition some of the infrastructure facilities had been constructed, as is demonstrated by the lighthouse which Gaius ordered to be built at Boulogne and which was very probably accompanied by extensive harbour works to make it suitable as the base port for the invasion force.[2]

Supplies and materials sufficient for the invasion force would have been gathered on Gaius' orders and warehouses erected and stocked. Hundreds of transports had undoubtedly been constructed and warships to protect them assembled. Many of these vessels would probably still have been available in 43, if somewhat dispersed and in need of repair. Having gone through the exercise once, any problems with organisation and logistical arrangements would have been identified and solutions formulated. The groundwork done by the general staff under Gaius was to serve Claudius well. It enabled him to respond quickly and effectively to a deteriorating political situation in Britain and to win military glory for himself at the rather shaky start to his reign. Cunobelinus, king of the Catuvellauni, died in 43 leaving his realm divided between his two sons Caratacus and Togodumnus. Young and ambitious, they made war on their neighbours including the Atrebates. Their king, Verica, had to flee for his life and as a Roman ally he naturally made his way to Rome to seek help from the emperor. As if this was not in itself a sufficient pretext for intervention it was followed by impudent demands for Verica's extradition. Non-compliance was followed by disturbances; probably attacks on Roman merchants in Britain and possibly even raids on the Gallic coast. Claudius had no choice, the invasion was on.

Although we would probably have more information about the invasion had the chapters of Tacitus' *Annals* covering the early years of Claudius' reign survived, nonetheless we do have the accounts of Suetonius and Cassius Dio which make use of contemporary sources. The invasion force, under the command of Aulus Plautius, consisted of four legions (*II Augusta, IX Hispana, XIV Gemina* and *XX Valeria*) together with a sizeable contingent of auxiliary troops. The total strength of the force is generally assumed to have been around 40,000 men who had to be transported across the Channel along with a minimum of several thousand slaves and servants, many hundreds of cavalry horses and pack animals, and the thousands of tons of equipment and supplies assembled over the preceding months. Although we are not told the main port for embarkation this was almost certainly Boulogne. Given the size of the operation some elements of the invasion fleet probably sailed from other ports nearby. Apart from *Legio IX Hispana* the legions involved in the invasion had previously been stationed at bases along the Rhine and some of their equipment and existing supplies were probably brought around to Boulogne by the *Classis Germanica*, perhaps for some vessels a repeat of a voyage they had made three years earlier (**23**).

After some initial dissent amongst the troops, who we are told were worried about campaigning in a land separated from the known world by the Ocean, the expedition set sail, as Dio describes it, 'in three divisions' (60.19). The ordinary soldiers' worries about the expedition at first seemed justified when they began to be blown back to port but they 'took heart when a bolt of light shot from east to west – the direction in which they were sailing' (Cassius Dio 60.19). This suggests that, either because of deliberate planning or because of the delay caused by the headwinds, the crossing occurred at night. The sources do not reveal the precise number of ships involved. A century earlier Caesar had 680 transports along with 200 commandeered merchant ships to convey a force of around 30,000 men along with their equipment and supplies across the Channel. The transports probably carried 80-120 men or 30 horses apiece.[3] On a proportional basis, and assuming Plautius' ships were of a similar size, then his fleet probably numbered around 1,000 vessels to which one might add an escort of 50-100 warships, most probably biremes. Other estimates have arrived at a similar figure and have also concluded that more than half of the total number of ships involved were required for transporting supplies and equipment, along with the pack animals to carry them following the landing.[4] There was no guarantee of obtaining food from local sources nor would any Roman military planner make such an assumption. Requirements would be calculated precisely with surpluses built in to allow for losses and other contingencies. Something of the order of 3,500 tons of grain would have been needed to feed the invasion force for the first three months, along with considerable quantities of meat, wine and other consumables. Stocks would also have to be built up to keep the army supplied throughout the approaching

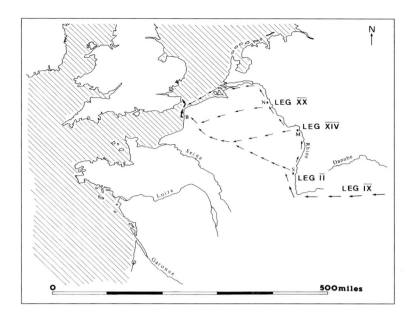

LEG XX

LEG XIV

LEG II

LEG IX

23 *Map showing movement of legions to assemble the invasion force of 43. While the majority of the troops may have travelled overland, much of their equipment could have been transported down the Rhine and then along the North Sea coast to Boulogne*

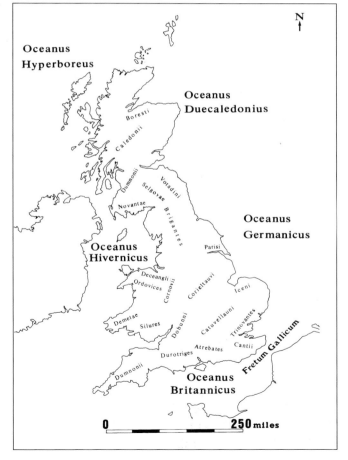

Oceanus
Hyperboreus

Oceanus
Duecaledonius

Boresti

Caledonii

Dumnonii

Voradini

Selgovae

Novantae

Brigantes

Oceanus
Germanicus

Oceanus
Hivernicus

Parisi

Deceangli

Ordovices

Cornovii

Corieltauvi

Iceni

Demetae

Silures

Dobunni

Catuvellauni

Trinovantes

Atrebates

Cantii

Durotriges

Fretum Gallicum

Dumnonii

Oceanus
Britannicus

24 *Names of the tribes of Britain and of the seas around her coasts*

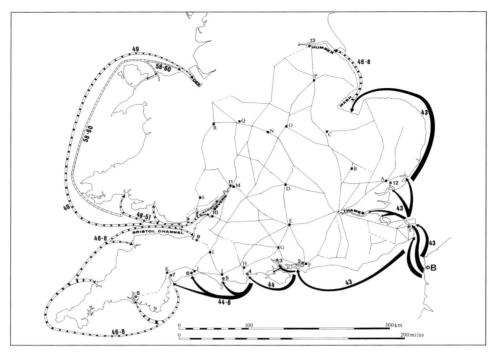

25 *Map illustrating the principal operations of the Roman fleet during the period AD 43-66 including location of known and probable legionary bases and military ports. KEY: Legionary bases: A - Colchester, B - Great Chesterton, C - Longthorpe, D - Alchester, E - Silchester, F - Chichester, G - Winchester, H - Wimborne, I - Dorchester, J - Axminster, K - Exeter, L - Ilchester, M - Kingsholm, Gloucester, N - Mancetter, O - Leicester, P - Lincoln, Q - Wall, R - Wroxeter, S - Usk. Military ports: 1 - Richborough, 2 - Fishbourne, 3 - Bitterne, 4 - Poole Harbour, 5 - Weymouth, 6 - Seaton, 7- Topsham, 8 - Plymouth, 9 - Bridgwater, 10 - Sea Mills, 11 - Kingsholm, 12 - Fingringhoe, 13 - Winteringham*

winter, and as Channel crossings after September were extremely risky there was a pressing need to get the supplies across to Britain (**24**). The equipment to be shipped included tents, artillery and replacement weapons along with wagons and carts to transport the bulky items. Comparison with the needs of early modern campaigning armies prior to the introduction of motorized transport suggests that around 10,000 mules would have been needed to move supplies inland as far as the Thames in the days following the landing (**25**).[5] They too would have needed feeding. Cassius Dio tells us that there were also a number of elephants attached to the expeditionary force.[6]

We do not have the degree of detail about the landing provided by Caesar's commentaries, but we do know that the delay in sailing caused by the soldiers' initial refusal to embark brought a bonus. The Britons, believing the Romans had abandoned the crossing, dispersed their forces and so landfall was made unopposed. The orthodox view of the landing is that it took place at Richborough. In the Roman period the Isle of Thanet was separated from the mainland by the Wantsum Channel, a sea channel up to three miles wide in places, which afforded an anchorage protected from strong winds (**26**).[7] Excavation here has revealed a sequence of Claudian installations interpreted as an initial defended beach-head perimeter succeeded by a stores base (**27**).[8] The reference to three divisions by Cassius Dio has led some to suggest that there were landings at three separate locations in east Kent.[9] The early surrender of the Gloucestershire Dobunni, coupled with the discovery of Claudian material at Fishbourne and neighbouring Chichester, encouraged others to conclude that the postulated three landings had been much farther apart or even that Chichester Harbour itself had been the landing place for the invasion force.[10] But splitting the army in this way would have risked disaster. If one division had been overwhelmed by superior enemy forces then the whole expedition would be in danger. Landings at three separate points far apart would also have complicated the logistical support required in the period immediately following the landing. To minimise the risks the power of the invasion force had to be concentrated at one point or at least along one sector of the coast.

Richborough still seems the most likely candidate, especially as this is where the great monument commemorating the conquest of Britain was later erected.[11] It should also be remembered that disembarking such a large force and its equipment would have taken a considerable length of time and the most likely interpretation is that the three divisions sailed sequentially, separated by

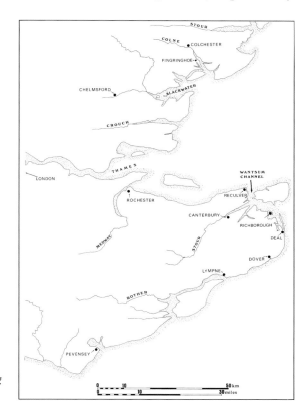

26 *Map of south-eastern Britain showing location of principal sites*

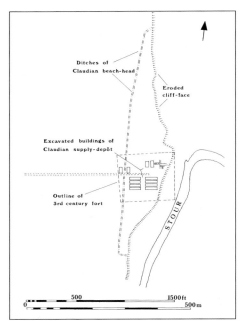

27 *Plan of the early military installations at Richborough*

intervals of a few hours. In this way the possibility of confusion and conges-
tion at the landing place, and the risks of having a large force waiting out to
sea would have been reduced without weakening the strength of the landing
force. The 'first wave' would have secured the beachhead and then moved
forward to establish a protective screen up to a mile inland, allowing the other
two 'waves' to disembark in relative safety. Those not involved in scouting or
securing the perimeter would have begun work on setting up the base camp.
Once it had safely delivered the invasion force, the fleet's task became one of
supply and support. There would still have been enormous quantities of
supplies and materials waiting to be brought over from Gaul. At this early stage
a constant supply of foodstuffs, especially grain, would have to be maintained
and stocks of weapons and missiles replenished. For the construction of the
earliest bases and forts which succeeded the tented encampments it is probable
that local timber was used, although it is not impossible that some elements
may have been prefabricated and brought across the Channel. Certainly, until
the works depots were up and running, nails, bolts and a wide variety of other
'specialised' materials would have been shipped across from Gaul. The earliest
Roman activity at Richborough is represented by two parallel ditches which
run for 2,100ft (640m) across the neck of the promontory accompanied by a
rampart and palisade on their east side (**27**). The extent of the area enclosed
cannot be determined with any precision owing to erosion but was probably
in the region of 100 acres (40ha). This is too small to have accommodated the
entire invasion force and the defences were presumably erected to protect the
ships and the steady stream of supplies that they brought.

After regrouping his forces Plautius advanced towards the Medway where the first major engagement with the British was fought somewhere near Rochester. Victory for the Romans was not gained easily for the battle lasted two days. The fleet probably kept in close contact with the land forces and the natural harbour at the mouth of the Medway near Rochester would have afforded a suitable location for another stores depot. British resistance stiffened after the death of Togodumnus in one of the many minor skirmishes and Plautius halted just south of the Thames at or near London. He was under instructions to send for the emperor at a decisive moment in the campaign and so the army rested for a period of six to eight weeks while Claudius made his way to Boulogne. His journey was mainly by ship; down the Tiber to Ostia, along the coast as far as Marseilles, and from there across Gaul partly by land and partly by river to the Channel coast. During this interval the navy would have continued to ship over supplies to the main base at Richborough, possibly Rochester, and perhaps up the Thames directly to the army encamped near London.

Claudius was ready to cross over to Britain in later August bringing with him his entourage, elements of the Praetorian Guard, other troops and a number of elephants. The journey across the Channel must have been a memorable experience for elephants and sailors alike. Notable among the imperial entourage was Publius Graecinius Laco, procurator of Gaul, to whom ultimate responsibility fell for keeping the invasion force supplied. Also present were a number of senators, some of whom the Emperor wished to honour and others that he was afraid to leave behind. Claudius led the advance towards the enemy capital *Camulodunum* (Colchester) and presided over its capture, an event which saw the collapse of much of the British resistance. The senate congratulated Claudius in a number of ways. They bestowed the title *Britannicus* on both him and his son, awarded him the right to hold a triumphal celebration, and also voted the construction of 'two triumphal arches, one in Rome, the other in Gaul, from where he had put to sea when he crossed to Britain' (Cassius Dio 60, 22). That at Boulogne has yet to be discovered, but fragments of the inscription from the one in Rome survive and it records that it was set up by the Senate and People to Claudius because he 'received the submission of eleven kings . . . and brought barbarian peoples beyond the Ocean under Roman rule for the first time'.[12] The emperor left Britain after staying only 16 days. Within six months he was back in Rome celebrating his great triumph which, as one would expect, had a strong maritime theme. 'Among the spoils of victory he had fixed a naval crown next to the civic crown on the pediment of the Palatine Palace as a sign that he had crossed and, as it were, conquered Ocean' (Suetonius, *Claudius* 17).

Colchester now became Plautius' headquarters, in effect the capital of the embryonic province. It was also to be the base of *Legio XX*, which began the construction of a fortress soon after the departure of Claudius (**28**). Quite apart from the political symbolism of establishing his headquarters in what had been the enemy's seat of power, the site had the great advantage from a logistical point of view of being accessible by sea. Although the River Colne was too shallow for large vessels to navigate up as far as the fortress, only a mile or so downstream it broadened out into a wide estuary, so landing and storage facilities were constructed at Fingringhoe (**28** & **colour plate 5**). From here goods could have been transported either overland or transferred to smaller, riverine vessels for the rest of the journey to Colchester.[13] Plautius would also no doubt have had a squadron of warships anchored in the estuary, for fast communication back to Boulogne and for reconnaissance up the east coast.

To the Severn and the Wash

Each of the other three legions became the spearhead of separate 'battle-groups' which fanned out to secure control of southern and central England (**25**).[14] The Ninth *Hispana* went north, skirting the friendly territory of the client-kingdom of the Iceni, and eventually established itself in a fortress at Longthorpe beside the River Nene.[15] Too small for the entire legion, the remainder was accommodated in one or more other so-called 'vexillation' fortresses in the East Midlands, possibly Leicester and/or Lincoln.[16] *Legio XIV* headed north-westwards into the heart of the Midlands finally taking up residence in a base at Mancetter. Earlier, part of it appears to have been based in a large fort at Alchester where during recent excavations tree-ring dating of timbers from one of its gateways indicated felling dates of autumn AD 44 and spring AD 45.[17] Another division of the Fourteenth was probably based at Great Chesterford.[18] The Second *Augusta* was selected for the toughest mission, the reduction of the still hostile tribes of the south-west. It was commanded by the future emperor Vespasian who, as Suetonius relates, during this campaign 'fought 30 battles, subjugated two warlike tribes, captured more than 20 *oppida* (towns), and took the Isle of Wight' (*Vespasian* 4). The rapid advance is explained by Roman control of the sea and the close support given to Vespasian's land forces by the fleet. Although there are no literary sources to provide the fine detail of the campaign, archaeology, especially discoveries made very recently, has revealed the general strategy on which it was based. Essentially, this saw the bulk of Vespasian's force moving westwards following a route only a few miles inland and with the major bases established at or very close to natural harbours to facilitate supply (**29**). Another part of his force may have gone north to establish a sizeable base at Silchester.[19] In some cases, the fleet may have been used to land a significant force in advance of the main battle-group in order to secure the anchorage and land supplies. The capture of the Isle of Wight would have seen the invasion repeated in miniature. Some years later naval forces were to play an essential role in securing Vespasian another victory, on that occasion the imperial throne itself.

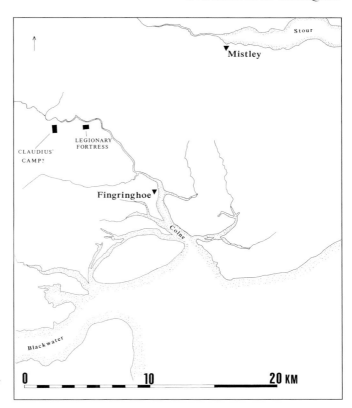

28 *Map showing location of principal early Roman military sites in the Colchester area*

Vespasian selected the fine natural harbour at Bosham near Chichester as his principal base to which supplies could be brought directly from Gaul. Storage buildings of early Claudian date found beneath the Flavian palace at Fishbourne suggest this was the location of the actual port and stores depot, while the fortress lay at Chichester where early military buildings associated with items of legionary equipment have come to light below buildings of the later Roman town.[20] This would replicate the relationship between Colchester and Fingringhoe. The assault on the Isle of Wight would have been carried out fairly early on in the campaign in order to secure the flank and prevent any interference with military shipping. The presence of Claudian pottery at Bitterne, 25 miles to the west at the head of Southampton Water, long ago led to the suggestion that this was the location of the next in the chain of port cum stores bases.[21] This now appears to have been confirmed by the discovery of storage buildings dating to the invasion period, very similar in type to those known at Richborough and Fishbourne, within the area of the later walled Roman settlement of *Clausentum* and occupying the tip of the Bitterne Manor peninsula.[22] There may have been a major camp nearby or, alternatively, this could have been located some distance inland, most probably in the vicinity of Winchester. In this case, supplies arriving by ship at Bitterne would have been transferred to smaller vessels for the journey up the River Itchen.

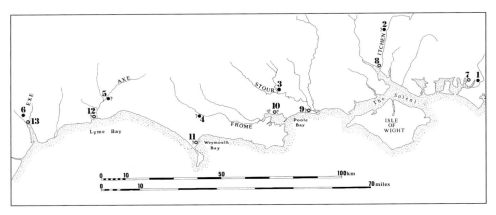

29 *Map of the south coast showing possible pairing of legionary bases and military ports/supply depots belonging to Vespasian's campaigns of AD 43-47. KEY:* Legionary bases: *1 - Chichester, 2 - Winchester, 3 - Lake farm, Wimborne, 4 - Dorchester, 5 - Axminster, 6 - Exeter.* Ports/supply bases: *7 - Fishbourne, 8 - Bitterne, 9 - Christchurch, 10 - Poole Harbour, 11 - Weymouth, 12 - Seaton, 13 - Topsham*

Another 25 miles or so on from Bitterne lies the partly excavated early vexillation fortress at Lake Farm near Wimborne in Dorset. Its accompanying port and supply depot could have been at Poole Harbour, a major port for at least a century before the invasion, where early samian has been found at Hamworthy.[23] Another possibility is Christchurch, a few miles to the east which would have enabled supplies to have been taken direct to the fortress by lighters operating on the River Stour. About 20 miles further on again lies Dorchester. Firm evidence for the early military base long suspected here is still lacking but the major Durotrigan stronghold of Maiden Castle nearby, with its dramatic evidence of siege and destruction by Roman forces, demands the presence of one of Vespasian's principal bases. Weymouth Bay a few miles to the south would have afforded a secure anchorage for supply ships. An alternative location for its port and stores depot would be Wareham at the west end of Poole Harbour. Although positioned somewhat to the rear of a base at Dorchester it would have had the advantage of a direct waterborne route for supplies via the River Frome.

Further west the next known legionary site is the fortress at Exeter. Although this was not founded until the early to mid-50s, an early naval base at Topsham, 4 miles to the south at the head of the Exe estuary, has long been considered a possibility because of finds of first-century material over an area of some 60 acres to the north of the modern town. In 2000 the south-east corner of a double-ditched military enclosure was discovered on the east bank of the Exe at Topsham and so it would seem the postulated base has at last been found.[24] There remains the long gap between Exeter and the suggested base at Dorchester. If there is another major camp or fortress to be found then perhaps it should be sought somewhere in the vicinity of the probable Neronian fort at Axminster.[25] A stores base of the invasion period on the coast at the mouth of the Axe, beneath or close to Seaton, seems a logical possibility.[26] The

alignment of the southernmost stretch of the Fosse Way suggests it may originally have run along the Axe Valley with the run to Exeter being a slightly
later addition. If so, then the base at Topsham may belong to the governorship
of Plautius' successor Ostorius Scapula (47-52) rather than that of Plautius.
Another fort of legionary vexillation size is known at Ilchester but its date has
yet to be determined.[27] Although well inland, this was accessible from the sea
via the Rivers Parrett and Yeo. Bridgwater, at the mouth of the Parrett, is a
likely location for another of the military ports established in the late 40s.

Vespasian's command continued until late in 47 when he returned to Rome
along with the departing governor Aulus Plautius. This meant he had four full
campaigning seasons to subdue the south-west. All of the bases just mentioned,
with the possible exception of Topsham, would have been constructed and held
during his term of office. The Second *Augusta* would have occupied several
fortresses simultaneously and even those left in the rear by the advancing battle-
group would have been maintained for several years. The fleet too would have
been dispersed along the south coast, constructing harbour facilities, bringing
in supplies to the chain of store depots and also carrying out reconnaissance
missions for the army. Beyond Exeter, it is difficult to believe that the protected
anchorages at Plymouth and Falmouth were not utilised in some way at this
time and indeed early material has been recovered from the Mount Batten area
of the former.[28] The military would have been eager to exploit the tin and
copper deposits of the Damnonii as soon as possible. Back at Richborough,
where the army had first set foot in Britain, the beach head compound had been
demolished within two years of the invasion and replaced by an even larger
stores compound and works depot covering more than 150 acres (62ha).[29]
Within this were at least nine granaries and the base was clearly a collection and
storage point for large quantities of corn (**27**). What cannot be decided as yet,
however, is whether this was being shipped in from the Continent to supply the
army in Britain, or exported from Britain to feed the army on the Rhine. The
second possibility has recently been emphasised by Bird who rightly points out
that grain was one of the main exports from Britain listed by Strabo.[30] This has
been taken further by Grainge who suggests that the warfare unleashed by
Caratacus and Togodumnus on their neighbours posed a threat to the supply of
grain from Britain to the Roman army on the Rhine and that this was one of
the prime reasons for the launch of the invasion.[31]

To 'the sea-facing Ireland'

By the time that Plautius left Britain the whole of the area south and east of a
line between the Severn and the Wash had been secured. Two client kingdoms,
the Iceni in East Anglia and the Atrebates in Sussex, retained a nominal inde-
pendence while a third – the Brigantes under Queen Cartimandua – acted as

a buffer between the Roman province and the hostile tribes to the north. However, Caratacus, the surviving son of Cunobelinus, had escaped into Wales and it was from here that the main threat to the province now came. Control of the Bristol Channel was essential both to prevent infiltration from Wales and to reconnoitre its southern coastline for potential landing-places. Even as consolidation of the line of supply along the south coast was proceeding, the fleet will already have rounded Land's End and begun to explore the Bristol Channel (**30**). Natural harbours such as the Camel, Taw and Parrett estuaries would have been used to anchor overnight and/or to shelter from stormy conditions and, as mentioned above, the last of these may well have been the site of a military port. Shipping along this treacherous coastline would have benefited from navigational aids and two signal stations were identified some years ago on the north Devon coast at Old Burrow and Martinhoe.[32] The first, and earliest, was that at Old Burrow positioned on a 1,000ft-high bluff. Martinhoe, 8 miles away, occupied a lower site less affected by hill mists and was built slightly later. More recently, two others have been located further to the south-west at Morwenstow and St Gennys.[33] Others must have existed but have either yet to be found or have been destroyed by coastal erosion. There may have been similar stations along the south coast of the south-west peninsula at places such as Star Point, The Lizard, Trevose Head and Bull Point. A small earthwork at High Peak near Sidmouth which has produced first-century pottery may have been one such station.[34]

Apart from a possible site at the mouth of the Parrett, the first major base along the north coast was established at Sea Mills, the Roman *Portus Abonae*, at the confluence of the Avon and Trym (**31**). Items of army equipment and a large number of Claudio-Neronian coins found on low ground near the confluence attest the existence of a military port and stores base although its precise form remains unknown.[35] With the beginning of the assault on Wales, Sea Mills was ideally positioned for the ferrying of troops and supplies across to the coastal plain on the opposite shore, in particular to the mouth of the Usk Valley, one of the principal routes into the interior. It is at this stage, the beginning of Ostorius Scapula's term of office that the surviving books of Tacitus' *Annals* take up the story. Arriving in the late summer of 47, Scapula found the province under attack from the Welsh tribes who had united under the leadership of Caratacus. He may even have managed to incite some of the tribes within the province to revolt. Scapula routed the force which had entered the province and then, to secure his flank, ordered the confiscation of arms from all of the tribes previously subdued, even the nominally independent client kingdoms. The Iceni rebelled at this but were soon defeated. The following year Scapula launched an attack against the tribe known as the Deceangli in North Wales, and Tacitus tells us that he had almost reached the sea-facing Ireland when a rising amongst the Brigantes forced him to withdraw.[36] Clearly Scapula was hoping to occupy the Cheshire Plain and thus

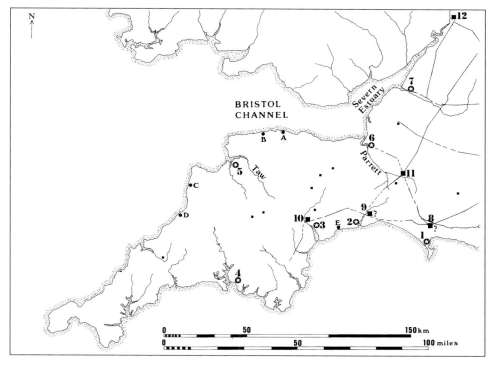

30 *Map of the south-west and the Bristol Channel showing location of early military bases and lookout/signal stations. KEY:* Military harbours: *1 - Weymouth, 2 - Seaton, 3 - Topsham, 4 - Plymouth, 5 - Barnstaple, 6 - Bridgwater, 7 - Sea Mills. Signal stations: A - Old Burrow, B - Martinhoe, C - Morwenstow, D - St. Gennys, E - High Peak. Legionary bases: 8 - Dorchester, 9 - Axminster, 10 - Exeter, 11 - Ilchester, 12 - Kingsholm. Auxiliary forts indicated by small squares*

create a bulwark of Roman power between the Welsh tribes and the anti-Roman elements of the Brigantes. However, the possibility of provoking all of Brigantia into open hostility was too great a risk as it would threaten the security of the entire province. Retreat calmed the situation and the rebellion lost impetus, enabling the ringleaders to be rounded up and killed. This episode raises the interesting possibility, indeed probability, that it was Scapula's intention to rendezvous with the fleet at some point on the North Wales coast, most probably a location on the west shore of the Dee estuary (**25**).

Scapula spent the rest of his governorship campaigning against the Ordovices and Silures in central and southern Wales respectively. In 49 the Twentieth Legion was moved forward from Colchester, which now became a *colonia*, at least part of it being based at Kingsholm near Gloucester.[37] This was the lowest bridgeable point on the Severn and, more significantly, was accessible by seagoing vessels, again emphasising the importance of maritime supply. Certainly there would have been a major increase in naval activity in the Bristol Channel at this time (**31**). Further north, part at least of *Legio XIV* was moved forward, probably accommodated in the 20-acre (8ha) fortress at Leighton near

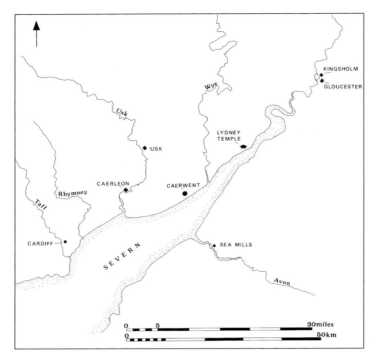

31 *Map of principal early Roman military sites beside the Severn estuary*

Wroxeter. Caratacus was captured in 51 but the war against the Welsh tribes continued. Under Scapula's successor Didius Gallus (52-7) the previously divided elements of both the Twentieth and the Fourteenth Legions were reunited in new fortresses, the former at Usk and the latter at Wroxeter. Although not on the coast, both fortresses were located on major navigable rivers – the Usk and Severn respectively – allowing supplies to be transferred from seagoing vessels and brought in by smaller river craft.[38] At the same time a substantial fort and/or stores base was built at Cardiff, at the mouth of the Taff, and another fort at the mouth of the Wye at Chepstow.[39] Both of these were again well sited to receive seaborne supplies for transport by river craft to other forts situated further up the valleys of these rivers in the Silurian heartland. It may also have been at this time that the fortress known to underlie the upper *colonia* at Lincoln was constructed by the Ninth *Hispana*. Here, too, supply by river craft was possible, in this case via the Witham which recent work has shown was much broader in the Roman period than today.[40] The Foss Dyke canal which linked the River Till with the Trent and thus the Humber is often assumed to be Roman, but its date is still open to question. The potential of the Humber estuary as the site for a future naval base may also have been recognised in this period and a fort may have been constructed on its south shore at Old Winteringham where Claudio-Neronian material has been recovered.[41]

Quintus Veranius succeeded Gallus as governor but died less than a year into his term of office. It is under the following governor – Suetonius Paullinus –

that the fleet next appears in the sources, in the context of his attack on the Island of Anglesey situated off the north-west tip of Wales (**25**). This was the centre of Druidic power and a boiling cauldron of hatred towards Rome and all things Roman, a refuge for all those rebels/freedom fighters who still refused to lay down their arms:

> So Suetonius planned to attack the island of Mona, which although thickly populated had also given sanctuary to many refugees. Flat-bottomed ships were built to contend with the shifting shallows, and these took the infantry across. Then came the cavalry; some utilised fords, but, in deeper water the men swam beside their horses. The enemy lined the shore in a dense armed mass. Among them were black-robed women with dishevelled hair like Furies, brandishing torches. Close by stood Druids, raising their hands to heaven and screaming dreadful curses. This weird spectacle awed the Roman soldiers into a sort of paralysis. They stood still – and presented themselves as a target. But then they urged each other (and were urged by the general) not to fear a horde of fanatical women. Onward pressed their standards and they bore down their opponents, enveloping them in the flames of their own torches. Suetonius garrisoned the conquered island.
>
> Tacitus *Annals* 14. 29-30

Before attacking Anglesey Tacitus tells us that Suetonius had spent two years (58-9) 'conquering tribes and establishing strong forts' (*Agricola* 14). The second season would have been occupied with the reduction of mainland Ordovician territory, probably including most of Snowdonia, as a prelude to the assault. Paullinus' campaign force would have consisted of the bulk of *Legio XIV*, based at Wroxeter, together with vexillations of *Legio XX* and a number of auxiliary units; a total of around 10,000 men. This was the force he rushed back with to the south-east in 60 on hearing of Boudicca's rebellion. The main campaign base appears to have been the 42.5-acre (17.2ha) site at Rhyn Park with the marching camps at Penrhos and Llanfor in the Dee valley indicating the line (or one of the lines) of advance taken in 59.[42] A lack of known sites means that the line of approach to Anglesey the following year can only be conjectured. The prevailing view for many years was that the ships used for the crossing (Tacitus uses the word *navis* – 'ship', and not *ratis* – 'raft', indicating that substantial oared transports were employed) were built in the sheltered estuary of the Dee, possibly somewhere in the vicinity of the later legionary fortress at Chester, with the main land advance following the North Wales coast.[43] Traces of two successive military bases have been found beneath the Chester fortress but neither is as yet susceptible to close dating.[44] The earlier, with a *titulum* protecting its south gateway, could well be a temporary camp of the Paullinian campaigns. However, be that as it may, an inland route to Anglesey is equally if not more likely and a location closer to the Menai Strait for the building of the ships is certainly more probable.[45] One possibility is down the Conwy valley, probably reconnoitred if not actually garrisoned the previous year, where the wide mouth of the estuary would have been an ideal spot for building the transports. The other would be along the Llanberis Pass reaching the coast at the south end of the Menai Strait near Caernarfon where the permanent fort of *Segontium* was to be erected a few years later. Although the mouth of the Seiont was much narrower, building the ships here meant that they did not have to risk the journey along the coast. Although the fleet is not mentioned specifically, and the shallows in the Menai Straits probably meant that warships could not be used to provide covering fire, its presence would have been vital. Firstly, to provide the shipwrights needed to build the transports probably together with the oarsmen to propel them; secondly, to assist in the provisioning of Paullinus' forces which by now lay at the end of a very lengthy overland supply line through extremely hostile territory; and thirdly, to patrol the waters around Anglesey to prevent the enemy's leaders escaping by sea.

No sooner had Paullinus occupied Anglesey than word came of Boudica's rebellion. Although ultimately successful, the Roman forces in Britain had suffered significant losses in the conflict, especially the Ninth *Hispana*. To bring them back up to strength 2,000 legionaries, eight auxiliary infantry units and 1,000 cavalry were transferred from Germany. This would obviously have been a significant naval operation but whether undertaken by the British or the German fleet, or both, is unrecorded. The devastation which Paullinus visited upon the tribal lands of the rebels attracted the disapproval of the Procurator Julius Classicianus who could see the potentially disastrous effects on future tax revenues. Paullinus survived an enquiry headed by the powerful ex-slave Polyclitus but was recalled shortly afterwards ostensibly because of an incident in which 'a few ships were wrecked on the shore and their crews lost' (Tacitus *Annals*, 14.39). Unfortunately we have no further information about this tantalising reference to naval activity.

Restoration and rebuilding within the province were the priorities following the suppression of the revolt and so completion of the conquest and occupation of Wales was postponed. However, while fleet activity off the west coast may have diminished in the immediate post-Boudiccan period, the number of merchant vessels plying the Irish Sea (*Oceanus Hivernicus*) probably increased. The exploitation of the mineral wealth of Deceanglican territory in north-east Wales may have been initiated in the 60s by private prospectors operating under government leases.[46] The ingots of metal are more likely to have been shipped out than transported overland. We also know from Tacitus' account of Agricola's campaigns in the late 70s that traders of all kinds had been conducting business in Irish ports for quite a number of years. Their knowledge of the Hibernian coast was to provide useful intelligence for the Roman military in its forward planning.

By the mid-60s, calm had been restored throughout the province, and in 66 Nero withdrew the Fourteenth Legion for service in the East. Three years later, during the period of civil war known as the Year of the Four Emperors, it was ordered back to Britain and the fleet transported it once more across the Channel.[47] In 70 the Fourteenth was on its travels again. This time the fleet conveyed it across the North Sea to the Rhineland to strengthen the forces engaged in the suppression of the Civilis Revolt. The fleet, too, was to assist in the campaign and this is the first time that the *Classis Britannica* is mentioned as such in the sources. Unfortunately its first appearance by name also marks one of the most ignominious episodes in its history. The commander of the Fourteenth, Fabius Priscus, instead of keeping legion and fleet together and attacking the Batavian heartland by amphibious assault, took the legion overland against the Nervii and Tungri. Although these capitulated to him another tribe – the Canninefates – attacked the fleet riding at anchor and destroyed or captured the majority of its ships.[48] The losses were made good during the ensuing autumn and winter, for in the following year Quintus Petilius Cerialis, who had crushed the Civilis Revolt, crossed over to Britain as its new governor accompanied by *Legio II Adiutrix*. Now was to begin the final phase of the conquest of Britain and it was one in which the British fleet, so recently humiliated, was to play a major role.

To the ends of Britain and beyond

While the Empire was undergoing the catharsis of civil war, Venutius had rebelled against his former wife Cartimandua, and this time, with the aid of anti-Roman elements from neighbouring tribes, he took control of the Brigantes and tore up the treaty with Rome. The Roman army in Britain, weakened by the departure of *Legio XIV* and by the withdrawal of vexillations from the other three legions during the civil war, could do no more than rescue Cartimandua and resist incursions into Roman territory. Although he could not have known it Venutius was playing right into the hands of Vespasian. The new emperor was very familiar with Britain, the collapse of the treaty relationship could not go unpunished, and it provided the opportunity for completing the conquest of a land begun by Claudius and left uncompleted by Nero. Thus could Vespasian establish the legitimacy of his new Flavian dynasty as rightful heirs to the principles and ideals set out by Augustus. The fact that he sent his ablest generals to Britain is a clear indication that this was to be a 'high profile' operation. It is made even clearer by the ceremony held in Rome in 75 presided over by Vespasian and his son Titus in which the sacred boundary of the city – the *pomerium* – was extended; a symbolic representation of a recent expansion of the Empire which, in the absence of conquests elsewhere, can only have been based on the victories in Britain. This had happened only twice before and was clearly a major propaganda exercise by the Flavians to demonstrate that under their guidance Rome was keeping to its 'divine mission' to rule the world.

The choice of the Second *Adiutrix* to accompany Cerialis to Britain was an obvious one. It had been raised largely from men serving in the Ravenna-based section of the home fleet which had played an instrumental role in securing the victory of Vespasian's forces in Italy.[49] As a reward they were formed into a legion with the higher status and extra privileges this brought. This legion was thus completely loyal to the Flavians – expressed in the legion's other titles of *pia*, 'loyal', and *fidelis*, 'faithful' – and therefore provided useful security for the first Flavian-appointed governor in a province where the other legions had supported rival candidates. The maritime experience of its men would also be useful in campaigns where seaborne operations were to play a significant role. Details of the conquest of northern Britain are preserved for us in the biography of Gnaeus Julius Agricola, the third of the great generals sent by the Flavians, written by his son-in-law Publius Cornelius Tacitus. As a eulogy to his father-in-law it was only natural that he should concentrate on the achievements of Agricola and if not exactly play down those of his immediate predecessors then describe them with an economy of words. He does tell us however that Cerialis

> . . . at once struck terror into their hearts by attacking the Brigantian nation, which is said to be the most populous in the whole province. After a series of battles, some not uncostly, he conquered much of Brigantia and overran more of it.
>
> *Agricola* 17

Understanding the extent of Cerialis' advance and just how much of Brigantia was actually garrisoned by him was for a long time impeded by a lack of evidence. However, archaeological discoveries and research in recent years have begun to show that Cerialis achieved rather more during his three years as governor than was previously thought (**32**).[50]

Immediately upon Cerialis' arrival *Legio IX Hispana*, of which incidentally he had been legate at the time of the Boudiccan Revolt, was ordered forward from Lincoln and set about constructing a new base at York. Again the fortress was situated beside a navigable river.[51] Its place at Lincoln, as evidenced by tombstones, was taken by the legion Cerialis brought with him, *II Adiutrix*. The future governor Agricola was also in Britain. He had been sent over the previous year to take over command of *Legio XX*, whose discipline and loyalty were both in question. Having served as a tribune of the Twentieth when Cerialis was in charge of the Ninth, he was well placed to undertake such a task. From what Tacitus tells us about Cerialis' strategy to reduce Brigantia it is clear that while he led one battle-group up the east side of the Pennines, presumably with his old legion the Ninth as the vanguard, Agricola led another up the west side spearheaded by the Twentieth. From what we know of the strategy employed in both previous and later campaigns we can be sure that the fleet was heavily involved in the advance (32). With much of the Twentieth absent from its base at Wroxeter, presumably accompanied by auxiliary units from in the region, Roman forces in the central and northern Marches would have been seriously depleted and possibly incapable of resisting a determined attack by the Ordovices. To counter this possibility, and also to establish a fleet base for naval operations along the north-west coast, Cerialis may have moved part of *II Adiutrix* to Chester at the head of the broad estuary of the Dee.[52] The rest of the legion would have remained at Lincoln to deal with any breakouts from southern Brigantia. The later and seemingly larger of the two pre-fortress bases at Chester would fit this context.[53]

Recent dendrochronological dating of timbers recovered from the south gateway of the fort at Carlisle, sited at the head of the Solway Firth, show it to

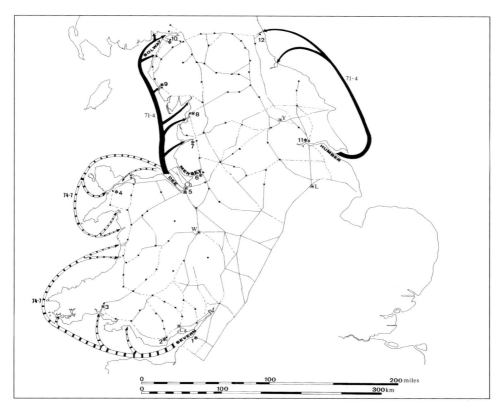

32 *Map illustrating campaigns of Cerialis and Frontinus (AD 71-7) and principal naval operations.*
KEY: Legionary fortresses: Ca - Caerleon, Ch - Chester, L - Lincoln, W - Wroxeter, Y - York.
Auxiliary forts indicated by small squares. Important military harbours: *1 - Sea Mills, 2 - Cardiff,*
3 - Carmarthen, 4 - Carnarvon, 5 - Chester, 6 - Wilderspool, 7- Kirkham, 8 - Lancaster,
9 - Ravenglass, 10 - Kirkbride, 11 - Brough-on-Humber, 12 - South Shields

have been constructed at the end of AD 72, rather earlier than hitherto suspected.[54] Other forts on the approach from the south, once thought to be Agricolan, are likely to be contemporary. These include Old Penrith, Brougham, Watercrook and Lancaster along with the probable fort sites at Walton-le-Dale, Wigan and Wilderspool (**33**). Kirkham and Ribchester on the Ribble also appear to have a Cerialian origin.[55] Many of these sites lie on estuaries thus enabling supplies and/or troops to be brought in by sea. The military sites at Ravenglass, Maryport and Kirkbride, lying at the mouths of the Esk, Ellen and Wampool rivers respectively, may also have come into being as links in this primary chain of safe havens and coastal supply dumps. The topography on the east side of the country did not permit regular contact between land and sea forces to the same degree as Cerialis' line of advance. Undoubtedly based on the route followed slightly later by Dere Street this crossed only two major rivers, the Tees and the Tyne. A fort built at the crossing of the first of these, at Piercebridge, could well have been supplied by river craft. In the case of the Tyne valley the importance of waterborne supply is clearer. A stores and works depot covering 20-30 acres (8-12ha) was built on the north bank of the river at Red House near Corbridge. This was obviously one of the key bases for the eastern force and once again some of its supplies could have been brought in by barge.[56] Its equivalent in the west is at present unknown although the largest of the military enclosures recently discovered at Dalston, 3 miles (5km) south-south-west of Carlisle, might fit the bill.[57]

Venutius' last stand was probably at Stanwick hillfort near Scotch Corner. With his defeat and death, Brigantian resistance faded away and by the time that Cerialis returned to Rome in 74 the whole of northern England, together probably with parts of southern Scotland, had been occupied. With the emergency over and victory won it fell to the next governor, Sextus Julius Frontinus (74-7), to remove the threat from Wales by completing its conquest. To achieve this and the garrisoning of the newly annexed territory in the North required a major redeployment of the forces in Britain which entailed the evacuation of any remaining forts in the south-east. The Second *Augusta*, which had been stationed at Gloucester since 66, was moved forward to begin the construction of a new fortress at Caerleon near the mouth of the River Usk. This site was far less susceptible to flooding than the earlier fortress at Usk itself and was much easier to provision by sea. The latter advantage was enjoyed to an even greater degree by the site at Chester where the whole of *II Adiutrix* was now brought together in another new fortress. Ten acres (4ha) or fully 20 per cent larger than its counterpart at either Caerleon or York, there is a strong possibility that *Deva* served, or was intended to serve, as the governor's headquarters in the Flavian era.[58] A network of forts was soon established throughout Wales including a number located on estuarine sites such as Caerhun, Caernarfon, Carmarthen, Conwy, Loughor, Neath and Pennal (**32** & **48**).

1 *A flotilla of triremes operating in British waters*

2 *Reconstruction scene depicting the Dover lighthouses*

3 *Sestertius of the reign of Hadrian. The scene shows a warship carrying the emperor who is seated between two standards at the stern. The prow is embellished with a figurehead taking the form of a large statue of a wind-god. Note what appears to be a ventilation course along the side of the vessel immediately beneath the projection. The coin was recovered from the River Tyne at Newcastle in the nineteenth century*

4 *Intaglio or gemstone carved with image of large merchant ship progressing to the right. The latter possesses not only the usual large square mainsail but also a smaller artemon or bowsail. To the right of the vessel is a representation of a lighthouse or pharos, perhaps one of the pair at Dover or that at Boulogne. Found at Caistor-by-Norwich in a mid-second-century context.* Norwich Museum

5 *Colchester. First-century lamp with image of a galley. The goose-head sternpost, more typical of a merchant ship than a warship, suggests the vessel is a merchant galley and that the projecting feature at the prow is a cutwater rather than a ram*

6 *Carnelian intaglio found on the foreshore at Southwark, London, in 1996. It depicts a warship in a very simplistic style with the oarsmen represented by four rowers. The overall form of the vessel is similar to those illustrated on the coinage of Carausius and Allectus – see illustrations **71-74** – and so the gemstone may be mid- to late third-century in date. The direction in which the vessel is sailing and the nature of the structures at bow and stern is disputed – Henig & Ross 1998 vs. Grainge 2002, 17-18.* Copyright Museum of London

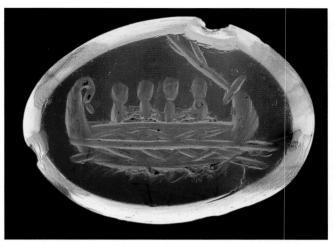

7 *Reverse of the gold medallion found at Arras, northern France. The scene depicts Constantius' triumphal entrance into London in 296 after part of his forces which sailed up the Thames rescued it from Allectus' retreating Frankish mercenaries. The guardian spirit of London kneels before the city gate to welcome Constantius who is hailed as redditor lucis aeternae – 'Restorer of the Eternal Light' – while his fleet is represented by a single ship in the lower part of the scene*

8 *Fourth-century mosaic floor in Low Ham villa, Somerset. The scene depicted is the mythological flight of Aeneas from Carthage but the ships are very probably modelled on contemporary warships protecting the shores of Britain*

9 *Chester. The so-called quay wall running along the eastern shoreline of the ancient harbour area (now the Roodee racecourse). The picture shows the best preserved section with nearly 10ft of the massive masonry standing above present ground level. Excavation in the nineteenth century proved it extends at least 14ft below ground. It is possible that, rather than a quay, it was in fact a late Roman defensive wall protecting a wealthy part of the civil settlement beside the legionary fortress. Alternatively, it may have begun life as a quay and then had further masonry added to make it into a defensive wall*

10 *Close-up of one of the 'pilaster-like' buttresses on the face of the Chester 'quay wall'. Too slight to perform any real structural purpose they may have been a decorative replication of the vertical retaining timbers typical of timber quaysides*

11 *Reconstruction model of quayside scene in Roman London.* Museum of London

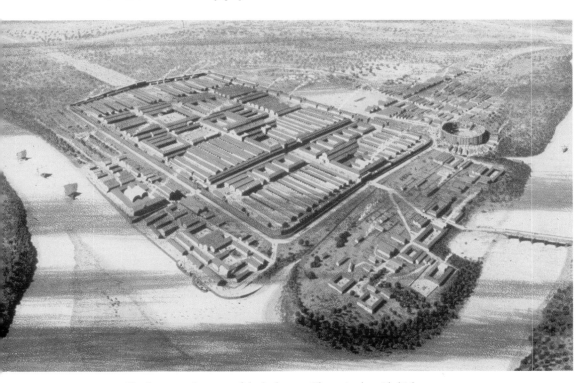

12 *Reconstruction scene of the harbour at Chester in the mid-third century*

13 *Wallsend. Reconstruction scene of fort and harbour in the early third century*

14 *Reconstruction scene of Portchester Shore Fort in the mid-fourth century*

15 *The eastern lighthouse at Dover. The lower three-quarters of the structure is Roman with the upper external masonry a medieval repair*

16 *West wall of the Shore Fort at Pevensey*

17 *East wall of Portchester Shore fort looking south towards Portsmouth Harbour. The projecting bastions are Roman, the square tower is medieval*

18 *Late Roman stone watch-tower on summit of Holyhead Mountain, Anglesey. View looking out over the Irish Sea*

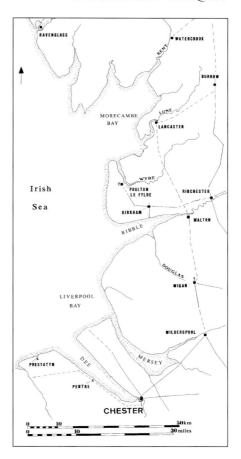

33 *Map of north-west England illustrating the placement of army bases in coastal/riverine locations*

Agricola took over as governor late in the summer of 77. Shortly before his arrival a squadron of cavalry had nearly been annihilated by the Ordovices. Agricola took swift and severe reprisals which included a lightning assault on Anglesey. So hasty was his action that there was not even time to order up the fleet and so his troops forded or swam across the Menai Strait, taking the enemy completely by surprise. By the following year he was ready to continue where Cerialis had left off and led his forces into Lowland Scotland, meeting little opposition and installing garrisons (**34**).[59] The two-column approach was used again, the western proceeding through Annandale to Clydesdale and the eastern through Redesdale to Lauderdale, routes soon formalised as permanent roads. Agricola's third season of campaigning

> . . . opened up new nations, for the territory of tribes as far as the estuary named Tanaus (the Tay) was ravaged. Our army was seriously buffeted by furious storms, but the enemy were now too terrified to molest it.
>
> Tacitus *Agricola* 22

The mention of furious storms could suggest transport by sea of part of the invasion force, while the choice of the Tay as a halting place for this season's campaign implies a rendezvous with the fleet in a set-piece combined forces operation. A spot somewhere in the vicinity of the early third-century legionary fortress at Carpow is one possibility for the year's ultimate camp although material of Flavian date has yet to be found (**37**). The 115-acre (47ha) camp at Abernethy a little to the west is another possibility, but again dating is difficult and there is also another camp on the opposite shore at Invergowrie, just west of Dundee. To the south, the Roman road known as the Devil's Causeway, which branches off from Dere Street just north of Corbridge, makes its way first to the Flavian fort at Learchild and then continues almost due north making for the mouth of the Tweed. Although yet to be found there can be little doubt that an early fort awaits discovery somewhere near Berwick, exploiting its strategic position and fine harbour. The fourth year of Agricola's term was spent consolidating the territorial gains already made with most of his men engaged in fort construction. The *Classis Britannica* must have been operating in strength as far north as the Solway estuary and Tynemouth since Cerialis' campaigns a decade earlier. To support Agricola's thrust into Scotland its numbers would have been greatly augmented, particularly so in the case of the squadron(s) on the east coast with the advance of the main body of the army to the Tay. As Tacitus tells us, the narrow neck of land separating the Forth and Clyde afforded a natural place at which to halt the advance, and this line was now secured by the construction and garrisoning of forts (*Agricola* 23). It also of course greatly facilitated supply operations, as the bulk of the goods needed by the campaign army could be brought in by ships operating along both the east and west coasts.

The fifth season of campaigning (AD 81) began with a sea-crossing followed by the successful and rapid subjugation of tribes hitherto unknown. Agricola then

> . . . drew up his forces along that part of Britain which faces Ireland, not in fear but in hope. If indeed it is true that Ireland lies between Britain and Spain and is conveniently placed for the Gallic sea it could be to our advantage to incorporate it into this strong part of our empire. [. . .] Its approaches and harbours are tolerably well known from our merchants who trade there. Agricola received one of the minor princes who had been expelled by a family feud and kept him with him with the appearance of friendship but also with an eye to opportunity. I have often heard Agricola say that Ireland could be conquered and garrisoned with a single legion and a few auxiliary units; and that it would serve as a useful tool against Britain if Roman arms were on every side and the prospect of freedom disappeared.
>
> *Agricola* 24

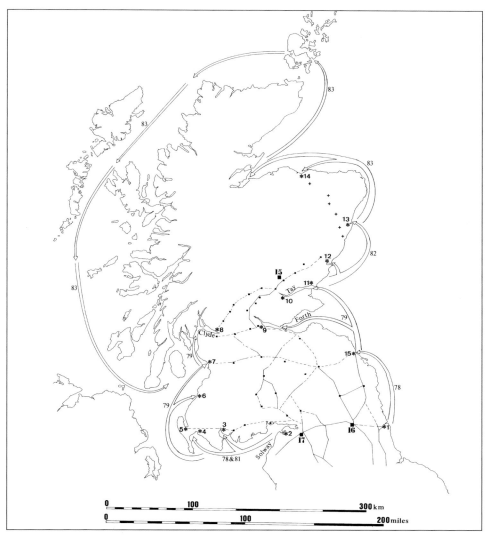

34 *Map of Agricola's campaigns in Scotland and the activities of Roman naval forces.*
KEY: *Known/probable main military ports: 1 - South Shields, 2 - Kirkbride, 3 – Newton Stewart, 4 - Glenluce, 5 - Stranraer, 6 - Girvan, 7 - Ayr, 8 - Dumbarton, 9 - Camelon, 10 - Carpow, 11 - Monifieth, 12 - Dun, 13 - Aberdeen, 14 - Bellie.* Legionary bases: *15 - Inchtuthil, 16 - Red House, Corbridge, 17 - Carlisle. Auxiliary forts indicated by small squares. Crosses indicate major marching-camps possibly belonging to the campaign of 83*

The conventional interpretation of this passage is that Agricola crossed the Solway Firth to reduce the area of Dumfries and Galloway, which had so far been bypassed by the main advance, and then set about organising his forces ready for a crossing of the Irish Sea. Others, however, have suggested the sea crossed was the Irish Sea and that Agricola actually carried out a Caesar–like reconnaissance in strength in 81.[60] For present purposes it does not really matter which view is correct, because of course a full-scale invasion never took place. What is clear however is that for Agricola to have been entertaining the idea of crossing the Irish Sea with an invasion force the concentration of naval power in these waters must indeed have been very considerable, possibly consisting of several hundred vessels. Furthermore, this was in addition to the squadrons carrying out supply and support operations on the east coast. The natural harbour at the mouth of the River Wampool, overlooked by the fort at Kirkbride, may have been the initial assembly point for the fleet. A number of marching-camps are known along the Dumfries/Galloway coast and appear to belong to a series stretching from the head of the Solway estuary as far west as Glenluce overlooking Luce Bay (**35**). Knowledge of more permanent installations is at present limited to a fort at Glenlochar and a fortlet at Gatehouse of Fleet. A road runs south from the latter and then turns to the west presumably making for either Glenluce or Stranraer at the head of Loch Ryan.[61] Forts at Stranraer and Newton Stewart further inland seem likely. The plan would have involved the invasion fleet assembling in either Luce Bay or Loch Ryan, or maybe even both, and thence making the 20 mile (32km) crossing to the upper reaches of Belfast Lough. Further north, Ayr, overlooking Irvine Bay (*Vindogara Sinus*), has also produced coins of this period and is another likely fort site.[62] There must surely have been a harbour of this period on the Clyde itself and a location close to Dumbarton is a possibility.

Although Agricola was obviously very taken with the idea of invading Ireland – if only because this would have put him on the same level as Aulus Plautius as the conqueror of a new land beyond the Ocean – and had clearly instructed his general staff to make all necessary preparations, the new emperor Domitian refused him permission directing him instead to subjugate the tribes north of the Forth-Clyde line:

> . . . he used his fleet to reconnoitre the harbours. It was first employed by him to bring his forces to the requisite strength. Its continued attendance on him made an excellent impression. The war was pushed forward by land and sea; and infantry, cavalry and marines, often meeting in the same camp, would mess and make merry together. They would boast, as soldiers will, of their various exploits and adventures, and match the perilous depths of woods and mountains against the hazards of storms and tides, the victories on land against the conquest of the Ocean. The Britons for their part, as was learned from prisoners, were stupefied by the appearance of the fleet. The mystery of their sea was divulged, their last refuge in defeat cut off.
>
> *Agricola* 25

That the 'hazards of storms and tides' were very real is demonstrated by a tombstone from Chester. This commemorates a man who '*naufragio perit*' –

perished in a shipwreck, quite possibly whilst taking part in Agricola's campaigns in the North (36). His name is not known as the relevant portion of the inscription is missing, but he had reached the rank of *optio* and was serving in the century of Lucilius Ingenuus. The regular formula HSE (*hic situs est* – 'his body lies here') lacks the first letter suggesting that his body was never recovered.[63] The historian Plutarch recalls meeting a man called Scribonius Demetrius in Athens in 83/4, at that time a schoolteacher, who had actually participated in one of the reconnaissance missions in the Western Isles a few years earlier.[64] Demetrius has been identified with the man of that name who dedicated two silvered bronze plaques at York. Both are inscribed in Greek; the dedication on one is to 'the gods of the commandant's residence', and that on the other, appropriate if it is the same man, to 'Ocean and Tethys'.[65]

During this sixth season of campaigning an event occurred which although incidental to the mainstream of events nonetheless provides us with the only information about the type of warship being employed in Agricola's operations. A cohort of Usipi, who had been levied in Germany and transferred to Britain, rebelled. They murdered the centurion and regular soldiers who were in charge of them and seized three warships. These are referred to by Tacitus as liburnians and confirms the general impression that by this period biremes had become the standard warship of the provincial fleets.[66] The Usipi set sail for home and Tacitus relates how they put into land on a number of occasions to grab what provisions they could, usually successfully but sometimes repulsed by the Britons. They managed to make it across the North Sea but not before they had been reduced to cannibalism. They eventually lost their ships through poor seamanship and

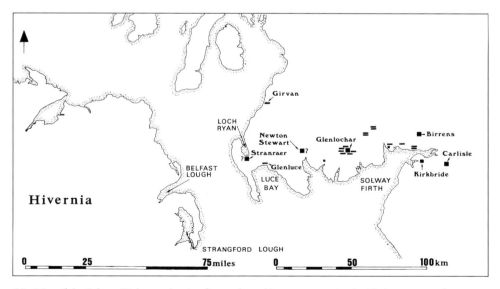

35 *Map of the Solway Firth area showing forts and marching-camps associated with the conquest of south-west Scotland and preparations for an assault on Ireland*

36 *Tombstone from Chester (RIB I 544) recording an* optio *who died in a shipwreck*

were attacked first by the Suebi and then the Frisii. Some of the survivors were sold on as slaves with a few eventually coming into the possession of the Roman garrison on the Rhine, whereupon their story was revealed.

The 'combined operations' which feature so prominently in Tacitus' narrative are as yet poorly represented in the archaeological evidence. Only one camp has been identified on the coast north of the Tay (**37**). This lies at Dun on the north shore of the Montrose basin, but with a size of only 8 acres (3.4ha) it was not a major site.[67] However, Ptolemy refers to a base somewhere in this general area called *Horrea Classis*, 'Granaries of the Fleet', which implies an installation of considerable size and importance.[68] Its location is unknown but the consensus of opinion favours the environs of Monifieth, on the north shore of the Tay just east of Dundee.[69] The site of the Severan legionary base at Carpow on the opposite shore is another possibility.

Agricola's seventh and final campaigning season began in much the same way as the previous year with the fleet being sent ahead to raid and plunder, spreading terror and uncertainty amongst the enemy. He knew only too well the effectiveness of this tactic as his mother had been killed and her estate plundered during a raid on the Ligurian coast by Otho's fleet during the civil war in 69. His employment of it now was geared to forcing the Caledonii and their allies into a pitched battle instead of using guerrilla warfare. In this he was of course successful, the decisive engagement taking place at the still unidentified location known as *Mons Graupius*. Some of the largest of the series of temporary camps known north of the Tay which skirt the eastern edge of the Highlands must belong to this campaign, most probably those of 100 acres or more such as Raedykes, Normandykes, Durno, Ythan Wells and Muiryfold (**34**).[70] After the battle,

Agricola took his army on a circuitous and leisurely march through the Highlands, possibly via the Great Glen, taking hostages from the various tribes as he progressed and eventually making his way back to base in Perthshire. To doubly emphasise the point that Roman arms now held sway over the whole of Caledonia, and thus the whole of Britain, he assigned troops to the fleet and sent it to navigate around the northern coast.[71] The camp of unknown size discovered at Bellie near the mouth of the River Spey, or the *Tuesis* as it was known to Ptolemy, was very probably one of the points where Agricola's army met up with his fleet. In the course of its voyage the fleet discovered and subdued the Orkney Islands and also sighted Shetland but did not land there as winter was approaching.[72] A harbour named *Portus Truculensis*, otherwise unattested, is cited as the place from which the fleet sailed and to which it returned after its voyage. Unfortunately, despite much research and discussion its identity is still unknown.[73]

Agricola was recalled in 83. The most conspicuously successful of the Flavian governors, he had built on the excellent groundwork of Cerialis and Frontinus. The achievements of these three men within the space of 12 years had more than doubled the size of the British province and each demonstrated a masterly appreciation of the capabilities of sea-power in extended military operations. Reconnaissance for potential landing-places, intimidating the enemy by appearing unexpectedly off their shores, dismaying them by the arrival of troops on land and by sea simultaneously, and keeping a large army in the field well supplied; all of these were employed to supreme effect. Large fleets had operated along the east and west coasts at the same time and, ultimately, Roman naval power had girdled mainland Britain. It was left to Agricola's unknown successor to carry out the consolidation of the newly won territory, but one of the last decisions he took before leaving the province was the siting of a new fortress for *Legio XX* at Inchtuthil, 10 miles north of Perth.[74] Unusually, this was one fortress that supplies could not reach directly by water. Although positioned on a plateau of sand and gravel beside the Tay, ships could not navigate any closer than about nine miles owing to rapids near Bertha. In this case a position closer to the potential threat from the Highland glens was considered more important than waterborne supply. At Richborough, at the other end of the province, work began on the construction of an enormous triumphal arch to commemorate the conquest of all Britain. Dismantled in the late third century, only fragments survive but these are sufficient to show it was clad with marble and embellished with bronze statuary.[75] As the site of the original landings and the main port of entry to the province, Richborough was the obvious location for such a monument. The total conquest of Britain was an achievement clearly deserving of commemoration in a substantive and permanent form. Propaganda for the Flavian dynasty was undoubtedly another factor. The triumphal arch erected at Richborough made a matching pair with that built at Boulogne by Claudius. Thus everyone entering or leaving the province would be reminded that although it was Claudius who had begun the conquest of Britain it was the

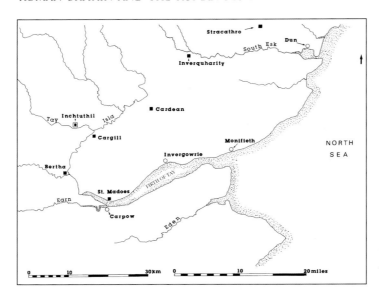

37 *Agricolan forts and possible harbours in the Tay area*

Flavian emperors who had completed it. The linking of the two dynasties through the medium of this architectural form was part of the propaganda campaign to show that the Flavians were the rightful heirs to the Julio-Claudians.

The tide ebbs

'*Perdomita Britannia et statim omissa*' wrote Tacitus – 'the conquest of Britain was completed and then let go' (*Histories* 1.2). Four years after Agricola left Britain, the fortress at Inchtuthil, not yet complete, was abandoned as part of a general disengagement from Scotland necessitated by the transference of *II Adiutrix*, probably along with a number of auxiliary units, for service in the Balkans. The Twentieth now returned to the region of its former service, taking the Second's place at Chester. What had been the most sustained period of action for the men of the *Classis Britannica* had now come to an end. Henceforth, apart from the odd expedition into northern waters, the role of the British Fleet was concerned with the more mundane duties of patrol, the transportation of men and material, and the carriage of important personages and communications to and from the Continent. With the end of the period of campaigning the time had come for a review of the naval forces attached to the province and the taking of decisions about their future organisation and location. The outcome of those deliberations is described in the next chapter.

7

THE MATURE CLASSIS BRITANNICA
*c.*AD 90-193

A permanent establishment

The decision to disengage from Scotland and abandon, at least for the time being, any idea of further conquest naturally led to a review of military deployment in the province. The three legionary headquarters henceforth were to be at Caerleon, Chester and York, while the auxiliary units withdrawn from Scotland were redeployed to existing or new forts in Wales and the Pennines. As regards the British Fleet its future role was seen mainly as providing the secure transportation of goods and materials to the army, conveying valuable exports such as precious metals to the Continent, and ensuring efficient government communications between Britain and Rome. Presumably it also had to maintain its military preparedness and capability through training and practice just as the army did in peacetime. There is now plentiful evidence to show that a major reorganisation of the infrastructure which supported the *Classis Britannica* was undertaken at the beginning of the second century. The bulk of the Fleet presumably returned to southern waters following the cessation of warfare in the North and the number of vessels is likely to have been reduced, most immediately by the scrapping of redundant troop-transports.

Biremes of *liburnian* type probably continued to be the most numerous heavy warship in the British Fleet although we know from a relief at Boulogne that there was also for a time at least one trireme.[1] This vessel, the *Radians* = 'Gleaming' or 'Resplendent', is one of only two vessels belonging to the *Classis Britannica* whose name has survived.[2]

The fleet headquarters at Boulogne (*Gesoriacum*)

Boulogne was where the embryonic *Classis Britannica* had first assembled in AD 43, and in keeping with its primary role of protecting both shores of the Channel this was where its headquarters continued to be located. Much of Roman Boulogne lies buried and inaccessible beneath the modern town but excavations in recent years have begun to elucidate some of the main features of the fleet base whose existence was already indicated by large numbers of tiles stamped with the letters CL.BR – short for *Classis Britannica* – and also by inscriptions set up by naval officers.[3] The latter provide some personal details of but a few of the thousands of men who once served in the British Fleet (see chapter 3). The defended core of the naval base stood on a prominent hill over-looking the natural harbour, and its defences, in their latest form, were partially incorporated in the walls of the medieval town (**38**). In outline it was much like any other military base of the period consisting of a rectangular enclosure with rounded corners. However, its large size, approximately 30 acres (12.45ha), shows beyond doubt that it was the headquarters of the British Fleet.[4] It was built in the opening years of the second century and was equipped with defences consisting of a stone wall with internal rectangular towers and an external ditch. Examination of the north-eastern portion of the interior, in what seems likely to have been the *retentura*, has disclosed the existence of barracks arranged in facing pairs mirroring the pattern in army bases (**39**). These were approximately 160ft long by 27ft wide (49 x 8.2m) and divided internally into 10 pairs of rooms with a larger apartment at one end for the officer(s). The total number of barracks and thus the overall number of men present is unknown but it seems very likely that at least 4,000 personnel were accommodated here, sufficient to crew 20 triremes or more than 60 biremes of liburnian type.

Cassius Dio records the construction of a triumphal arch here to celebrate Claudius' victory. As yet however the site of the first-century naval base has

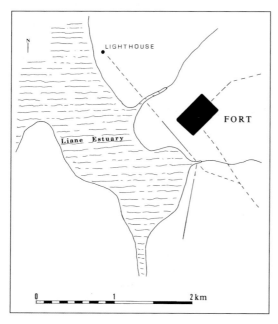

38 *Roman Boulogne. General plan*

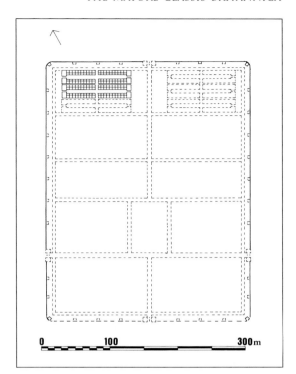

39 *Boulogne. Plan of the headquarters fort of the* Classis Britannica. *After Gosselin & Seillier*

0   100   300m

still to be located, a task made more difficult by the fact that silting over many centuries has obscured the original topography of the harbour area. It may have stood on the lower ground to the south or south-east of the later fort. To guide ships to the harbour entrance a lighthouse (*pharos*) was built on high ground about 1 mile north-west of the fort. Known as the Tour d'Ordre, this was demolished in the sixteenth century. Early descriptions mention tile-bonded masonry typical of the later Roman period which might suggest that the original structure, built on the orders of Caligula in AD 40, had subsequently been reconstructed.[5] Stamped bricks and tiles of the fleet have also been found some distance inland at Desvres, but the nature of the installation here is unknown; possibly it was the production centre for this material.

Dover (*Dubris*; *Novus Portus?*)

For 50 or so years after the invasion, Richborough continued to be the main naval port but now, perhaps because of silting in its harbour or approaches, the decision was taken to make Dover (*Dubris*; also possibly Ptolemy's *Novus Portus*)[6] the main base for the British Fleet on this side of the Channel (**40**). A conventional shaped fort like Boulogne but much more modest in size, it was discovered in 1970 and occupied a small promontory on the west side of the

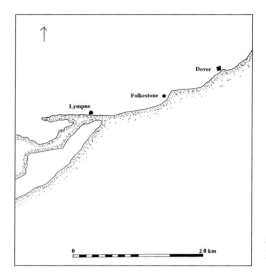

40 *Location of the* Classis Britannica *forts at Dover and Lympne, and of the villa at Folkestone*

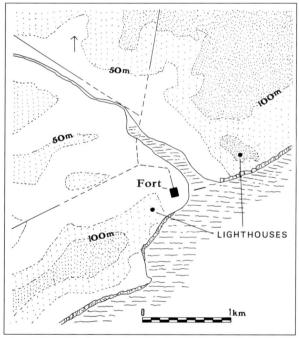

41 *Roman Dover. General plan*

River Dour close to the point where it flows into a wide shallow bay (**41**). This was the only break in more than 12 miles (20km) of chalk cliffs which rise almost vertically for more than 330ft (100m). The coastal landscape has changed considerably over the last two thousand years but various studies have revealed what it was like in the Roman period.[7] Opposite the fort lay a spit of shingle which reduced the mouth of the river to a width of about 165ft (50m). This gave access to a wide, shallow basin. Long since obliterated by marine transgression and silting this was probably occupied largely by mudflats even in the Roman period and unusable as a haven.[8] Dover also lies at the shortest crossing-point from Britain to the Continent and was thus naturally predisposed to become the principal port of entry to the province, taking over that role from the invasion port of Richborough around the beginning of the second century. Construction of the initial fort began around AD 116 but this was left unfinished, most probably because the fleet was needed in the north to aid in the suppression of a revolt the following year.[9] The west wall of this fort has yet to be discovered but its overall size was in the region of 2.5 acres (1ha). Like its successor, the initial fort was enclosed by a stone perimeter wall, but like army bases of the period this was not accompanied by a rampart nor by internal corner and interval towers. The internal buildings too were to be of stone, and those found in the eastern portion of the interior (probably the *praetentura*) have the appearance of barrack accommodation divided into eight identically-sized rooms.

Work on the construction of the second fort here began *c*.AD 130, presumably when the *Classis Britannica* was free of its commitments associated with building of the Hadrianic frontier system. The second fort was built precisely over the levelled remains of its unfinished predecessor and the opportunity was taken to enlarge it slightly to 2.6 acres (1.05ha). Again it was enclosed by a stone defensive wall which lacked towers and a rampart but it was equipped with an external ditch (**42**). Both the north and the east gates have been excavated and both were twin-portalled affairs. The east gate (*porta praetoria*), however, was given special treatment, befitting its role as the main gate into the fort from the harbour, having two projecting D-shaped towers instead of the ordinary square type like the north gate. As to internal buildings, two small granaries have been identified in the north-west quadrant while the *praetentura* was occupied by what have been interpreted as ten barrack blocks.[10] Administrative buildings have yet to be found as has the residence of the commander or *navarch*. This fort was rebuilt around AD 160, abandoned again *c*.AD 180, and experienced a final phase of intensive occupation in the first decade of the third century after which it was disused and possibly demolished.

As at Boulogne measures were taken to provide guidance for ships out at sea making for the harbour. Here though there was not just one *pharos* but two, built on each of the chalk headlands flanking the naval base at an elevation in both cases of around 295ft (90m). That on the Eastern Heights, on Castle Hill, was subsequently enclosed by the medieval castle and still stands to a height of about 62ft, of which 43ft (13m) is Roman work, the rest together with most of the external facing being medieval.[11] Its counterpart on the Western Heights, recorded on eighteenth-century prints, was destroyed by the construction of additional fortifications in the nineteenth century. Its foundations, seen when the redoubt was built in 1861, seems to have included reused materials suggesting it may have been later than its counterpart on Castle Hill. The

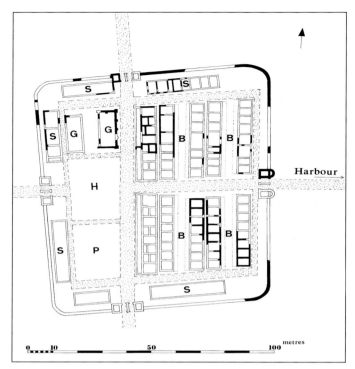

42 *Plan of the second-century fort of the* Classis Britannica. *KEY:* B = *barracks,* G = *granaries,* H = *headquarters,* P = *commandant's residence,* S = *stores.* After Philp

preserved lighthouse has a rectangular ground-plan internally, but octagonal externally, with an overall width close on 40ft (13m). Its walls are 13ft (4m) thick at the base, narrowing progressively upwards in a minimum of four stages. There may have been a total of eight stages originally with the *pharos* having an overall height in the region of 80ft (24.4m) (**45, colour plates 2 & 15**). The facing consists of greensand and tufa ashlar with bonding courses of two layers of tiles at regular intervals. In the chamber at the summit of each tower there would have been a fire-beacon, the light from which may have been amplified by reflectors of burnished copper or even silvered bronze. Because of their elevation these beacons would have been visible from far out in the Channel under reasonable conditions. Indeed, it is interesting to speculate on the possibility that the lighthouses at Dover and Boulogne could communicate by some form of signalling. An impression of one of these towering structures appears together with an image of a merchant ship on an intaglio found at Caistor-by-Norwich and now in Norwich Museum (**colour plate 4**).

To create a safe and protected anchorage it was necessary to modify the inlet formed by the mouth of the Dour by means of major engineering works (**41**).[12] In 1855 a 100ft (30m) length of a massive breakwater or mole was found about 750ft (230m) east of the fort. Consisting of huge timber-framing with an infill of shingle this appears to have run transversely across the mouth of the inlet. A probable continuation of this feature was found in the 1920s. A short distance inland from this, timber piles, groynes, and mooring-rings were found around 1860. Both of these features are thought to be of second-century date. Substantial stone-built structures found at various points along the west side of the inlet seem likely to represent the harbour-side below the fort. A 50ft (15m) length of chalk-block masonry found in 1956 was interpreted as a quay with a timber jetty nearby. A similarly constructed and deeply-buried structure found in 1974 much closer to the mouth of the inlet probably represents a continuation of the harbourside.

Ports such as Dover, along with most major towns, contained comfortable lodgings for travelling government officials and couriers. These large, usually courtyard-plan buildings, were called *mansiones* (singular = *mansio*) and the building known as the Painted House situated immediately outside the north gate of the Dover fort undoubtedly performed this function. The portion of the building excavated was erected *c*.AD 200 but there must be a predecessor somewhere in the close vicinity. If at no other time than the beginning and end of each incumbent's term of office the *mansio* at Dover would have accommodated the provincial governor and his entourage. In this connection it is interesting to note the altar found close by the Painted House in 1976 which records a dedication to the Mother Goddesses of Italy by one Olus Cordius Candidus who held the office of *strator consularis* – transport officer for the provincial governor.[13]

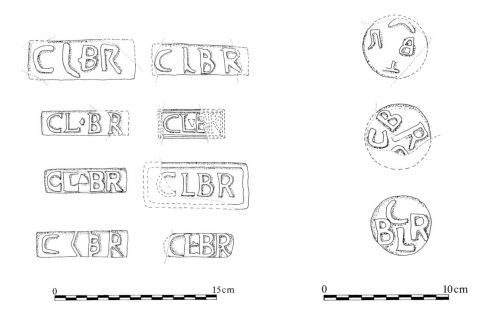

43 (Left) *Brick/tile stamps of the* Classis Britannica. After Philp
44 (Right) *Brick/tile stamps of the* Classis Britannica. After Philp

0   10   **40** feet
0   **10** metres

45 *Reconstruction drawing of the eastern lighthouse at Dover*

Lympne

The existence of the as yet unlocated *Classis Britannica* fort here is indicated by an altar set up by Lucius Aufidius Pantera *Praefectus Classis Britannicae*, who held this post in the late 130s, along with CL.BR stamped tiles.[14] Other tiles and reused masonry can be seen incorporated in the surviving fabric of the late-third-century Shore Fort. The altar, dedicated appropriately enough to Neptune, had clearly lain underwater or on the shore as it had become encrusted with barnacles before being salvaged for reuse in the Shore Fort's east gate, and this may indicate that the earlier fort stood on lower ground.

Pevensey

Like Lympne the walls of the Shore Fort at Pevensey contain reused tiles which petrological analysis has shown are identical to *Classis Britannica* tiles.[15] Five CL.BR stamped bricks have also been found along with second-century pottery.[16] The existence of a fleet base here is thus a distinct possibility but at present no more than that.

Other potential fleet-bases in the south-east

Richborough and London have each produced a few CL.BR stamped tiles (**47**).[17] While ships of the *Classis Britannica* undoubtedly called at both ports, and there would probably have been at least one vessel stationed more or less permanently at London at the disposal of the provincial governor, there is no supporting evidence for an actual fleet base. The villa at Folkestone excavated by Winbolt in 1924 yielded a number of CL.BR stamped tiles, including four complete examples, giving rise to the suggestion that it was the residence of the Prefect of the British Fleet on this side of the Channel.[18] However, as Peacock has pointed out, the number is small compared to the amount of tile recovered and the majority are of a very different fabric.[19] Perhaps, therefore, the CL.BR tiles are more likely to be reused material imported from elsewhere, perhaps from the lighthouse at Folkestone postulated by Rigold.[20] At Reculver, more than 40 Roman tiles made of the same clay as that used for CL.BR tiles elsewhere (the variant known as Fabric 2) can be seen built into the fabric of St Mary's Church, and others are built into the east gate of the Shore Fort.[21] Only the sides of the tiles are visible and so it is impossible to determine if any are stamped. If not imported from some distant site they could be contemporary with the known fort which was built in the opening decades of the third century. Alternatively they might derive from an earlier fleet base in the vicinity.

46 Bronze model of a galley-prow from London (RIB II 2432.1). It bears the inscription, in retrograde, 'Ammilla Augusta, the Fortunate'. Possibly a votive object, the vessel depicted seems to be an imperial warship

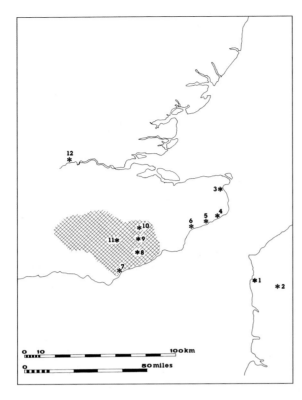

47 *Distribution of sites which have produced CL.BR bricks/tiles and location of ironworking industry in the Weald. KEY: 1- Boulogne, 2 - Desvres, 3 - Richborough, 4 - Dover, 5 - Folkestone, 6 - Lympne, 7 - Pevensey, 8 - Beauport Park, 9 - Bodiam, 10 - Cranbrook, 11 - Bardown, 12 - London. Shaded area = approximate extent of Weald ironfield*

The Weald Iron Industry

As already mentioned, the *Classis Britannica* was heavily involved in the exploitation of the iron deposits in the eastern sector of the Weald. Like many other metal-producing areas in the Empire it was probably sequestered immediately following the invasion and made into an imperial estate administered by a *procurator* who was in turn answerable to the provincial *procurator*. Supplying the army was one of the latter's chief responsibilities, and the military required vast amounts of iron not just for weapons and tools but for a wide range of everyday articles encompassing everything from nails to wagon fittings. Research by Gerald Brodibb and Henry Cleere over many years has revealed the extent of the operations in the Weald, identifying production centres at Bardown and Beauport Park, an administrative complex at Cranborne, and an export depot on the River Rother at Bodiam (**47**).[22] Production accelerated in the last quarter of the first century, probably to satisfy the increase in demand generated by the conquest and garrisoning of northern England and Scotland, and continued at a high level into the opening decades of the third century. The scale of production can be gauged from the discovery at Beauport Park of a slag heap 50ft (15m) high covering 2 acres (0.8ha).[23]

The fleet itself would have required iron for use in shipbuilding, but in what quantities is uncertain. As far as transports and cargo ships were concerned the Romans certainly adopted features of the local shipbuilding tradition in order to produce vessels sufficiently sturdy to cope with the rougher seas around Britain. The same may also have been true of their warships. As the remains of the Blackfriars I and County Hall vessels from London and the St Peter Port I ship from Guernsey demonstrate, the strength of such vessels was achieved by the extensive use of large section iron nails to fix the hull planking to the framing (see chapter 4). It seems likely therefore that cargo vessels of the Roman period continued to incorporate many of the features of the Venetic ships of Caesar's day, presumably to the extent of including anchor cables of iron chain rather than rope, like the example in Dorchester Museum.[24] Consequently the amount of iron needed by the *Classis Britannica* itself may have constituted a higher percentage of the annual production than one might at first think. Furthermore, given the unlimited supply of good quality timber afforded by the Weald it might have made sense to concentrate the fleet's shipbuilding activity on the edge of the Weald, perhaps along the shores of the Rother estuary.

In addition to organising transport of the iron to destinations far afield, the British Fleet also undertook the construction of some of the infrastructure at the refining centres including, for example, the construction of the bath-house at Beauport Park, near Battle. The *Classis Britannica's* presence is indicated by the large number of stamped bricks and tiles found at these sites. More than 1,600 examples have been recovered from the Beauport Park bath-house alone. A number of separate stamps were used. Some of these are represented by hundreds of tiles but others only by single specimens; 33 of them unparalleled elsewhere. This implies production on a large scale. Research by Professor David Peacock has demonstrated that the clay used for the bulk of the tiles ('Fabric 2') was derived from a division of the Hastings Beds known as Fairlight Clay and that the kilns, still to be located, were probably sited somewhere in the central Weald.[25] The other type of clay ('Fabric 1') was also found to predominate amongst the tiles from Boulogne and was apparently obtained from the valley of the Liane. The stamp dies at Boulogne are also different and so there was clearly a centre of brick and tile manufacture on each side of the Channel. Yet about one third of the material recovered from Boulogne was in the British fabric. Rather than carrying raw clay across the Channel it is likely that bricks and tiles were carried back and forth as ballast.

Beyond the Fretum Gallicum

The extent of the *Classis Britannica's* involvement in waters beyond the Channel once the era of Flavian conquests had ended is easy to imagine but difficult to prove. Stamped bricks and tiles of the *Classis Britannica* are restricted to the area

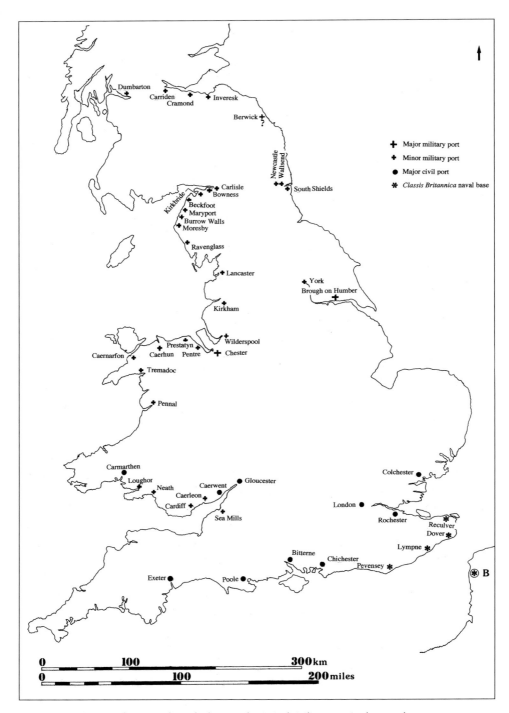

48 *Map showing military harbours and principal civilian ports in the second century*

Key:
- ✚ Major military port
- ✜ Minor military port
- ● Major civil port
- ✳ *Classis Britannica* naval base

Dumbarton
Carriden
Cramond
Inveresk
Berwick
Newcastle
Wallsend
South Shields
Carlisle
Bowness
Kirkbride
Beckfoot
Maryport
Burrow Walls
Moresby
Ravenglass
Lancaster
York
Brough on Humber
Kirkham
Wilderspool
Prestatyn
Caerhun
Pentre
Chester
Caernarfon
Tremadoc
Pennal
Carmarthen
Loughor
Neath
Caerleon
Caerwent
Gloucester
Cardiff
Sea Mills
Colchester
London
Rochester
Reculver
Dover
Lympne
Pevensey
Bitterne
Chichester
Exeter
Poole
B

0 100 300 km
0 100 200 miles

between Pevensey and London but of course this does not, and surely cannot, mean that there were no naval forces elsewhere in Britain. A number of warships would undoubtedly have been required for patrol and reconnaissance duties on both the east and west coasts (**48**). This would perhaps have been particularly important as regards the waters off southern Scotland during the gradual withdrawal to the line of the Stanegate at the beginning of the second century. Keeping a watch on enemy shipping and reminding the northern tribes that Rome still controlled the sea as well as the land during this potentially vulnerable period would have been an advisable strategy. Naval vessels would also have been needed to transport despatches and personnel and, above all, supplies. The absence of CL.BR bricks/tiles from the north presumably reflects the fact that the British Fleet did not have to build any facilities of its own here, whereas in the south-east by contrast it was the sole military presence with the exception of the Governor's bodyguard in London. Flotillas could have been present in the north and west which made use of harbours constructed by the army (in other words the legions) and with any accommodation necessary built with army-supplied materials and situated for example in a special compound beside forts and fortresses. In this way modest detachments of the *Classis Britannica* could have been based near the mouth of the Tyne, possibly at the suspected predecessor of the mid-Antonine fort at South Shields and, on the west coast, somewhere on the south side of the Solway Firth, initially perhaps Kirkbride.[26] Further south, Chester is an obvious candidate as a regular port of call for naval vessels if not the actual base of a flotilla. The Bristol Channel too may have been the subject of regular patrols while on the east coast Brough-on-Humber has been proposed as a naval base.[27]

Travelling by sea was not of course without its perils, a fact illustrated by a fragmentary tombstone found at the legionary fortress at Chester which commemorates a centurion's second-in-command or *optio* who '*naufragio perit*' – perished in a shipwreck (**36**).[28] Although both men are usually regarded as legionaries they may in fact have been naval personnel given that a ship's complement was also organised as a century. Another inscription from Chester perhaps records a more successful voyage. This is in the form of an altar dedicated to Fortuna Redux ('Fortune the Home-Bringer') and to Aesculapius and Salus – the gods of Healing and Health – by the freedmen and slave-household of the imperial legate (whether legionary commander or provincial governor is open to debate) Titus Pomponius Mamilianus Rufus Antistianus Funisulanus Vettonianus.[29] Fortuna Redux is particularly associated with sea journeys and the altar in question, thought to be of early second-century date, was found in a large building interpreted as a large baths complex beside the harbour. Perhaps it records the safe return of the legionary commander from a voyage of inspection to the coastal auxiliary forts in his command area.

For the transportation of certain categories of supplies, especially those imported from other provinces the army, or rather the provincial procurator who was responsible for procuring supplies for the military, placed contracts with traders (*negotiatores*) who either owned their own ships or hired those of commercial shippers (*navicularii*).[30] Goods in this class would have included the thousands of *amphorae* variously containing wine, olive oil, figs, fish sauces and other products imported every year from Spain, Italy, Greece and North Africa.[31] Some of this traffic passed through the Straits of Gibraltar and up the Atlantic coast. The rest followed an inland route via one or more of the major river systems of Gaul to the Atlantic coast. Other consignments consisted of fine pottery such as samian from Gaul and colour-coated beakers from Germany, the latter perhaps shipped along with the barrels of wine depicted on carvings from the Mosel valley.[32] Lyon has a fine collection of inscriptions which provide details of shippers, traders and guilds of river boatmen.[33] At York we have the names of three *negotiatores* who probably made their fortunes from the import/export trade: Marcus Aurelius Lunaris, Lucius Viducius Placidus and Marcus Verecundius Diogenes. Lunaris set up an altar at Bordeaux on which he describes himself as *sevir Augustalis* (priest of the cult of the emperor) at both York and Lincoln.[34] Placidus, whose homeland was the region around Rouen, paid for the construction of an arch and shrine at York[35] and is probably the same Placidus who dedicated an altar to the goddess Nehalennia at her shrine near the mouth of the Rhine.[36] Diogenes, another *sevir Augustalis* of the York *colonia*, hailed from the territory of the Bituriges Cubi in Aquitania.[37] All three men cited were in business during the decades immediately following AD 200 but we can be sure that the trade which made them rich had been developing rapidly throughout the previous century.

At least in the early years of the occupation it would have been necessary to ship in even basic foodstuffs for the garrisons in Wales and the north. While in time agricultural production in some regions of the 'Military Zone' – such as perhaps the Solway Plain and Eden Valley – may have developed to the point where it was capable of supplying the staple foodstuffs required by the military garrisons, this would not have happened quickly and in some places perhaps never. It is interesting to note that the legionary fortress at Caerleon has yielded evidence that grain was imported from as far afield as the Mediterranean although one assumes that the bulk of the grain requirement would normally have been shipped around the coast from the south-east.[38] As the civilian pottery industry developed and expanded during the second century the army bought more and more of its ordinary ceramics on the open market rather than producing their own. These too would have been shipped around the coast to the north from places such as Poole Harbour, the centre of Black-Burnished Ware production.[39] The majority of goods like these which basically required transportation from the south to the north were probably carried on ships of the *Classis Britannica* rather than those of private shippers.

Some materials, however, may have been carried by military cargo vessels. The initial construction and subsequent rebuilding of the many army bases throughout Wales and northern England required vast amounts of raw materials. This was particularly so in the case of the three great legionary fortresses. The basic building materials such as stone, timber, clay and sand were generally readily to hand. Others, however, such as lime and especially the metals needed had to be obtained from further afield. Chester affords a useful insight into how this was achieved and how sea transport was involved (**49**). Large quantities of lead were needed for the water supply and distribution system serving the fortress and official extramural buildings.[40] The galena or lead ore was extracted from the Flintshire lead-field running in an arc 15 to 25 miles (24-40km) to the west. A number of refining centres operated under direct imperial control and supervised by the legion were established, one of which lay on the south-western shore of the Dee estuary near the modern town of Flint.[41] From here the ingots of lead were transported by ship to Chester where at least one – manufactured in AD 74 – was lost overboard as the consignment was being unloaded at a timber jetty in the harbour west of the fortress.[42] A more serious loss, possibly encompassing not just some of the cargo but the vessel itself, is represented by a group of 20 such ingots found on the south shore of the River Mersey near Runcorn in the sixteenth century.[43] This consignment, despatched during the reign of Domitian, was presumably destined for the industrial complex at Wilderspool. There was further imperial interest in lead-mining because of the silver which could be

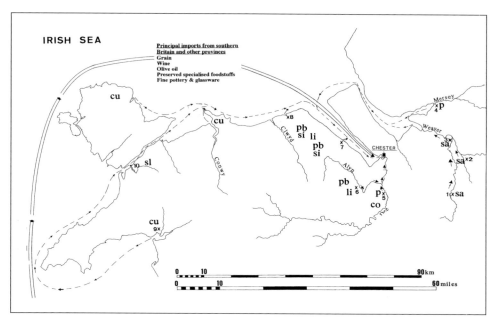

49 *Map showing origins of principal commodities imported by ship to the legionary fortress at Chester.* KEY: *Sites = 1 - Nantwich, 2 - Middlewich, 3 - Northwich, 4 - Wilderspool, 5 - Holt, 6 - Ffrith, 7 - Pentre, 8 - Prestatyn, 9 - Tremadoc, 10 - Carnarvon.* Commodities = *co - coal, cu - copper, li - limestone, p - pottery, pb - lead, sa - salt, si - silver, sl - slate*

extracted from the lead ore. Waterborne transport of lead was also employed at the Caerleon fortress. Lead-mining centres were set up at Risca and Draethen/Lower Machen approximately 6 miles (10km) west of the fortress. Both were sited beside rivers – the Ebbw and Rhymney respectively – and it is clear that the ingots were taken by boat down to the coast and then up the Usk to Caerleon (**50**).[44]

Copper was another important commodity required in bulk by the legions. In Chester's case it was won from mines at the Great Orme near Llandudno, on Anglesey, and in southern Caernarfonshire.[45] As to the third metal needed in great quantities – iron – we have already seen that the *Classis Britannica* was itself heavily engaged in its production in the Weald and also presumably in its distribution to the army. Another major centre of iron production was the Forest of Dean and neighbouring areas around the head of the Severn estuary, ideally situated for sea transport to the legionary garrisons at both Caerleon and Chester as well as other military consumers in the north and west.[46] There was also traffic in the reverse direction with the products of the legionary workshops – such as weapons, specialised equipment and building materials – at all three fortresses being sent by ship to the auxiliary forts in their respective command areas. The occurrence at auxiliary forts of bricks and tiles bearing the legionary stamp is one illustration of this.[47]

Each legion would have required something like 2,800 tons of grain per annum (based on 2lb per day and 7,000 men in total including servants and, in the first century, a squadron of auxiliary cavalry). So if all its grain had to be imported by ship this would mean 28 shiploads if the vessels used had a 100-ton carrying capacity. The quantities of wine, olive oil and other products carried in *amphorae* required each year are unknown but were presumably considerable. Add in the shiploads of metals, pottery and all manner of other goods imported each year then the total number of annual ship-movements concerned with supply alone to a fortress like Chester would probably have numbered at least 100. Also, the vast majority of voyages would be concentrated in the period April to September to take advantage of the (usually) kinder sailing conditions. Given that there were in fact three legions as well as scores of auxiliary units to be supplied, and with a high proportion of those supplies very probably carried by ship, then one begins to appreciate the scale of the *Classis Britannica*'s workload and importance.

Legionary fleets?

There may have been fleets – unattested in the surviving literary sources and inscriptions – other than the *Classis Britannica*. A *Classis Ivernica* operating in the Irish Sea is one of the more obvious possibilities. However, the complete invisibility of the *Classis Britannica* from the archaeological record in the north

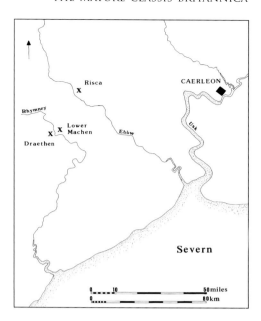

50 *Waterborne supply of certain metals to the legionary fortress at Caerleon*

and west can be explained in other ways. During the conquest of the area that was to become Rome's northern provinces we have seen from the sources that large fleets were regularly constructed by the army. Tarruntenus Paternus, the praetorian prefect under Commodus and a respected military jurist, whose writings have survived in part in the *Digest*, lists shipwrights as well as pilots among the specialists in a legion.[48] From Novae, the base of *Legio I Italica* in Moesia, there is a whole series of bricks and tiles on which the legionary stamp is contained within a frame which is clearly intended to represent the outline of a warship, most probably a bireme of Liburnian type (**51**).[49] The lower reaches of the Danube and the northern sector of the Black Sea were the preserve of the *Classis Moesica* but it would seem that the stretch of the river near Novae was patrolled by a flotilla operated by the legionary garrison. A similar situation seems likely to have existed on the upper Rhine. The headquarters of the *Classis Germanica* was at Alteburg near Cologne in Germania Inferior and its operations were centred on the lower Rhine and the North Sea.[50] At the double legionary fortress at Mainz on the upper Rhine, tile stamps of one of the resident legions, *Legio XXII Primigenia*, include variants depicting a ship similar to those from Novae.[51] There are also three inscriptions from here which refer to men of the same legion working in the *navalia* or shipyards.[52]

There were clearly situations where a legion could build and operate a fleet which included warships as well as transports. Perhaps a similar arrangement was adopted for the unusual and unique circumstances of the island province of Britain. The headquarters of the *Classis Britannica* were established at Boulogne with the main subsidiary base on this side of the Channel at Dover.

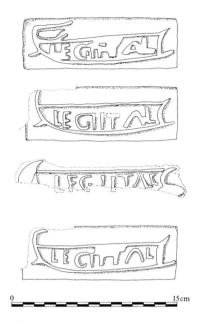

0   15cm

51 *Ship-shaped stamps on bricks and tiles of the* Classis Moesica. After Sarnowski

Yet the military forces in Britain lay largely on the far side of the island or much farther to the north. Detachments of the *Classis Britannica* could have been out-stationed in the north and west but it is equally possible that the legions at Caerleon, Chester and York each possessed a small fleet of their own. These would have sufficient warships to carry out routine naval patrols together with the transports and cargo vessels needed to move men and materials within the limits of their command area. The bulk of supplies brought in from outside the region would still have been transported by the *Classis Britannica* or *navicularii*. Only in times of crisis or the undertaking of major enterprises such as punitive campaigns and, as we shall see, the construction of new frontier systems would the *Classis Britannica* have been present in strength. The putative Chester flotilla could have operated from the harbour close to the fortress. At Caerleon it may have been necessary to anchor some distance downstream and there may well have been a secondary base on the opposite side of the Bristol Channel at Sea Mills.[53] The fortress at York was situated much farther inland, and although attainable by smaller merchant vessels and river craft, warships would have been stationed closer to the coast, most probably somewhere near the head of the Humber estuary and perhaps at Brough-on-Humber, suggested as a naval base by Wacher.[54]

An arrangement along the lines just suggested would have a number of advantages. It would achieve the most efficient use of resources by avoiding duplication of facilities and also simplifying administration and provisioning. The chain of command would be more straightforward, and the potential for friction and misunderstandings reduced, by placing some naval forces under the direct control of the regional commander (i.e. the legionary legate) rather than the Prefect of the *Classis Britannica* in faraway Boulogne.

Ports and harbour facilities

Although army bases situated either on the coast, beside major estuaries, or on navigable rivers must have possessed port facilities of varying complexity, detailed information about actual structures is still very rare. As regards legionary sites, excavations at Caerleon (*Isca*) in the 1960s located traces of a quay beside the former course of the Usk about 1,650ft (500m) out from the south-west gate (*porta principalis dextra*) of the fortress (**52**).[55] Here the riverbank had been cut back and a wall some 3ft (1m) thick built to retain a stone platform behind it. This had subsequently been extended and the new work included a timber stage 5ft (1.5m) wide along its face, presumably to counteract the silt which inevitably accumulated against the face of the quay wall. The original construction is dated to the beginning of the third century and so the quays operational at the time of the fortress' foundation have yet to be located, although traces of earlier timber structures were found during the excavation. The fragmentary remains of a simple stone building positioned end-on to the quayside have been interpreted as an open-sided boat-house with internal dimensions of 18ft 3in (5.6m) by at least 34ft 4in (10.6m). Toft has recently suggested that the Caerleon quay was above the tidal reach of the river which may explain its comparatively insubstantial construction.[56] That ship-building facilities were located somewhere along the Severn estuary is a

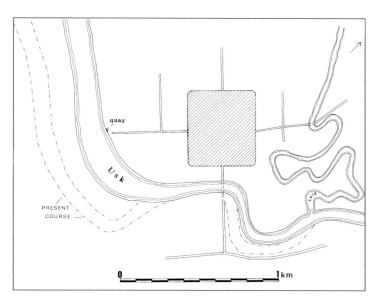

52 *Plan of the legionary fortress at Caerleon showing location of known quays*

123

strong possibility given the intensity of maritime activity here and the plentiful supplies of iron and timber available locally.

For the harbour at Chester, sited at the head of the Dee estuary, the Roman legionary engineers made use of a large bowl-shaped area lying west of the fortress carved out by the river at the end of the last Ice Age. The harbour disappeared long ago owing to silting of the river channel, and the reclaimed land which now occupies its site (known as the Roodee) has been used as a racecourse since the sixteenth century. The estuary itself also suffered severely from silting and indeed the present course of the Dee for 10 miles below Chester is the result of a canalisation project undertaken in the mid-eighteenth century in an attempt to revive the fortunes of the port. Renewed interest in the maritime role of Roman Chester in recent years has led to a reassessment of nineteenth-century discoveries in the area resulting in a clearer picture of the port's development.[57] Initially a very substantial jetty was constructed which ran out from the eastern shore across an area of shallows/mud-flats to the deep-water channel beside the opposite bank, a distance of some 1,150ft

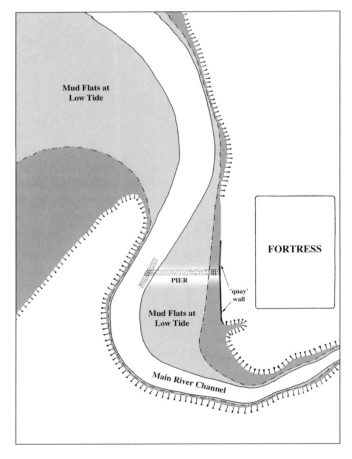

53 *Plan of early harbour installations beside the legionary fortress at Chester*

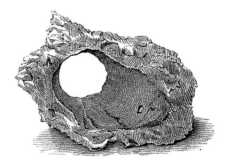

IMPRESSION OF IRON SHOE OF OAK PILE.

POINTED END OF IRON SHOE.

54 *Chester. Drawing of iron sheaths used to clad tips of timber piles belonging to early jetty*

(350m) (**53**). This enabled ships to dock under all tidal conditions. Portions of this jetty have been encountered on a number of occasions, most spectacularly when a section near its western terminus was exposed in the 1880s by ground-works for the construction of a gasometer. Timber piles about a foot in diameter and still surviving in lengths of 10ft (3.3m) or more were found. These had had one end shaped to a point and then encased in an iron sheath to ensure they did not sheer off during the pile-driving process (**54**). Concrete was poured around the piles as an added reinforcement.[58] In addition to much Roman pottery in various wares, an ingot of lead datable to AD 74 and two human skulls were retrieved from the detritus which had accumulated in the vicinity of the piles. Whether all this material had resulted from accidental losses during offloading/loading or whether the jetty had eventually collapsed or been destroyed in a freak accident is an open question.[59] Elements of a substantial wall found nearby might belong to a stone mole which replaced the jetty, although there is as yet no certainty of a Roman origin.

Another wall, this time of undoubted Roman origin, runs along the east side of the 'Roodee' at the foot of the ancient river-cliff below and a little in advance of the medieval city wall. Built of large blocks of local sandstone averaging 1ft 3in (0.37m) in height and up to 5ft (1.5m) in length, the visible masonry runs for a distance of around 130ft (40m). The wall has in fact been traced over a total of 820ft (250m), running more or less parallel with the southern sector of the western fortress defences. It generally stands just over 3ft (1m) proud of modern ground level but at one point the masonry survives to a height of 10ft (3.3m) (**colour plate 9**). Excavations in 1884 revealed the wall to be 8ft (2.4m) thick, with an additional backing of concrete, and that it carried on down below modern ground level for at least another 15ft (4.5m).[60] What are referred to as 'pilaster-like buttresses' were encountered at regular intervals along its face, and some of these can still be seen on the below-ground section left on public display (**colour plate 10**). This wall is popularly referred to as the 'quay wall' and with its massive-block mode of construction it is reminiscent of the ancient quay walls found in many ports around the Mediterranean. Indeed, the 'pilaster-like buttresses', which in fact are too slight to have performed any real buttressing function, recreate the pattern formed by the vertical timbers used to revet wooden quaysides. However, the precise course of the river in the Roman period is still open to debate and it is doubtful if it came anywhere near the supposed quay wall. Its interpretation is thus in doubt and, rather than a quay wall, it may instead have been a late defensive wall built to protect the wealthy suburbs lying between the fortress and the harbour (**colour plate 12**).[61]

The legionary fortress at York stood on the north-east bank of the River Ouse just upstream of the point where it was joined by the Foss. The civil settlement which was later promoted to the rank of *colonia* stood on the opposite side of the Ouse. Situated more than 15 miles (24km) inland from the head of the Humber estuary, it is likely that a significant proportion of the goods coming to York by sea were offloaded onto lighters somewhere in the estuary (perhaps at Brough) for the final leg of the journey to the fortress (**55**). Knowledge of the port facilities is very limited. Quays and wharves must have lined the Ouse but as yet no positive traces of these have come to light. The Foss, whose course has been greatly modified since the Roman period by damming, land reclamation and canalisation, was originally much wider than at present and ran conveniently close to the east angle of the fortress. Traces of riverside structures have come to light on a number of occasions, the most impressive located on its west bank and discovered during building works for a telephone exchange in 1951-2 at Garden Place.[62] Fronted by a double row of piles which probably supported a landing-stage was a 12ft (3.65m) thick platform of uncertain length built of large stone blocks. Behind this again was a rectangular stone structure with walls 5ft (1.5m) thick. Hints of additional jetties and quays have been found on both sides of the Foss and it was clearly a major focus of port activity (**56**).

Of the relevant auxiliary forts in Wales and north-west England, only at Caerhun, situated just under 6 miles upriver from the mouth of the Conwy, is there any tangible trace of Roman waterside structures (**57**). About 800ft (250m) from the north-east corner of the fort there is a rectangular depression opening from the river which is flanked on its south side by a stone-faced quay which projects some 25ft out into the river channel. Having all the appearances of a silted-up dock the quay wall was investigated in the 1920s, and although no conclusive dating evidence was retrieved, its constructional style was adjudged similar to that of other examined extramural Roman structures.[63] Aerial reconnaissance in the 1970s identified traces of an extensive *vicus* lining the road running north-eastwards from the fort along with signs of possible structures associated with the dock.[64]

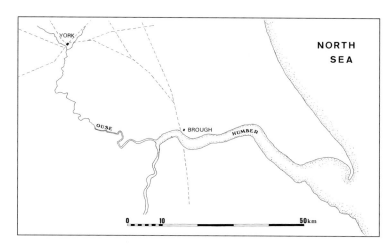

55 *Map showing location of Brough-on-Humber and York*

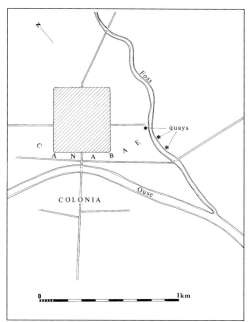

56 *Plan of the legionary fortress at York showing location of known quays and jetties*

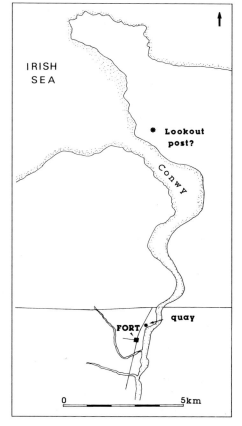

57 *The auxiliary fort at Caerhun and its quay, and the possible late Roman look-out post constructed within the Iron Age fort at Deganwy overlooking the mouth of the Afon Conwy*

A return to northern waters; 'all ashore that's . . .'

It was apparent from the 1970s excavations that construction of the naval fort at Dover had been interrupted long before it was nearing completion. This was probably caused by the need for the fleet to assist in the suppression of a revolt in the north which began in AD 117, continued into the following year, and perhaps persisted as late as 120.[65] A tombstone recently discovered at *Vindolanda* commemorates a centurion in charge of the garrison who was killed in this war.[66] Further evidence of the seriousness of the situation and the scale of the losses suffered by the Roman forces is indicated by the drafting in of 3,000 men from the legions in Upper Germany and *Hispania Tarraconensis c.*AD 120.[67] They were landed at Newcastle where, during disembarkation, Iunius Dubitatus dropped his shield into the Tyne, a loss for which he was surely chastised and fined.[68] The *Classis Britannica* was probably involved in bringing at least some of these men across from the Continent, and in 122 it had the important task of carrying the Emperor Hadrian himself across the Channel along with his entourage (**colour plate 3**). Hadrian's decision to build a linear barrier from the Tyne to the Solway, with a westwards extension down the Cumbrian coast, prolonged the fleet's stay in the north. The legionary vexillations and other units engaged in its construction all had to be supplied with provisions. Any agricultural surplus in the region would already have been earmarked for the existing garrisons in the area and so most of the foodstuffs needed by the construction force would have been brought in by sea from other parts of Britain. From now on both the eastern and western seaways saw a significant increase in traffic brought about by the need to service the northern frontier garrisons (**60**).[69] Newcastle was the site of one of the main bridges over the Tyne, hence its name of *Pons Aelius*. The latter was built by *Legio VI Victrix*, brought over from *Vetera* in Lower Germany to replace the Ninth *Hispana* at York, and its men set up two altars in a shrine located on the bridge itself; one dedicated to Neptune and the other to Oceanus, deities presiding over the river and the tidal waters of the sea respectively.[70]

That the men of the fleet for a time left their ships behind and actually took part in the construction of the Wall is attested by three inscriptions. Two record their building of a length of the Wall near Birdoswald while the third commemorates their construction of one or more granaries at Benwell.[71] Given the fleet's regular involvement in the transport and storage of grain they presumably possessed considerable expertise in the construction of this type of building. Following their participation in the construction of the Wall and its forts, some elements of the fleet were apparently formed into one or more infantry cohorts. This is indicated by the existence of the unit designated *Cohors I Aelia Classica* – 'The First Cohort of the Aelian Fleet'; the title *Aelia* indicating its creation during the reign of Hadrian. This cohort appears in a list of units mentioned on a discharge diploma dating to AD 146 found at the Wall-fort at Chesters.[72]

That it was based at Ravenglass (*Tunnocelum/Itunocelum* rather than *Glannoventa* as previously thought)[73] on the Cumbrian coast by AD 158 is suggested by the discharge diploma of one of its number found on the beach below the fort in 1995 and also by a lead sealing bearing its stamp found inside the fort during excavations in the 1970s.[74] In all probability it was stationed here right from the time of its creation, perhaps from the force of marines who helped build the Wall. It is interesting, given its background, that this unit should be posted to a coastal fort, and Hind has speculated that it might have retained some form of naval capacity.[75] This seems eminently possible given the nature of the Cumberland coast system and the threat it was designed to counter.

The Cumberland coastal defences consisted of towers and mile-fortlets with forts at intervals, as on the Wall itself. Although, on the latest analysis, lacking a connecting feature such as a palisade or ditches, the system was nevertheless designed to be continuous.[76] The impetus for its construction was obviously the threat of sea-raiders crossing the Solway Firth, either directly from Novantian territory or indirectly from Northern Ireland after having negotiated the North Channel and hugging the coast of what is now Dumfries and Galloway. In some stretches it runs very close to the shoreline but in others it has been pulled further back to higher ground, apparently to facilitate the inter-visibility of sites and their capacity for signalling one to another. The forts too occupy prominent positions. The system was designed to keep a close watch on the shore for illicit landings as well as observing what was happening at sea. Extending the line of installations so far down the Cumberland shore meant that raiders would have to sail a long way before reaching an unprotected stretch of coast. Forced to make part of their voyage during daylight, they would be spotted before making landfall and arrangements made to intercept them. The system could easily be breached by a substantial landing-party, as happened on a number of occasions in the later Roman period, but reinforcements would soon be on hand to deal with them. This defensive system would have been incomplete without an accompanying naval presence, needed not only to detect and destroy raiding parties while still at sea, but also to protect from piracy the considerable number of army supply and commercial vessels servicing the garrison of the Wall. The *Cohors I Aelia Classica* at Ravenglass may have had such a role with perhaps other modest flotillas based at places such as Maryport and Moresby. The soldier of this unit whose discharge diploma was found in 1995 was a cavalryman. The *Cohors I Aelia Classica* was thus well equipped for its coastal defence role, possessing cavalry which could respond swiftly to sightings of raiders who had already made landfall.

Another discharge diploma, this one found at Wroxeter, bears a list of units from which time-served men were discharged on 14 April AD 135.[77] One of these units is described as *naut(arum)* = 'marines'. Only one letter – *n* – survives of the rest of its titles but the unit is most likely to be the *Cohors I Me[n]ap(iorum)*.[78] The Menapii inhabited the region now encompassing the coast of northern France, Belgium and Holland. Like their neighbours, the Morini, they were famed for their seafaring abilities, their most famous – or perhaps infamous – citizen being the late third-century usurper Carausius. We have no idea where these marines were stationed but it is likely that their unit served in the command area of *Legio XX Valeria Victrix* based at Chester and so presumably garrisoned one of the forts on the coast of north Wales or north-west England.

Little is known of the port facilities which served the Wall itself. The sea-port at South Shields underwent its major development in the opening years of the third century when the fort was enlarged to become a stores base and trans-shipment depot to serve Severus' campaigns in Scotland. Before this any harbour facilities probably served the fort alone. Ships carrying supplies destined for garrisons further along the Wall probably docked at Wallsend or Newcastle where their cargoes could be transferred to barges for the final leg of the journey up the Tyne. At Wallsend (**colour plate 13**) an extension of the Wall ran down to the river from the south-east corner of the fort. Recently, defences consisting of a rampart and ditch system have been found heading down to the Tyne from the Wall itself about 212ft (65m) west of the fort, returning eastwards on a line some 245ft (75m) out from and parallel with the fort's south side.[79]

The area between the fort and the river is known to have been the site of the extramural settlement or *vicus* and is also the most likely location for harbour facilities. It is unusual for such settlements to be equipped with defences and these may have been provided because the area also contained warehouses for army supplies in transit. From here barges could have navigated the Tyne as far inland as the forts at Corbridge and Chesters (**58**). The fort at Newcastle on the north bank of the Tyne was not built until AD 150/60 but it may have had a predecessor on the south side of the river.[80]

At the west end of the Wall ships presumably navigated up the Eden to dock either at Carlisle or below the fort at Stanwix on the opposite bank (**59**). Again information about harbour structures is lacking. Netherby, the first outpost fort north of Carlisle, was sited beside the River Esk several miles upstream from the Solway coast. That some of its supplies also came by ship is implied by the comments of the sixteenth-century antiquarians John Leland and Reginald Bainbrigg, who both mention the discovery of ship's timbers as well as iron staples or mooring rings in walls, while in 1726 Gordon refers to the finding of an anchor.[81] Harbours further south on the Cumbrian coast would have afforded havens for vessels plying the west coast (**60**).

A (brief) return to the home port

The evidence at Dover suggests the base there was completed in the early 130s which would accord well with the coming to an end of the fleet's involvement in the actual construction of the Wall.[82] In fact the opportunity was taken to

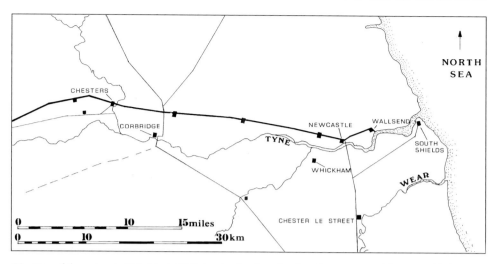

58 *Map of the east end of Hadrian's Wall showing location of main military ports and forts accessible by river*

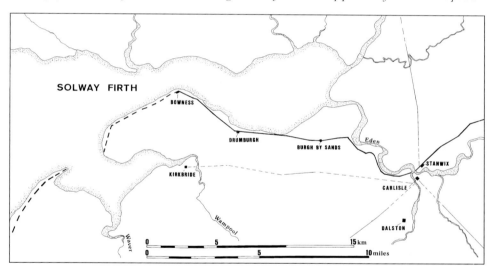

59 *Map of the west end of Hadrian's Wall showing location of main military ports and forts accessible by river*

enlarge the fort slightly and to effect a number of other modifications. As a consequence the excavator designated this to the *Classis Britannica II* fort. Not long after finishing this work, however, the fleet was recalled to the north. Within a year of Hadrian's death his successor Antoninus Pius ordered his governor in Britain Quintus Lollius Urbicus to begin preparations for a reoccupation of southern Scotland, possibly in response to disturbances there. These began in 139 with the refurbishment of the fort at Corbridge and the outpost forts at Risingham and High Rochester. Coins issued late in 142 or early 143 commemorate a great victory in Britain. Given the speed with which old Flavian fort sites were rebuilt or new ones constructed the strength of

131

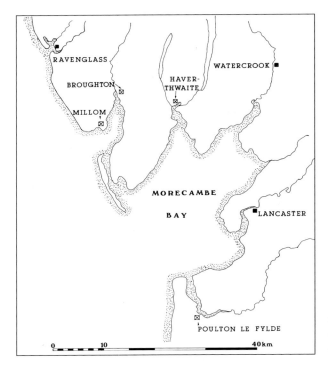

60 *Map of known and possible coastal fort sites in the Morecambe Bay area*

opposition to the Roman advance may have been quite modest. The new linear barrier of the Antonine Wall was built 80 miles (125km) north of its Hadrianic predecessor, taking advantage of the narrowing of the mainland created by the estuaries of the Clyde and the Forth as well as the means of seaborne supply which they afforded. The fleet may well have had a military role in the advance. A squadron of large warships sailing up both coasts simultaneously would have demonstrated the power of Roman arms, while oared transports may have been employed to effect the landing of substantial advance parties on the shores of the Clyde and the Forth to establish supply depots and base camps. As with the construction of Hadrian's Wall 20 years earlier, the main function of the navy thereafter would have been the import of supplies and equipment, initially for the legionary construction gangs and then for the garrisons of the forts.

Although the western terminal fort lay at Old Kilpatrick this cannot have functioned as the main port in the west as the Clyde was not navigable this far until the eighteenth century.[83] A road has been found running out through the west defences of the annexe south of the fort and this could have led to a harbour at Dumbarton where the Leven flows into the Clyde (**61**).[84] On the south shore of the estuary, there was a large fort at Bishopton and beyond it fortlets at Lurg Moor and Outerwards. There may well have been other fortlets and/or signal-towers watching over the estuary. Beyond the eastern terminus of the Wall there were forts at Cramond and Inveresk on the south shore of the Forth estuary (**62**). Both of these had quay facilities, as did Carriden, the fort at or close to the east end of the Wall.[85] It was presumably the potential for commercial activity at the main port in the east that led to the growth of a sizeable civil settlement beside the fort at Carriden whose inhabitants – the *vicani consistentes Castello Veluniate* – commissioned an altar to Jupiter Optimus Maximus.[86] The forts at Cramond and Inveresk were also accompanied by substantial extramural settlements.[87] The presence of the *procurator Augusti* Quintus Lusius Sabinianus at Inveresk might suggest that, as the first port for ships making their way up the coast from South Shields, it was a particularly important link in the supply-chain for the Wall garrisons.[88] The Agricolan road

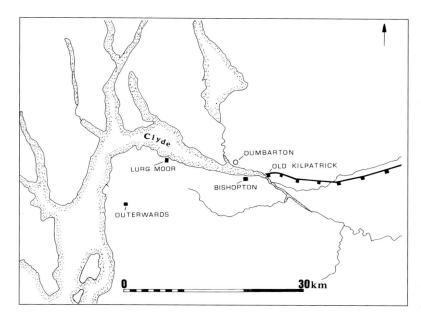

61 *West end of Antonine Wall showing the location of main military ports*

62 *East end of Antonine Wall showing the location of main military ports*

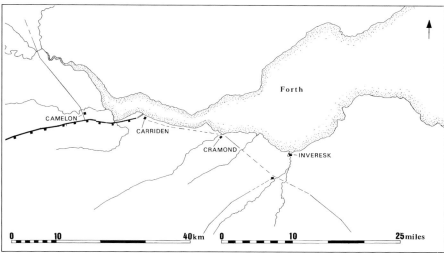

north of the Wall was also re-garrisoned with forts. These were placed at Camelon, Ardoch, Strageath and Bertha. The first of these lay beside the River Carron not far from the Forth estuary, and the last was positioned at the confluence of the Tay and Almond, and thus both were accessible from the sea. Further, it has been suggested that Camelon, rather than Carriden, was the main port of supply for the Antonine Wall.[89]

Troops were sent from Britain in the mid–140s to assist in a campaign against the Moors and were presumably transported there and back by the *Classis Britannica*, a rare excursion to warmer climes.[90] Warfare again erupted in the north in the mid-150s and once more reinforcements were sent for all three British legions from the armies of both Upper and Lower Germany. These men disembarked at Newcastle where they set up a dedication to Antoninus, probably in the shrine on the bridge over the Tyne.[91] The Antonine Wall was abandoned *c.*AD 165 and it is around this time that the *Classis Britannica* fort at Dover was rebuilt, presumably prompted by the return of sections of the fleet which had been operating in the north. Approximately 10 years later the British Fleet was involved in a major transportation exercise when 5,500 heavily armoured cavalry, supplied by the Sarmatians as part of a treaty agreement, were transported across the Channel.[92] The death of Marcus Aurelius in 180 coincided with an outbreak of serious warfare in Britain. Cassius Dio states that enemy tribes crossed the Wall that divided them from the Roman garrisons, ravaged widely and cut down a 'general' along with the troops accompanying him.[93] Most probably it was the abandoned but still standing Antonine Wall that was being referred to while the 'general' may have been a legionary legate. Ulpius Marcellus was despatched as the new governor charged with restoring order, and Dio's comments imply the undertaking of punitive expeditions in the far north which would undoubtedly have been supported by the fleet. An inscription from Carlisle of this period which refers to the 'rout of a huge multitude of barbarians' may be commemorating such an expedition.[94] Victory had been achieved by 184 and soon afterwards the *Classis Britannica* undertook the transfer of two of the British legions to Gaul to suppress a rebellion in Brittany.[95]

8

DRAMA AND TRANSITION
AD 193-276

Civil war: the invasion in reverse

The years around AD 200 saw the *Classis Britannica* fully engaged in a number of operational theatres. The assassination of the Emperor Commodus on the last day of 192 ushered in a period of civil war. One of the rival claimants for the throne was the governor of Britain, Clodius Albinus. He came to an agreement with one of the other contenders Lucius Septimius Severus, who commanded all 16 legions stationed along the Rhine and Danube, whereby he gained the title of Caesar and the implied right of succession which went with it. However, once Severus had disposed of his other main rival, Pescennius Niger, governor of Syria, he sent agents to assassinate Albinus. The latter survived the attempt and decided that he now had no option but to take the war to Severus by crossing over to the Continent, which he did in the autumn of 196. To have any hope at all against the numerically far superior forces of Severus, Albinus must have stripped Britain of practically every available soldier. This is implied by the prolonged period of campaigning in the north that was required in the wake of the Albinian episode. The *Classis Britannica* would obviously have been fully occupied with the transportation across the Channel of Albinus' army which possibly numbered as many as 40,000 men, an exercise of a magnitude not seen since the invasion of 43, and one which in all probability necessitated the rapid construction of new transports as well as the requisition of every available merchantman. The sources do not relate if there were any naval engagements between the two sides. The decisive battle was fought near Lyon in February 197. Both armies suffered very heavy losses but the forces of Severus won the day and Albinus committed suicide. That there was no attempt by the remnants of his forces to continue the war indicates the scale of their defeat and demoralisation.

On this occasion there are no surviving inscriptions recording the despatch of vexillations to reinforce the British legions, but this must surely have happened, not only because of the scale of their losses but also to ensure the loyalty of the army in Britain to the new Severan dynasty. It is also possible that some of the remnants of Albinus' army were transferred to other legions. Bringing the army in Britain up to strength appears to have taken some time as the new governor Virius Lupus had to buy peace from the Maeatae, a confederation of certain of the tribes in central Scotland, who had taken advantage of the weakness of the Roman forces to attack the province. The decade following the violent events of 197 was taken up with a major programme of repair and renewal of the military infrastructure of the province, a process which encompassed a further rebuilding of the *Classis Britannica* fort at Dover.

Caledonia revisited

While this work was proceeding Severus was making plans to exact revenge on the Maeatae and their allies. By 208 preparations had been completed for a major assault. Granaries at Corbridge had been rebuilt while the fort at South Shields was extended and converted into a supply-base. Initially it was intended to add 13 new granaries to the existing pair, but before these could be completed there was a change of plan and the number of granaries was increased to 24. Lead-sealings bearing portraits of Severus and his sons Caracalla and Geta datable to AD 208-11 provide useful confirmation of the context for this supply-base.[1] The scale of the work, along with the capacity of the South Shields depot – where it has been estimated the granaries could hold rations sufficient for a force of 40,000 men for three months – clearly show that this was not for the purpose of a single campaign but for a permanent reoccupation of a major part of Scotland in which supply by sea was evidently intended to play a major role (**63**). Cassius Dio says that Severus was intent on conquering the whole of the rest of Britain, although subjugating might be a more accurate term as extensive garrisoning was not the intention.[2]

Herodian tells us that the governor, Lucius Alfenus Senecio, wrote to the emperor stating that he lacked the requisite forces to punish the northern tribes and requesting reinforcements or, better still, an imperial expedition led by Severus in person.[3] The request was of course the result of prior instructions from the emperor himself as the scale of the preparations indicates. Although physical infirmity forced him to travel in a litter, Severus was still ambitious for personal military renown. Also, realising that he probably had but a few years left, he wanted his sons Caracalla and Geta to gain military experience under his direct tutelage, and thus forge a personal bond with the army and secure the future of the dynasty. It was the army that had gained Severus ultimate power and his keenness to see that his sons realised the importance of its continued support after his passing is indicated by his words to them on his deathbed: 'Live in harmony with one another; enrich the soldiers, and ignore everyone else' (Cassius Dio 76.15.1-2).

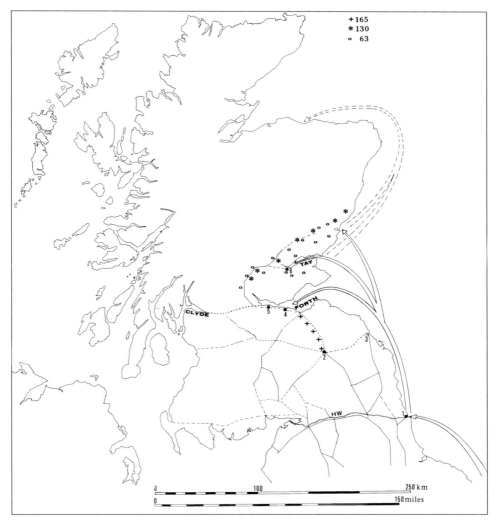

63 *Map of Severus' campaigns in Scotland and supporting naval activity. Marching-camps shown in groups of 165, 130 and 63 acres. KEY: 1 - South Shields, 2 - Newstead, 3 - Berwick, 4 - Cramond, 5 - Carriden, 6 - Carpow*

Thus it was that in 208 Severus, his sons, the imperial court, and many high-ranking senators (the last included to prevent them making trouble while the Emperor was away) arrived in Britain where a headquarters was established at York. Severus brought large reinforcements with him which included legionary vexillations.[4] An inscription from Rome of this period has been interpreted as recording the combination of the fleets of Germany, Moesia and Pannonia under one command with the *Classis Britannica*.[5] Given the developments at South Shields and the size and direction of Severus' campaigns up the east coast of Scotland this is surely the only possible context for such an extraordinary concentration of naval power. Coins of 208 record the *Profectio*

137

Augustorum – the Emperors setting out on campaign – while two interesting issues of this and the following year depict two different types of bridge. The first illustrates a permanent bridge with towers at either end while the other shows a bridge of boats with the legend '*Traiectus*' – a crossing-over. The image of a galley with standards at the stern appeared on Caracallan bronze *asses* of 207-8 and was used again on silver and bronze issues of 210.[6] Other issues of the period 209-11 portray Oceanus and Neptune, a further indication of the important role of the navy in Severus' assault. According to the historians Herodian and Cassius Dio the first objective was the Caledonii. They were the focus of the campaign in 208 and 209 during which 'Severus did not give up until he neared the furthest point of the island where in particular he observed with great accuracy the change in the sun's motion and the length of days and nights in both summer and winter' (Cassius Dio 76.13). The Caledonians were forced to sue for peace and ceded a large sector of their territory.

A series of remarkably large marching-camps, forming three sub-groups 165, 130 and 63 acres (65, 53 and 25ha) in size, considered to belong to this period illustrate the progress of the campaign force (**63**).[7] From a marshalling-point near the outpost fort at Newstead, now recommissioned, the army proceeded to a crossing of the Forth near Stirling. Five camps of 165 acres, indicating a force some 25-30,000 strong, mark its advance up Dere Street to the vicinity of Inveresk. Beyond the Forth only 130- and 63-acre camps occur, and it appears that a detachment was left behind to safeguard the Forth-Clyde line. The distribution of 63-acre camps, which have been proven to be earlier than the 130-acre type, suggests the rest of the force split into two battle-groups of equal size, reuniting for the campaign of 209 which advanced up the eastern coastal plain at least as far as Inverbervie. The Tay was crossed at Carpow where a new fortress was shortly to be built (**64**). The first installation to be constructed here though was a multi-sided enclosure at least 70 acres (28ha) in size.[8] It was very probably the Tay crossing that consisted of the pontoon bridge depicted on contemporary coins, and this enclosure may have been built to protect the bridgehead. However, a far more likely interpretation in view of the involvement of elements of four fleets in this campaign is that this was a beachhead established by the navy. Supplying an army of the size deployed by Severus, a large section of which may well have over-wintered north of the Forth, obviously had to be carefully planned. The assembling of such a strong naval force was clearly a crucial part of the overall strategy and it seems very likely that it was intended to use it not simply in a support role but also to provide a marine force sufficiently powerful to establish an advance base in enemy territory ready for a rendezvous with the rest of the army marching overland. The size of the enclosure, allowing for the fact that a significant proportion of the interior would be taken up with stores, implies a force at least 8,000 strong which probably included cavalry. The bringing together of four fleets suggests the amphibious assault force may in fact have been far larger. Perhaps Severus, knowing that his health was failing, employed this 'leap-frog' tactic in order to secure victory as soon as possible. It is also clear that he and/or his generals had been assiduous in their reading of Tacitus' *Agricola*.

New installations intended to be permanent were seemingly few and restricted to the east coast. The strategy was apparently to dominate the Maeatae and Caledonii from a small number of strong bases positioned so that they could protect and control the agriculturally productive coastal plain and which could also be supplied and easily reinforced by sea. Thus the Antonine fort at Cramond on the south side of the Forth was recommissioned as a link in the supply chain probably along with the putative and intermediate Roman base at Berwick at the mouth of the Tweed. A much larger base was established at Carpow on the south shore of the Tay estuary (**64**). About 28 acres (11.5ha) in size, inscriptions and stamped tiles show that this was built and garrisoned by detachments of *II Augusta* and *VI Victrix*.[9] Comparatively little of the interior has been examined and so the size of the garrison is unknown but it seems likely to have numbered at least 3,000 men.

The Maeatae revolted in 210 and this time the campaign to suppress it was led by Caracalla as Severus was too ill to travel. The trouble continued into 211 and Severus was preparing to lead another expedition personally when he died at York on 4 February. As Caracalla and Geta did not arrive back in Rome until late that year the planned expedition may actually have taken place especially as their victory in Britain was still being commemorated on coins issued in 212. A building inscription of that same year, or possibly a little later, shows

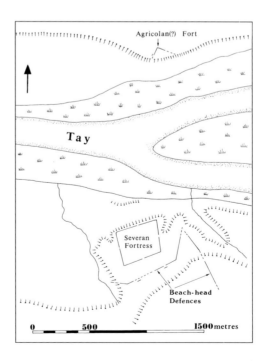

64 *Plan of Carpow on the Tay estuary showing site of legionary base and other military constructions*

that construction of the Carpow fortress continued after the new emperor's departure from Britain, but both it and Cramond were soon abandoned.[10] By contrast, the recently constructed supply base at South Shields continued in use.[11] It now became the chief granary for the garrisons along the eastern half of Hadrian's Wall with ships bringing grain up from ports along the south and east coasts. From here it was transported to the forts, most likely by rivercraft operating on the Tyne. The abandonment of installations beyond and including Newstead demonstrates the success rather than the failure of Severus' work as the treaty arrangements made with the Maeatae and Caledones remained in force for more than 80 years. The army now settled down to an extended programme of rebuilding and refurbishment work at its forts and fortresses throughout the province. For the *Classis Britannica*, however, the evidence suggests that the period immediately following the end of the Severan campaign in Scotland was one of reorganisation and role-change.

Reorganisation

That the *Classis Britannica* of earlier times underwent a fundamental change in the wake of Severus' Scottish expedition is clear from a range of evidence (**65**). Most obvious is the abandonment of its headquarters fort at Dover which has produced plentiful evidence for demolition *c.*AD 215. So efficient was its removal in fact that the later Saxon Shore fort here was built completely without reference to the outline of its predecessor. The iron-making establishments at Bardown and Beauport Park also ceased production around this time.[12] The bath-house at the latter was systematically stripped of materials such as lead piping and window glass which could be reused elsewhere. The latest coins from Bardown belong to the reign of Caracalla (211-17) and those from Beauport Park to that of Severus Alexander (222-35). However, the *Classis Britannica* clearly continued in existence under that name, for some decades later it is mentioned on an inscription from Arles dating to the reign of Philip (244-9), which records one of its officers by the name of Saturninus.[13] It may be mere coincidence but it is noteworthy that the *Classis Germanica* disappears from the record in much the same period so it would appear that whatever reorganisation affected the navy was not confined to Britain. Obviously a substantial naval presence in British waters was still essential and indeed there are literary references to its employment on a number of occasions during the last 150 years of Roman rule in Britain. Determining the organisation, deployment and strength of naval forces in later Roman Britain however is fraught with problems. Overall, understanding has been impeded by a straightforward lack of clear and unambiguous evidence; no inscriptions or stamped tiles to indicate fleet activity and only occasional references in the literary sources which largely describe the situation at the close of the fourth

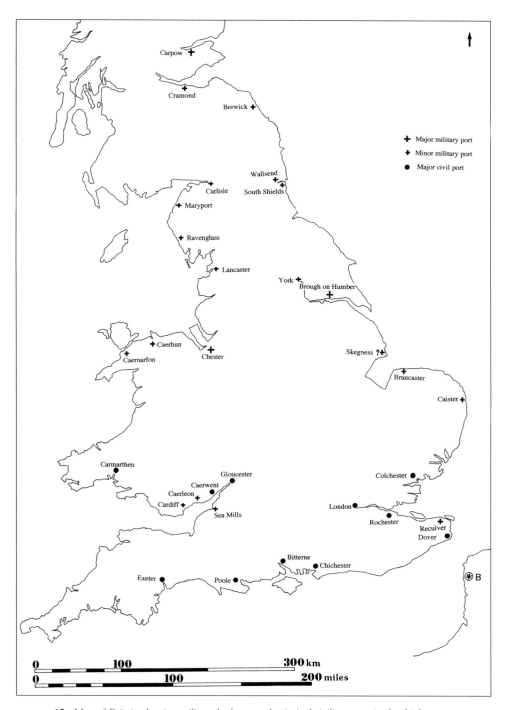

65 *Map of Britain showing military harbours and principal civilian ports in the third century*

century. Then there is the matter of the true purpose of the coastal installations which have come to be known as the Saxon Shore Forts and the entrenched opinions which have grown up around that question. To these can be added a general tendency to concentrate attention on the south and east coasts to the detriment of appreciating naval strategy for late Roman Britain as a whole.

What is perfectly clear though is that during the course of the third century the role of the *Classis Britannica* changed significantly. Previously, apart from involvement in a major offensive operation once every 30 or 40 years, much of its time was taken up with supplying the army, maintaining communications with the Continent, and assisting with the exploitation of the island's mineral resources. From about the middle of the third century, however, it took on the additional and increasingly onerous tasks of combating seaborne coastal raiders and protecting merchant shipping from piracy. Whereas in earlier times, life for the *nautae milites* had been very largely one of peaceful routine disturbed by occasional bouts of manic activity, it soon became a matter of constant patrolling punctuated with violent action. By the end of the third century the military activity of the fleet was focused on catching and eliminating opponents whose principal objectives were robbery, murder, hostage and slave-taking, and terrorism in contrast to the large-scale, set-piece manoeuvres against a conventional enemy of earlier times. Punitive expeditions involving significant naval forces were still occasionally undertaken, but use of the fleet for conquest had come to an end; offence had given way to defence. Although the numbers of sea-raiders would have been very small, in the beginning successful raids would soon have spurred on others to try their luck. As we know only too well from events in our own times the degree of alarm and insecurity generated by a few acts of terrorism can be out of all proportion to the scale of the atrocities. Furthermore to mount an adequate response to such terrorism the protecting military power always has to deploy forces far greater than those ranged against it.

During the Severan period, most probably under Caracalla, the administrative arrangements for Britain underwent a major reorganisation. Britain was divided into two provinces, *Britannia Superior* in the south and *Britannia Inferior* in the north with the boundary roughly following a line drawn between the Mersey and the Wash. This was part of an empire-wide reform introduced by Severus with the aim of preventing any single provincial governor having control over an army large enough to contest the throne. This probably had little if any direct impact upon the organisation of the *Classis Britannica*. The inscription from Arles mentioned above suggests the original fleet arrangements were still intact at least as late as *c.*AD 247. Armed forces from Upper Britain could certainly serve in Lower Britain, as is demonstrated by the continuing presence at Corbridge and Carlisle of detachments of both the Second and Twentieth Legions. Perhaps, therefore, the *Classis Britannica* remained as a unified command with ultimate control residing with the Prefect in *Superior* but with vessels/flotillas serving in

Inferior under the operational control of the governor who was also commander of *Legio VI* at York. If, however, the legions had their own naval squadrons as suggested in chapter 6 then there would have been no major administrative changes to the *Classis Britannica*. That said, there certainly were changes to its physical deployment.

The fact that the fort at Dover was demolished, and not just abandoned as had happened on earlier occasions, shows that whatever changes were introduced around AD 220 were intended to be permanent. The same conclusion is indicated by the deliberate dismantling of facilities at the Bardown and Beauport Park depots in the Weald. Any other bases of the *Classis Britannica*, such as that which very probably existed at Lympne, were presumably affected in the same way. About the same time as these installations were closed down, at least three new coastal forts were constructed further around the coast to the north, the first to be built in this region for more than a century (**65**). The northernmost lay at Brancaster on the north Norfolk coast overlooking the Wash and the approaches to the Ouse, Welland and Witham river-systems which afforded access into the Fenland, East Anglia, the Midlands and Lincolnshire (**66**). The second was built 50 miles (80km) further along the East Anglian coast at Caister-on-Sea, close to the mouth of the River Yare which led inland to *Venta Icenorum* (Caistor-by-Norwich), the *civitas* capital of the Iceni (**67**). The third was sited at Reculver (*Regulbium*) on the north Kent coast, overlooking the approaches to the lower Thames estuary (**68**).[14]

All three forts were approximately square in plan and very similar in size at 7.14, 6.47 and 7.56 acres (2.89, 2.62 and 3.06ha) respectively. They were of traditional form with rounded corners and internal towers and each was equipped with a stone perimeter wall nearly 10ft (3.05m) thick backed by an earth rampart. At Caister there was an initial phase when the turf rampart had timber gates and towers. None has been investigated to any extent but excavation at Reculver and aerial photography at Brancaster indicate internal buildings of normal type while finds from both forts and their surroundings indicate a construction date in the 220s or 230s. Furthermore, a fragmentary inscription from Reculver records the construction of the '*aedes principiorum cum basilica*' (the shrine in the headquarters with a cross-hall) during the governorship of a man called Rufinus whose term of office occurred some time in the late second or early third century.[15]

The fact that the construction of these new coastal forts occurred around the same time as the demise of the earlier *Classis Britannica* installations has given rise to the suggestion that they were the new bases for the British Fleet.[16] Stamped tiles from primary contexts at both Brancaster and Reculver show that the original garrisons were units of auxiliary infantry, the *Cohors I Aquitanorum* at the first and the *Cohors I Baestasiorum* at the second.[17] That at Caister is unknown. At Reculver, however, there is a definite link with the *Classis Britannica* as more than 40 Roman tiles made of the same clay as that

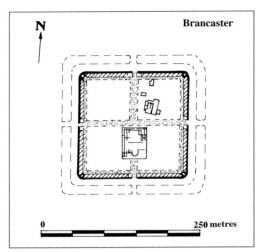

66 *Plan of the third-century fort at Brancaster*

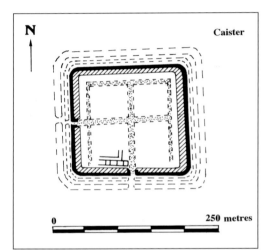

67 *Plan of the third-century fort at Caister-on-Sea*

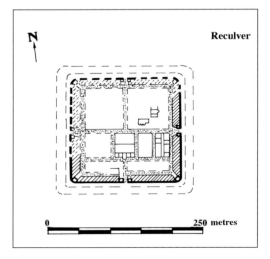

68 *Plan of the third-century fort at Reculver*

used for CL.BR tiles elsewhere (the variant known as Fabric 2) can be seen built into the fabric of St Mary's Church, and others are incorporated into the east gate of the fort.[18] They could of course have been imported to the site as building material or, then again, they might derive from an earlier fleet base in the vicinity. Yet there is at least a possibility that part of the British Fleet was based here, and at the other new forts, alongside the army units known to have been in residence. Certainly the new forts are rather large for a single infantry unit 480 strong – 3-4 acres would normally be ample – so theoretically at least they were quite capable of additionally accommodating naval personnel.

It was suggested long ago that this apparent redeployment of the *Classis Britannica* was in response to the beginnings of the barbarian piracy and coastal raiding that were to become a real threat to maritime commerce and supply by the 280s.[19] Although these attacks are first mentioned in the sources towards the close of the third century they would need to be occurring on a significant scale in order to attract the attention of contemporary writers. The probability is therefore that they had been developing and increasing in intensity over a considerable period. It is quite possible for example that sea-raiders from north of Hadrian's Wall first made an appearance during the troubles which preceded Severus' Scottish expedition. Brancaster and similar sites would thus have been positioned so as to prevent raiders entering the major river systems on the east coast in order to attack rich sites inland, and for this purpose a mixed garrison of land and sea forces would have been appropriate.

Developments at Richborough towards the middle of the third century imply it was added to this embryonic coastal defence system. The Flavian triumphal arch was surrounded by an earthwork enclosure about 1 acre (0.4ha) in size. This had an earth rampart fronted by a triple ditch system interrupted by a single gateway of timber in the middle of the west side (**69**). It would appear that the venerable monument was being used as a look-out post. There may have been other forts in this defensive chain. Coastal erosion has destroyed large tracts of land in this region since the fifteenth century and a number of substantial settlements have been lost to the sea. At Skegness, occupying a strategically important location opposite Brancaster on the north side of the Wash, much of the old town had been washed away by the mid-sixteenth century including a 'castelle' which might conceivably have been a Roman fort in origin.[20] Dunwich, near Blythburgh, possibly the site of *Sitomagus* listed on the late fourth-century map of the Roman world known as the Peutinger Table, has been put forward as another candidate (**75**).[21]

Like many inland towns, a number of those on the coast received earthwork defences for the first time in the late second century, subsequently strengthened by the addition of masonry fortifications in the third. Rochester was one such town, with a defended area of 23 acres (9.5ha). Where it has been sectioned the rampart here has been found to consist largely of turf work laid on a stone base.[22] This is a constructional method typical of military sites,

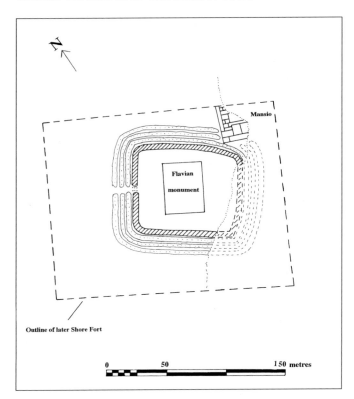

69 *Plan showing conversion of Flavian monument at Richborough to look-out post and enclosure within earth fort in the mid-third century*

Within the plan:
Mansio

Flavian monument

Outline of later Shore Fort

0   50   150 metres

contrasting with the usual dump method found in civic fortifications, a fact which gave rise to the suggestion that the defended area at Rochester was a naval base.[23] However, while harbour facilities undoubtedly existed here and may well have included a naval dockyard, the defended area is too large for a fleet base. Possibly naval personnel stationed here assisted with the design and construction of the defences around the core of the town.

Moving north of the Wash it has already been described how the Humber estuary is an obvious candidate for some form of naval station throughout the Roman period. At Brough (*Petuaria*) a circuit of defences enclosing an area in excess of 15 acres (6ha) was erected over the site of the earlier fort and supply-depot in the mid-second century. Around AD 200 these were replaced by a new defensive system on a different line delimiting an irregular rectangle of 12.5 acres (5ha). Two later phases of work saw the addition of a stone curtain wall and then a series of bastions. An inscription of AD 140-4 found reused in the fabric of a fourth-century building inside the settlement records the construction of a new theatre stage paid for an *aedile* of the *Vicus Petuarensis*. As in an ordinary *vicus* the elected officials normally consisted merely of a pair of magistrates (*magistri*); the presence of an *aedile* was interpreted to mean that Brough had become the capital of the local tribe known as the Parisi.[24] The most recent excavator at the site, however, has consistently put forward the view that the succession of defended enclosures had been used as a naval base and that the *vicus* referred to was the suburb outside it.[25] The less than regular layout of the interior along with the sheer size of the area enclosed tends to imply a civilian rather than a military function while the nature of the extra-mural settlement does not match up to what one would expect of a *civitas* capital. The idea that the defended area was a naval base must therefore be rejected. Yet the location of Brough in relation to the overall defensive needs of the coastline and the natural harbour facilities afforded by the Humber estuary make it very likely that a naval flotilla, whether part of the *Classis Britannica* or under the control of the provincial governor at York, was based somewhere near Brough. This was certainly the case in the first half of the fourth century as will be seen in the next chapter.

The northernmost naval station and military port lay at South Shields at the mouth of the Tyne.[26] This had long been the main port of entry and exit for troop units travelling between Britain and the German frontier, and with the increasing number and severity of the attacks on the latter during the third century, the volume of traffic will have increased considerably. At nearby Wallsend the port area was enclosed by defences at the beginning of the third century (**70**). No Roman port is known along the 100-mile stretch of coastline between Brough and South Shields and indeed there are few natural havens where one could exist. The Tees estuary, however, is an obvious candidate and one suspects a Roman harbour will one day be found somewhere in the vicinity of Middlesbrough, assuming it has not been entirely destroyed by coastal erosion.

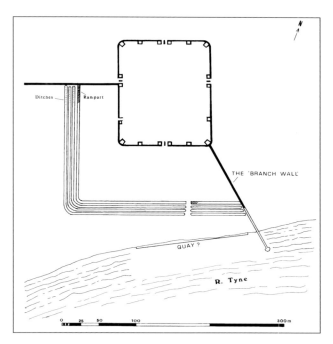

70 *Plan of the fort and defended harbour at Wallsend*

There are no signs of new naval installations anywhere else on the British coast and it would seem that it was only the *Classis Britannica* in the east and south-east that was redeployed. What had begun as sporadic instances of piracy and coastal raiding by Picts, Saxons and Frisians multiplied rapidly after *c*.AD 230. The reasons for the general upsurge in attacks on the Roman frontier have been much debated but probably included population pressure, deteriorating climate – which for the Saxons ultimately resulted in the inundation of coastal settlements because of a rising sea-level – along with improved military organisation and tactics. A new confederation of Germanic tribes known as the Alamanni began to cause serious trouble in the 230s, and they were joined by the Franks in the 250s. For the successful campaign against them in 255, legionary vexillations, probably accompanied by other units, were despatched from Britain.[27] A few years later, however, the Franks gained a firm foothold in central and eastern Gaul as well as north-eastern Spain, while the Alamanni penetrated as far south as Italy itself. The psychological impact of these successful breaches of the Empire's defences was far greater than the actual physical damage. Quite understandably the general population was becoming more inclined to support a local leader who could protect their own particular region rather than the legitimate emperor at his distant court and this led to a number of secessionist movements in the ensuing decades. Gallienus, co-emperor with his father Valerian, defeated the invaders but then had to turn his attention to the Danubian provinces. The troops from Britain that accompanied him never returned as in 259, Postumus, commander of part of the Rhine army, was hailed as emperor by his troops and established the so-called Gallic Empire consisting of Germany, Gaul, Britain and parts of Spain. This was to endure for 14 years until the defeat of its last ruler – Tetricus – by Aurelian in 274.

Although the garrison of Britain was depleted by further troop withdrawals during the *Imperium Galliarum*, the northern frontier was troubled by neither rebellion nor incursion. However, the reduction in manpower might well have impeded the maintenance and upgrading of military installations. While there is no mention in the literary sources of naval forces in this period, the frequent depiction of warships on the bronze coinage of Postumus illustrates the importance he attached to the fleets under his command which would of course have included all naval forces in both Britain and Germany.[28] They would have been vital for supporting his campaigns across the Rhine, ferrying troops from Britain to the Continent, maintaining communications between the constituent provinces of the Gallic Empire, and controlling the Atlantic seaboard. With this probable upsurge in naval activity the fleet dockyards would have been working flat out to satisfy the demand for extra ships.

9

PIRATES, SEA-RAIDERS AND USURPERS

Carausius, Allectus and Constantius: secession, murder and recovery

In 276 disaster befell Gaul. The Alamanni launched a major attack across the Rhine frontier and ranged widely throughout Gaul sacking 60 towns. The Emperor Probus (276-82) recovered the situation but Gaul was never the same. In the wake of the disaster all the important towns and cities, or rather in most cases their central core areas, were encircled with new fortifications.[1] The restoration of Gaul was interrupted in 281 by yet another revolt when a Roman general named Bonosus rebelled against Probus to avoid the consequences of his carelessness in allowing the Rhine fleet based at Cologne to be burnt in a German attack. He was soon defeated, but the following year Probus had to send a Moorish officer named Victorinus to Britain to deal with a rebellion by one of its governors. That there was warfare in the island soon afterwards is indicated by the assumption of the title *Britannicus Maximus* by the emperor Carus (283-5), indicating a victory in Britain. A contemporary poem praising the victorious campaigns of Carus' eldest son Carinus refers to their being won beneath the Northern Bear *'sub Arcto'*.[2] This phrase is a reference to the Pole Star and was used to indicate 'the far north'. The Pole Star was also the mariner's guide and its use may hint at a naval campaign.[3] These constant disturbances must have had a detrimental effect on military building programmes, not to mention morale and public confidence.

In 285 Diocletian appointed one of his senior officers Marcus Aurelius Valerius Maximianus as his deputy and emperor-designate with the title of 'Caesar', charged with particular responsibility for defending Italy and the western provinces. In the following year he was made co-emperor. One matter requiring Maximian's urgent attention was the swarms of Saxon and Frankish raiders who, as both Aurelius Victor and Eutropius tell us, were infesting the sea off the coast of both Belgica and Armorica – that is from Brittany to the mouth of the Rhine (**88 & 89**).[4] Clearly the raiders had not only become far more numerous than before but had also broken through and were ranging far beyond the narrow and theoretically easily patrolled 'neck' formed by the Straits of Dover. To clear the seas of this menace Maximian appointed Marcus Aurelius Mausaeus Carausius, a man who had grown up in the region of Menapia on the coast of Belgica, served as a river pilot as a young man, and then joined the army where he served with distinction. The comments of Aurelius Victor and Eutropius reveal that he was put in charge of assembling a fleet which, under direction from his headquarters at Boulogne, achieved notable success against the sea-raiders.[5] The implication is that both the *Classis Germanica* and the *Classis Britannica*, if the latter was still known as such, had been incapable of dealing with this problem for some considerable time. Despite his success, or perhaps because of it, the suspicion began to grow that Carausius had prior knowledge of the raids and was using this to his personal advantage by letting the barbarians attack and only intercepting them once they had set off on their homeward journey laden with plunder, which he then confiscated and kept for himself. Maximian ordered his execution but Carausius, forewarned, sought refuge in Britain and set about recreating the *Imperium Galliarum*. The events of this period are related in the works of highly partisan panegyricists – poets at the imperial court of the legitimist emperor who made their living by composing works which heaped praise on the actions of their master. One such, written in 297 describes Carausius' secession thus:

> In that vile act of brigandage the fleeing pirate first seized the fleet which once protected the provinces of Gaul, built many more ships besides in Roman style, seduced a Roman legion, cut off divisions of provincial troops, recruited Gallic merchants to his service, won over hordes of barbarous forces by spoils from the provinces them-selves, and through instruction by supporters of that disgraceful act he trained them all for naval duties.

> *Pan. Lat.* viii(v) 12.1. *Panegyric for Constantius Caesar* Anon.
> 1 March 297

As we have only the biased accounts of the court poets for information, the true reasons for Carausius' defection remain a mystery; possibly there was disagreement between him and Maximian about resources and priorities. Carausius' primary power-base was the fleet which he soon augmented with additional ships and personnel and which he soon employed to great effect (**71, 72, 73** & **74**). However, he also continued to hold Boulogne and a consider-able portion of northern Gaul where a mint issuing Carausian coinage operated at Rouen. Among the coins issued during his reign is a series commemorating no fewer than nine legions supporting the Carausian cause. These were not in fact full legions but vexillations which had been assembled for special campaigns in the Rhineland and which were the first to declare for

71 *Silver coin of Carausius (RIC 560) showing warship proceeding right*

72 *'Aurelianus' coin of Carausius (RIC 649) depicting warship proceeding right*

73 *Quinarius of Allectus (RIC 124) with image of warship proceeding right*

74 *Quinarius of Allectus (RIC 128) showing warship proceeding left*

Carausius. The only entire legions under his control were the three in Britain perhaps together with *XXX Ulpia Victrix* at Xanten, this last possibly the 'seduced' legion of the Panegyric. Carausius also seems to have enjoyed widespread popular support both because of his success against the sea-raiders and because he was a local man who could provide strong and able leadership to protect the interests of the north-western provinces.

It was not until 289 that Maximian was ready to move against Carausius. He sailed down the Rhine with a newly-built fleet and apparently managed to break out into the North Sea. The court poets wrote presumptuously of Maximian's forthcoming victory:

That pirate must now lose heart, when he sees that your armies have almost entered those straits which alone have postponed his death until the present, that his men have abandoned their ships and have followed the retreating sea. Is there now any more distant island he can hope for, any other Ocean? How can he escape punishment for treason, without being swallowed by an earthquake, or swept by a hurricane on to lonely reefs? Splendid fleets were built and equipped, which would head for Ocean simultaneously by every river; men not only competed in their labours to complete them, rivers suddenly rose to receive them. For almost a whole year, Your Majesty, when you needed good weather to build shipyards, to fell timber, to invigorate the workers to keep their hands from idleness, hardly a day has been spoiled by rain. Even winter copied the mildness of spring. Now we thought we were not living in the north; we felt the clemency of a southern sky as if stars or countries had changed places. This river of ours, having for a long time lacked a supply of rain, could not carry the ships; it only brought down the timber for your shipyards. But suddenly, when the warships had to be launched, the earth produced abundant springs for you, Jupiter poured out masses of rain, and Ocean flooded whole river beds. And so the ships attacked the waters that came beneath them of their own accord, ships moved by the slightest effort of their crews; the happiest of beginnings that needed a sailor's shanty more than his hard work. Your Majesty, how prosperous an outcome will follow you upon the sea, when even the weather obeys you at the right moment.

Pan. Lat. x (ii).11.7.
Panegyric in honour of the Emperor Maximian Mamertinus 21 April 289

However, the same sources are notably silent about its outcome and it is clear, given that an agreement was made with Carausius immediately thereafter, that Maximian's expedition failed miserably. Another panegyric, delivered some years later, hints that this may have been caused by bad weather as much as the prowess of the usurper's fleet.

Your troops in contrast, though in valour unsurpassed, were none the less unused to naval action. And so we heard that from a shameful act of brigandage the evil threat of war had sprung, sure though we were of its outcome. On top of, this, the crime so long unpunished had fanned the insolence of those reckless men to boast that roughness of the sea, which by constraint of fate delayed your victory, was a cover for your fear of them. The war had been abandoned in despair, so they believed, not just postponed by act of policy.

Pan. Lat. viii(v).12.1-2, Anon.

Although Carausius appears to have believed that Maximian would abide by whatever agreement had been concluded, the latter was clearly intent on recovering Carausius' breakaway empire. Its continued existence was not only an affront to Maximian's authority and an encouragement to others to secede but also Britain was considered a very valuable resource to the central empire. Having escaped the ravages which had affected the neighbouring provinces on the Continent, it was a valuable source of men, foodstuffs and minerals. Early in 292 the campaign against Carausius was placed in the hands of Flavius Valerius Constantius, Maximian's recently appointed deputy. Constantius' previous position of praetorian prefect was taken over by Julius Asclepiodotus. As a panegyric of 297 tells us, Constantius moved quickly the following year, appearing outside the walls of Boulogne and taking the garrison completely by surprise.[6] Despite lacking a fleet, or at least one which he thought could compete successfully against that of Carausius, he besieged the city. To prevent the possibility of reinforcement or flight by sea he made the harbour unusable by building a mole across its entrance formed of driven piles heaped around with boulders. The defenders were trapped and soon surrendered. Constantius then attacked and defeated Frankish forces occupying the Rhine mouth area who may well have been allies of Carausius. The latter did not survive these two reverses and soon after the loss of Boulogne he was murdered and replaced by Allectus, his finance minister.

Three years were to pass before Constantius moved against the rump of the rebel regime in Britain. This delay can be accounted for partly by his first having to deal with more pressing problems along the Rhine frontier and partly, as the panegyrists are keen to explain, in order to build a fleet of the size and strength which would ensure there was no repeat of the embarrassing failure of 289. When the invasion force finally began its journey across the Channel in the summer of 296 it must have been an extremely imposing sight. We have no figures for the size of Constantius' army but on the reasonable assumption that he took as much care in assembling his land forces as he did in building the fleet, one is drawn to conclude that it must have numbered at least 20,000 men. The fleet therefore would probably have consisted of more than 500 vessels. It sailed in two divisions: one from Boulogne, under the command of Constantius himself, which set off first; and the other from the mouth of the Seine further south led by Asclepiodotus. Constantius' division encountered bad weather and rough seas and made headway but slowly. Asclepiodotus was more fortunate. He reached the Isle of Wight and managed to slip past Allectus' waiting fleet in a thick sea-fog. His forces disembarked, Asclepiodotus ordered his boats be burned and headed inland. On learning of the Solent landings Allectus left the port where he was staying, and where a second fleet was based, and hastily tried to assemble his forces. He was apparently unaware of Constantius' approaching division. Not yet properly organised, Allectus' army encountered Asclepiodotus' force sooner than expected and was thoroughly routed. Allectus himself perished in the battle.

Little is said about what Constantius' fleet was doing while events were unfolding. However, one part of his force achieved a spectacular rescue of London from disaster. Separated from the main body of the fleet in the fog, they managed to reach London. Here they found that some of the Frankish warriors from Allectus' recently defeated army, keen to make some profit from their stay in Britain before they returned home across the North Sea, were on the point of sacking *Londinium*. Constantius' soldiers fell upon them and slaughtered them in full view of the citizenry; as the poet Eumenius puts it 'not only rescuing the provincials but giving them a gladiatorial show into the bargain'. Constantius himself arrived soon after and was awarded a triumphal welcome. This is the scene depicted on the impressive gold medallion found near Arras (**colour plate 7**). The obverse shows Constantius as the great general in armour on horseback with, above him, the words *Redditor Lucis Aeterna* – 'Restorer of the Eternal Light'. Below is the fleet, the instrument of reconquest, represented by a single war galley crammed with soldiers. London, in the form of its *tutela* or spiritual personification, kneels before the gates of the city with her hands raised in gratitude for her deliverance. The recovery of Britain was important but so too was the regaining of control over the seas as the words of the anonymous panegyrist of Constantius make clear:

> What a manifold victory, one marked by countless triumphs! By it Britain was restored; the power of the Franks eradicated; obedience imposed on many other tribes found guilty of complicity in the crime; and the sea cleansed for eternal peace. You may boast, invincible Caesar, you have discovered another world when, by restoring to the might of Rome its naval prestige, you added to her empire an element greater than all lands. You have, I say, invincible Caesar, ended a war that seemed to threaten every province, that could have spread and flared up anywhere that the Ocean laps the land . . .

> *Pan. Lat.* viii(v). 17-18. Anon.

Constantius stayed in Britain until the following spring, surveying its defences and initiating a programme of restoration and rebuilding along with the construction of new large forts in the North such as those at Piercebridge and Newton Kyme. It would have been most unwise to leave the garrison of the Rhine frontier depleted for any longer than absolutely necessary, so the fleet assembled for the re-taking of Britain would soon have been busy transporting most of Constantius' army back across the Channel. Constantius returned to Britain's shores nine years later, in 306, by which time he had become the senior Augustus, Diocletian and Maximian having retired the previous year. The purpose of his visit was leadership of a campaign into Scotland; possibly the Picts (a generic term now applied to the Caledonii and neighbouring tribes) had been stirring up trouble. However, it is possible that attacks had been made on the province itself not just the protectorates to the north of Hadrian's Wall. Recent excavations at South Shields for example have revealed that part of the fort was burnt down around this time, apparently as a result of enemy action which could have taken the form of a sneaky seaborne raid right into the harbour.[7] Nothing is known of the campaign in detail but the words of the panegyrist imply that the very north of Scotland was reached:

> In that last great campaign of his he did not seek for British trophies, as is generally believed, but with the gods already calling him he drew close to the furthest limit of the earth. And yet, with deeds so many and so various already performed, he did not seek to occupy the forests and marches of the Caledonians and other Picts, not to mention nearby Ireland and furthest Thule and the Isles of the Blessed, if they exist. Rather, something he wished to tell no man, though he was about to join the gods, he went to gaze upon the Ocean, that father of the gods who restores the fiery stars of heaven, so that as one about to savour endless light he might already see continuous day.

Pan. Lat. vi(vii). 7.1-2. *Panygeric for the Emperor Constantine AD 310*

Early fourth-century pottery found at both Cramond and Carpow suggests that Severus' amphibious tactics were repeated.[8] If so, the resident naval forces in Britain may have been temporarily and massively augmented. A brilliant victory had been won by midsummer after which Constantius returned to York where, on 25 July, he died. His son Constantine was, illegally, proclaimed Augustus, receiving official recognition as such the following year. In assembling forces to depose his rival Maxentius, Maximian's son, Constantine drew levies from Britain, and once again the Channel fleet(s) would have been busily engaged in ferry duties. There is evidence that Constantine returned to Britain on a number of occasions during the years leading up to his becoming sole emperor in 324. These visits were perhaps inspired by the desire to ensure there was no repeat of the Carausius episode by elements still committed to the secessionist cause.

New coastal installations and the fleet

The most recent analyses of the available dating evidence suggest that it was during the general period of the Carausian episode that the eight new forts which are the most impressive members of the series known as the Saxon Shore Forts were built along the south-east coast of England (**75**).[9] They were distributed along the coastline from East Anglia to the Solent and, ironically in view of their abandonment 60 years earlier, included new forts on the sites of

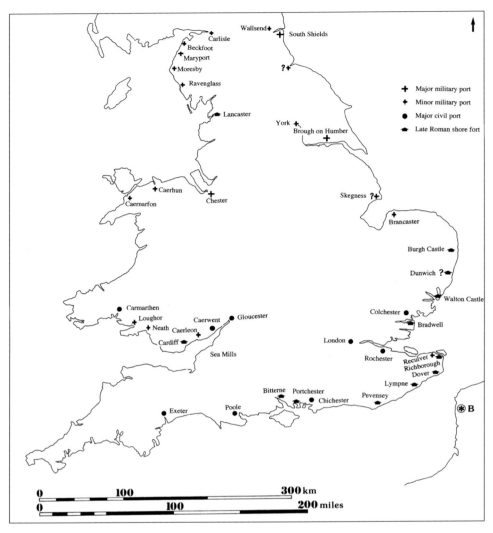

75 *Map of Britain showing new Shore Forts as well as existing military harbours and principal civilian ports in the fourth century*

the former fleet bases at Dover and Lympne. The term Saxon Shore Forts stems from the fact that they, together with some forts of earlier origin, appear in the late Roman document known as the *Notitia Dignitatum* as belonging to the forces of a military commander known as the *Comes Litoris Saxonici* or 'Count of the Saxon Shore'. Detailed discussion of each fort has appeared in a number of other works and so here it is merely necessary to summarise their principal and common characteristics.[10] Their military architecture was of the same style as the fortifications built around the core areas of many urban centres in Germany and Gaul around this time. They were equipped with a thick, freestanding, perimeter wall, projecting bastions at regular intervals, and narrow, heavily defended entrances. In terms of ground plan, the majority were either square or rectangular although at least one (Lympne) was pentagonal while one other (Pevensey) was oval. As to size, they lie within the fairly narrow range of 6 to 8½ acres (2.4–3.45ha). At few of these forts has the interior been excavated to any significant extent. What is perfectly clear though is that they were not crammed with buildings like the forts of the first and second centuries. Masonry buildings were few and far between and seemingly often restricted to a modest bath-house. There was a tendency to place buildings against and under the lee of the perimeter wall and large areas appear to have been left as open ground. This impression may be somewhat misleading, however, as it is clear from excavations at both Dover and Portchester that many buildings were constructed of timber in the later Roman period and have left few if any traces in the ground.[11] Also, the large numbers of rubbish pits and wells found peppering the interior of some of these forts along with the very considerable assemblages of coins, pottery and other artefacts show that they were intensively occupied albeit intermittently.

Now that the processes of coastal change and their effects on individual sites are better understood it is clear that at the time they were built all of the forts were positioned 'in sheltered, tidal environments that lay close to, but not directly on, the open sea'.[12] In many cases they were situated at the main entrance to a major river system which gave access to important settlements far inland. The northernmost of the new forts, Burgh Castle, probably replaced the nearby and earlier fort at Caister-on-Sea and was positioned on an elevated site at the head of the then broad estuary of the River Yare known as Breydon Water (**76**). This provided a large and sheltered anchorage and the site was well chosen to guard the river approach to the Icenian capital at Caistor-by-

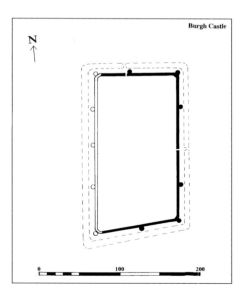

76 *Plan of Burgh Castle Shore Fort*

Norwich. To the north, the existing fort at Brancaster was retained in use. Proceeding south from Burgh, the next lay at Walton Castle, near Felixstowe. Nothing now remains of the fort but its former existence is recorded in eighteenth-century documents and by prints and sketches. Built beside an earlier and long established settlement with an excellent harbour, the new fort stood on the cliffs about 100ft above the sea. This stretch of the coast is heavily indented by the mouths of three rivers, the Deben, the Orwell and the Stour, which afforded easy access to the northern approaches to the *colonia* at Colchester. The southern approaches to Colchester, and also waterborne access to *Caesaromagus* (Chelmsford) via the Chelmer, were protected by the next fort in the series at Bradwell positioned at the tip of a promontory on the south side of the Blackwater estuary (**77**). Like most of the forts in this group it has been seriously affected by coastal erosion. Traces of what may be harbour walls have been noted in the marshland in front of the fort. Fourth-century material recovered from a number of other sites along this stretch of coast suggests the possibility of accompanying lookout towers (**78**).

South of the Thames, the earlier fort at Reculver continued in use and was supplemented on the east Kent coast by a new fort at Richborough; to accommodate this the mid-third-century earthwork enclosure was levelled and the great Flavian monument itself dismantled (**79** & **80**). At Dover the full plan of the Saxon Shore fort has still to be defined although it is known to have

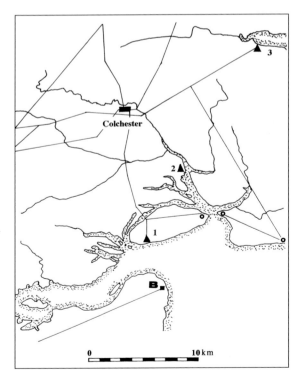

77 *Map of Colchester area showing location of Bradwell Shore Fort and possible look-out posts. KEY: Harbours: 1 - Mersey, 2 - Fingringhoe, 3 - Mistley. B = Bradwell Shore Fort. Small open circles denote possible location of fourth-century signal-stations*

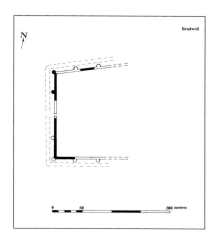

78 *Plan of Bradwell Shore Fort*

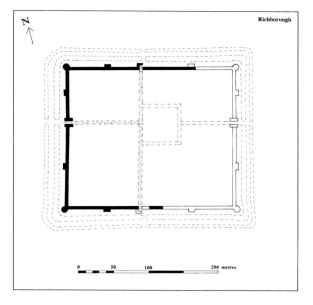

79 *Plan of Richborough Shore Fort*

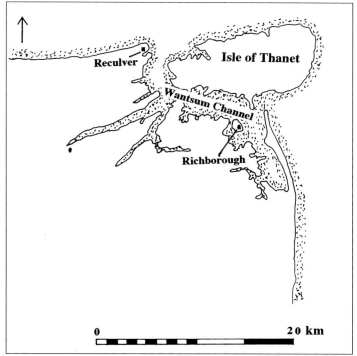

80 *Setting of
Richborough and
Reculver forts*

overlain the north-east quadrant of the earlier *Classis Britannica* fort. A position closer to the harbour appears to have been an important consideration as a number of well-appointed houses were demolished to make way for the new installation (**81**). Lympne fort, also known as Stutfall Castle, was sited on a hill overlooking the mouth of the River Rother which, until affected by silting in the late Roman period, afforded an ideal natural harbour (**82**). Its relationship with the earlier *Classis Britannica* base is unknown as the latter has still to be located. The fort was affected in late Roman and post-Roman times by severe landslips which distorted its outline, but which is believed to have been pentagonal. Further along the coast is Pevensey (**83** & **colour plate 16**), occupying a promontory of higher ground surrounded by marshes and unusual in that the defended area is oval in plan, and Portchester, standing on low-lying ground right next to the sea at the head of Portsmouth Harbour (**84, 85** & **colour plates 14** & **17**).

When added to the earlier forts and fortified towns and ports these new bases formed a continuous chain of strongholds from the Wash round to the Solent. There may in fact have been an additional fortification at Bitterne (*Clausentum*) on the outskirts of Southampton where a walled enclosure of uncertain size was erected over a partially abandoned earlier settlement towards the end of the third century. Occupying land formed by a bend in the River Itchen, its walls are built in the style of Pevensey's and were equipped with projecting bastions.[13]

Across the Channel, the *Classis Britannica* base at Boulogne had large, square projecting towers added to the front of its defensive wall at some time after AD 270. A little later on, a completely new wall replete with projecting semi-circular bastions was built further out, using the ditch of the earlier circuit as a foundation trench (**86**).[14] Very precise dating is impossible, but the earlier of the two schemes might represent Carausian measures, and the later a thorough remodelling following Boulogne's recapture for the Empire by Constantius in 293. Further up the coast a new fort was built at Oudenburg (*Portus Aepatiaci*) while a small fortlet was constructed on the island of Alderney at some stage in the late Roman period (**104**).[15] Many other coastal settlements received defences towards the end of the third century but investigation has been so limited at many that it is unclear whether they were forts or fortified towns (**87**). To a certain extent this is irrelevant as it became increasingly common as the fourth century progressed to station military units in towns as the deployment set out in the *Notitia Dignitatum* demonstrates. Most likely to be new forts of this period, however, are the late fortifications at Blaye (*Blabia*) on the Garonne estuary, Brest (*Osismis*), and Aleth (*Aletum*) overlooking the Bay of St Malo.[16] Two other stations listed in the *Notitia* – *Marcis* and *Grannona* – also probably came into existence in this period. The location of neither site is known for certain, but Marck or Marquise in the Pas de Calais are thought likely candidates for *Marcis* while Le Havre has been proposed as the site of *Grannona*.[17]

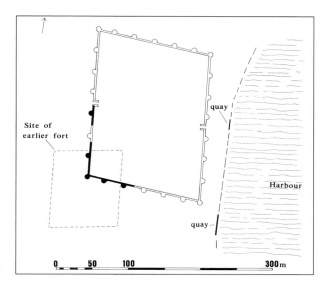

81 *Plan of Dover Shore Fort*

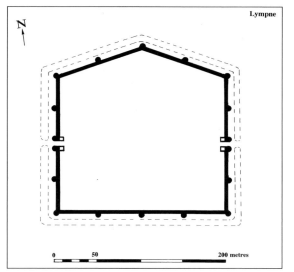

82 *Plan of Lympne Shore Fort*

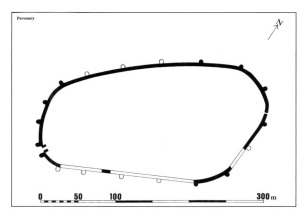

83 *Plan of Pevensey Shore Fort*

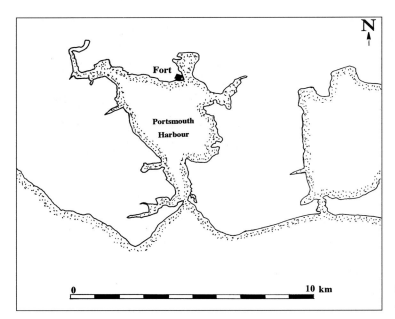

84 *Setting of Portchester Shore Fort*

85 *Plan of Portchester Shore Fort*

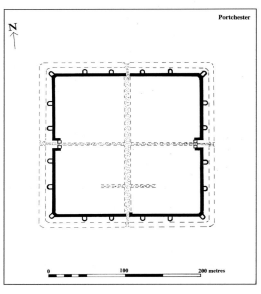

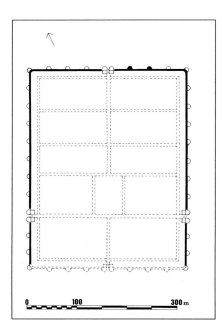

86 *Plan of Fleet Headquarters fort at Boulogne as remodelled c.AD 300*

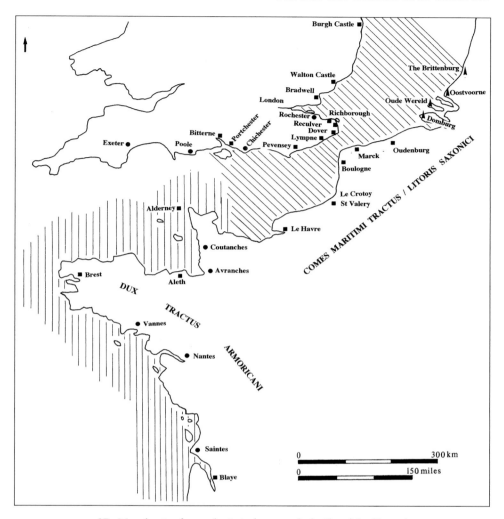

87 *Map showing forts and principal ports on both sides of the Channel*

The origins and purpose of the Saxon Shore Forts on this side of the Channel have been much discussed. The oldest and most widely held opinion is that they came into being as one of a number of measures designed to counter piracy and seaborne raiding.[18] An alternative interpretation was put forward by D.A. White who suggested they were built by Carausius to defend the coast against attack by the forces of Maximian.[19] However, while they may have been utilised by the breakaway regime, the design if not the implementation of the system almost certainly pre-date Carausius. They would also be of little purpose in repelling a determined invasion force which would simply by-pass them. More recently, some writers have drawn attention to the possible role of these forts, along with other military posts and fortified ports around the British coast, in the economy and military supply system. Rather than

163

simply military bases they are seen as secure depots where goods and supplies in transit could be stored temporarily before either being taken on to army units inland or shipped around the coast to garrisons in the North or across the sea to Gaul and Germany.[20] This seems eminently plausible given that the various crises from the mid-third century onwards not only meant that the army had to re-deploy units at short notice, but also that its normal supply lines and sources were frequently disrupted. The design of the forts, with their massive defences, large open spaces and apparently modest accommodation, would fit with a scenario in which considerable quantities of goods regularly had to be stored for short periods (possibly in nothing more substantial than a wagon-park) in secure conditions but protected by a garrison of modest size. The same environment would also serve as a protected bivouac for troop units in transit from one troublespot to the next. Whether naval defence or naval supply was the primary concern 'operations by sea were clearly central to the whole functioning of the Saxon Shore'.[21] Cotterill has taken this idea further, contending that the forts had no role at all in combating sea-raiders because the length of time it would have taken the ships of the Germanic seafarers to travel the distances involved would have made raids on the British coast completely impracticable.[22] He also points out that the units based in the Shore Forts as listed in the *Notitia Dignitatum* are completely unsuited to the role of intercepting coastal raiders in that there are no naval flotillas and no cavalry.

Cotterill's view is surely too extreme. We know from Carausius' appointment that the seaways between Britain and the Continent were infested with barbarian vessels by the 280s and this is not the sort of phenomenon that develops overnight. It is true that there are no earlier references to this problem in the sources, but then surviving accounts from the middle decades of the third century are very few. Similarly, while attacks on the British coast are not mentioned specifically, and none may actually have taken place, the threat was obviously very real. The conversion of the triumphal monument at Richborough to a lookout-post surely reflects this concern. The simple fact that the Shore Forts were not only built but also maintained thereafter proves that they were a response to a tangible and continuing danger. As to the capabilities of the ships of the Franks and Saxons, our information is restricted to a small number of vessels such as the three late fourth-century vessels found at Nydam in the 1850s and the early seventh-century boats found at Sutton Hoo and Snape in this country, and the contemporary vessels discovered at Kongsgarde and Gredstedbro in Denmark. The largest vessel at Nydam, the so-called oak ship, was sunk in a bog laden with war booty as a votive deposit, while that at Sutton Hoo was of course a regal burial. [23] The Nydam oak-boat was an open boat, over 70ft (20m) long and 12ft (3.60m) broad. It was constructed of five, broad, overlapping planks per side, riveted together with iron clench-nails with lashings used to fasten the reinforcing ribs to the sides and to the broad flat keel plank. The ship had a crew of 30 oarsmen whose oars pivoted on hole pins fastened to the gunwales. Steering was effected by a side rudder. The later and larger Sutton Hoo vessel was 90ft (27m) long and 14ft (4.20m) wide, again clinker-built with a flat keel ideal for beaching. Calculations have shown that such vessels, if propelled by oars alone, would have made extremely slow headway in the North Sea and thus it has been suggested – in the context of the fifth-century migrations – that instead of voyaging directly from Jutland to the east coast of Britain a far more likely approach would have been to travel down the continental coast to make a much shorter crossing in the English Channel.[24] Return voyages would have taken several months and would have involved escaping detection by Roman naval patrols. Even if they did manage to complete the Channel crossing successfully the effort needed by the rowing crew would have necessitated their resting up before making a raid.

However, our knowledge of Germanic ships of this era is meagre and those types which are known to us may not be representative of the largest ships of the period. Even understanding of the ships which have been discovered is imperfect, as Haywood has demonstrated.[25] For example, a number of objects found lying loose in the Nydam oak-ship have been convincingly interpreted by Akerlund as supports for a hogging truss designed to give the hull extra longitudinal strength.[26] This would have greatly improved its seaworthiness and the ability of ships like this to carry a mast and sail, a facility which would have transformed their performance. Unfortunately those parts of a ship which could provide information on this vital point are usually the least likely to survive. In the case of the Sutton Hoo ship, for example, the burial chamber was sited in the central part of the ship and the mast and step, had they existed, would have been removed to make way for it. With the tenth-century Ladby ship, preserved in the same form as the Sutton Hoo ship, all traces of mast and step had disappeared, the fact that it had been a sailing vessel indicated solely by the presence of eight shroud rings.[27] The flat keels of these early ships have been regarded as too weak to support a mast, yet the later boat from Graveney with such a keel was equipped with sail.[28] It is also perfectly possible that other types of barbarian ships existed of which examples have yet to be found.[29]

Roman sources from Caesar's day onwards record the seafaring prowess of the peoples along the Atlantic coast, tribes such as the Veneti, Morini, Menapii, Chauci, Frisii, Usipi and Canninefates. The first of these nearly defeated Caesar in 56 BC while the last inflicted several reverses on Roman naval forces during the Civilis Revolt of AD 69-70. The seafaring skills of these peoples were not lost with the advent of Roman supremacy. They joined the Roman navy, possibly in significant numbers, with others participating in the enormous volume of mercantile trade in the North Sea area which developed in the following centuries. Even those tribes beyond the frontier would have been well aware of developments in ship design and performance, as well as the weaknesses of the Roman fleets. Who was it after all in the 280s

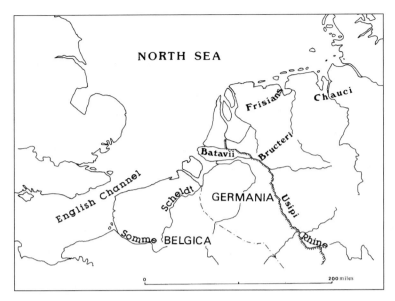

88 *Map showing homelands of seafaring tribes of the North Sea coast in the second century*

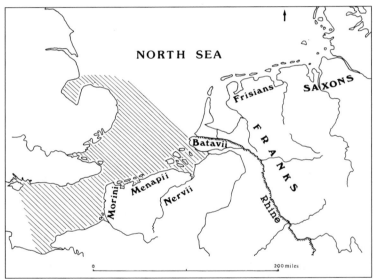

89 *Map showing location of tribes involved in piracy and sea-raiding from c.AD 250 onwards*

that the Roman high command enlisted to defeat the pirates? Carausius, a Menapian. It is inconceivable that the Saxons, Franks and others who indulged in piracy and raiding did not possess ships powered by both oars and sail. Although not a technical source, the late fifth-century poet Sidonius Apollinaris tells us that Saxon warships had sails while the comments of Ammianus suggest this was so a century earlier.[30]

Equipped with even a primitive sail, the performance of ships like those just described would have been completely transformed. It has been estimated that under oars alone a boat could make 36 nautical miles in a day, but only under favourable conditions – i.e. no storms or even headwinds – and the crew rowing for 12 hours before putting into shore for the night. However, with a simple sail and a following wind the same boat could travel at least four times as far, without exhausting the crew and without having to make landfall for the night.[31] A vessel thus powered could achieve a voyage in a few days that would take weeks in a rowing boat. The necessity for frequent landfalls to rest and obtain supplies would be avoided, as would the high risk of detection and interception. Passing unseen through the Straits of Dover in the course of a single night would have been perfectly possible. It is surely this capability that explains both the initial inability of the Roman naval forces to counteract Saxon and Frankish sea-raiding and the scale of the measures eventually taken in response.

As to examples of barbarian vessels plying the western ocean, a gold model of a boat from Broighter in Co. Derry provides a clue as to the type of ship used by the Scotti in their raids on the west coast of Britain. Dating to the first centuries BC/AD, this shows a vessel equipped with eight pairs of oars, a steering-oar, and a mast.[32] It would seem to represent a boat about 50ft long manned by a crew of perhaps around 30 strong. Boats with seven oars per side are mentioned in the Senchus fer nAlban document describing the mustering of forces in the seventh-century Scottic kingdom of Dalriada in west central Scotland. Other literary references indicate many such boats were of the curragh type, consisting of a wooden framework covered with hides and perhaps coated with pitch.[33]

To summarise, the Saxon Shore Forts, on present evidence, seem best interpreted as a chain of coastal strongholds constructed in response to the increasingly insecure conditions in the Channel and North Sea caused by piracy and raiding. They should be viewed as multifunctional structures in that while they served as garrison posts they may also have provided secure compounds for government goods in transit waiting to be shipped elsewhere in Britain or to the Continent. In this regard it is worth noting Libanius' comment about the regular shipping of grain from Britain to the forces on the Rhine in the first half of the fourth century.[34] If, as is suggested below, the forces originally assigned to the forts included naval as well as army personnel, then the ample space within many of them may also have been required for the storage, repair and perhaps even manufacture of ships, gear and rigging.

Cotterill is correct in pointing out that the infantry units which the *Notitia* places at the Shore Forts lack the mobility required to deal with raiding-parties but of course the *Notitia* is describing – with many flaws and inaccuracies – the situation prevailing *c*.AD 400 when the garrison of Britain had been subjected to repeated depletions. The deployment of forces a hundred years earlier could have been and no doubt was very different. There are a few scattered pieces of evidence which allow a tentative reconstruction of the garrison arrangements made for coastal defence at the beginning of the fourth century (**87**). Evidence relating to Pevensey confirms the general impression that the operational effectiveness of the system was based on the co-deployment of land and naval forces at each fort and/or fortified port. At the time of the *Notitia's* compilation Pevensey was occupied by the *Numerus Abulcorum*. However, two units recorded at bases on the Continent can be identified from the place-name incorporated in their titles as the original garrison of Pevensey (*Anderitum*). These are the *Milites Anderetiani* at *Vicus Julius* in the command of the *Dux Mogontiacensis*, based at Mainz, and the *Classis Anderetianorum* at Paris. A similar pairing of army regiment and naval flotilla can be postulated at the other forts. The defensive tactics are clear. Small scouting vessels patrolled a certain distance out to sea keeping a lookout for approaching raiders. It would not have been necessary to patrol the entire coastline, only key areas such as estuaries and the approaches to exposed settlements right on the coast along with regular 'shipping lanes'. However, the speed and capability of the raiders' vessels as described above would mean that such patrols would have to be constant and perhaps even continued during bad weather which the Saxons apparently would use as cover.[35] The lighthouses at Boulogne and Dover would presumably have now taken on the additional role of look-out posts. A graphic description of how such operations were conducted is given by Vegetius, writing at the end of the fourth century:

> As for size, the smallest warships have a single bank of oars . . . . Associated with the larger warships are scouting skiffs, which have around twenty oarsmen per side, and which the Britons call *Pictae* (painted ships). These are used on occasion to perform descents or to intercept convoys of enemy shipping or by studious surveillance to detect their approach or intentions. Lest scouting vessels be betrayed by white, their sails and rigging are dyed Venetian Blue, which resembles the ocean waves; the wax used to pay the ship's sides is also dyed that colour. The sailors and marines wear Venetian Blue uniforms also, so as to to lie hidden with greater ease by day as by night.
>
> *Epitoma Rei Militaris* 4.37

Clearly the patrols sometimes dealt with the enemy directly and sometimes merely observed them, reporting back to the flotilla so that the larger warships could then make ready to intercept.

The form of the larger warships referred to can only be conjectured. They could have been biremes as in earlier times. Yet the larger warships depicted on the coinage of Postumus, Carausius, Allectus and Constantius and the Low Ham villa mosaic, although retaining the high up-curving prow and stern of early Imperial warships, are all single-banked galleys (**71-74** & **colour plates 6, 7** & **8**). This might simply be due to the fact that the image was so small that

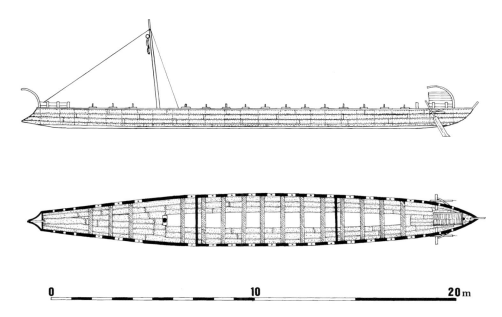

90 *Reconstruction of late Roman river patrol boat – navis lusoria – based on wrecks found at Mainz*

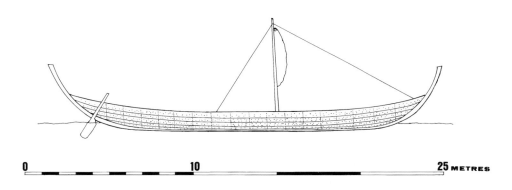

91 *Reconstruction of seagoing ship of type used by Saxon and Frankish raiders*

the artist could only represent the oars in a very simplistic manner. Then again if, as seems likely, the general reorganisation of the naval forces attached to Britain implemented at this time saw them divided up into many small flotillas deployed at a greater number of bases, it would have made sense – in view of the type of enemy they were confronting – also to increase the number of vessels in each flotilla by reducing the number of biremes in favour of more monoremes. To use a modern parallel, they had fewer battleships and cruisers but more destroyers and corvettes.

The 'descents' which Vegetius refers to – the word used is *superventus* literally 'coming from above' – are surprises or ambushes.[36] As will be seen shortly this term occurs in the title of a unit originally stationed at Brough-on-Humber in this period. It is also used in the *Notitia* to describe troops based at Nantes in the later fourth century – the *Milites Supervenientes*.[37] Patrols must have involved a number of vessels so that a watch could be maintained on the raiders leaving one or more *pictae* free to head back to base to raise the alarm. It is also clear, as one would expect, that patrols were mounted after dusk as moonlit nights were no doubt a favourite time for raiders to make landfall. In case the latter should make it ashore the army element of the fort garrisons would in theory already be waiting for them and the warships would close in behind them or catch them when they tried to escape. Completing the naval element at each base would have been a number of merchantmen used for the transport of supplies and, on occasion, troops.

Perhaps when a sufficient quantity of supplies had been amassed, small convoys of cargo vessels would set off accompanied by one or more escorting warships. Because of the frequent need for rapid deployment, mounted or part-mounted regiments would seem the most appropriate unit type to place in these forts and indeed cavalry are listed in the *Notitia* at both Brancaster (*Branodunum*) and Burgh Castle (*Gariannonum*); the *Equites Dalmatae Branodunenses* at the first and the *Equites Stablesiani Gariannonenses* at the second. Cavalry was essential in these cases, of course, because they had to cover the wide open coast and countryside of East Anglia. At Reculver (*Regulbium*) by contrast, the First Cohort of Baetasians continued in residence throughout the fourth century. In the *Notitia*, Richborough (*Rutupiae*) was occupied by a detachment of *Legio II Augusta* and as the legionary commander or *Praefectus* was present (by this period the equestrian prefect had replaced the senatorial legate) this suggests that Richborough was now the legion's head-quarters. At less than 7 acres (2.85ha) in size however it is clear that only a fraction of the legion was here. Vexillations may have been transferred to other provinces, although this is not certain, while another may still have been resident in the old legionary fortress at Caerleon and yet another in the new fort at Cardiff (see below).[38] Completing the list, but not necessarily the original garrisons of the early fourth century, were the *Numerus Fortensium* at *Othona* (Bradwell), the *Milites Tungrecanorum* at *Dubris* (Dover), the *Numerus Turnacensium* at *Lemannis* (Lympne) and the *Numerus Exploratorum* at *Portus Adurni* (Portchester).

Evidence for the garrisons of the Gallic coastal stations again comes almost exclusively from the *Notitia*. Only one unit of cavalry is listed, the *Equites Dalmatae* at *Marcis*, the others being old-fashioned cohorts or *milites*. The exception is the *Classis Sambricae* commanded by a *praefectus* stationed at a place described as *loco Quartensi sive Hornensi* – 'the place Quartensis or Hornensis'. The unknown base of this Sambrican Fleet was long thought to lie somewhere near the mouth of the River Sambre. Johnson, however, argued persuasively that *Sambrica* should be emended to *Samarica* as a *Classis Samarica* is attested by tiles bearing the stamp CLSAM found at Etaples in 1890.[39] This fleet would thus be based on the River Somme either at neighbouring St Valéry or Le Crotoy.[40] It is unlikely this unit was created before *c*.AD 250 because the *Classis Britannica* was still in existence at that time and with its headquarters still at nearby Boulogne.[41] Equally, the practice of stamping tiles seems to have ceased by the end of the third century. Perhaps therefore the *Classis Samarica* came into being as part of the reorganisation following the devastations of either AD 260 or 276 when the process of splitting the British Fleet into small flotillas based at a greater number of bases apparently began.

Naval units were also stationed at bases further up the east coast of Britain. A unit recorded at Malton in the *Notitia* bears the title *Numerus Supervenientium Petuariensium*. Clearly this unit had previously been stationed at Brough and must have been there for some considerable time to incorporate the place-name in its titles. Mirroring the situation at Pevensey there would have been a *Classis Petuariensium* to provide the complementary naval element of the 'surprise'. This Humber flotilla would presumably have been equipped with larger warships which did most of the intercepting as well as the *pictae*. The transfer of the *Supervenientes Petuarienses* to Malton was probably brought about by silting, which reduced the usefulness of Brough as a harbour in the later fourth century. Another joint unit may have been based in the Tees estuary and there would certainly have been a substantial presence at the mouth of the Tyne. The stationing at South Shields of a unit of Tigris Boatmen/Lightermen – the *Numerus Barcariorum Tigrisiensium* – is recorded in the *Notitia*. The *barca* was a small vessel used for transferring a ship's cargo to land when it was not possible for the ship itself to get close to the shore. Leaving aside whatever their personal feelings were about the change in climate compared with that of their homeland, South Shields was a very appropriate posting for them given the vast amount of supplies for Hadrian's Wall coming into this port. However, the light, shallow-draughted *barcae* could also if necessary be used in a fighting role. The arrival of the *numerus* at South Shields is indicated by a rebuilding and rearrangement of the accommodation inside the fort which included an opulent, east Mediterranean-style residence for the commandant.[42] As this occurred immediately after what appears to have been an enemy attack on the fort around AD 300, when more than a few buildings were destroyed by fire, it may indicate that the attack had come from the sea and that the *numerus'* transfer here was as much to do with bolstering naval defence as with the movement of supplies.

On the west coast the military installations along the Cumbrian shore had of course been designed to counter seaborne infiltration right from their inception, and as one would expect in this period of increased sea-raiding, the forts here continued to be garrisoned throughout the fourth century. Less clear though is to what degree elements of the system of milefortlets and watch-towers which linked them were either still in use or recommissioned. Tower 2b (Campfield), west of Bowness, appears to have been in use at the end of the third century,[43] and the larger than average Milefortlet No. 5 (Cardurnock) was certainly occupied in this period and throughout most of the fourth century, presumably because of its position guarding the mouth of the Wampool estuary.[44] There is also a small amount of fourth-century pottery from Milefortlets 12 and 20.[45] We have already seen in chapter 7 that the *Cohors I Aelia Classica* based at Ravenglass may have continued to have some form of maritime role after its formation from the marines of the *Classis Britannica*, and the *Notitia Dignitatum* shows this unit was still here at the end of the Roman period. Interestingly the garrison of the fort of *Glannoventa*, as yet unlocated but possibly situated at the mouth of the River Ehen north of Ravenglass, is listed in the *Notitia* as the First Cohort of Morinians, a unit originally recruited from the seafaring tribe living in the vicinity of Calais and Boulogne. Perhaps they too had a naval as well as a terrestrial role.

The situation further south on the west coast is less clear. New defensive installations in coastal locations were certainly constructed in the late Roman period if not perhaps in the integrated and contemporary manner observable on the south-east coast. The very nature of the coastline, with its numerous indentations and river mouths, the lower density of major settlements, and the lack of an obvious approach route made it impossible to defend in quite the same way. But these potential difficulties for the defenders were offset by the dangerous nature of the coastline and the small number of worthwhile targets. The fact that the *Hiberni* are listed as one of the principal enemies of the Britons in the *Panegyric to Constantius* (11.4) suggests that Irish sea-raiders were also becoming a problem in the last quarter of the third century. Collectively the tribes of Ireland were known to the Romans as the *Scotti*, a term meaning 'plunderers', and it is as sea-raiders that they are most frequently mentioned in the classical sources. This was presumably the context for the construction of a Saxon Shore-style fort at Cardiff at some time after *c*.AD 268 (**92**, **93** & **94**).[46] Quadrangular in plan and enclosing an area of 9 acres (3.57ha), it was equipped with the usual thick curtain wall and projecting bastions. Its garrison is unknown but may well have included part of *Legio II Augusta*, transferred from the nearby fortress at Caerleon which shows evidence of less intensive occupation after *c*.AD 275. The Cardiff fort presumably accommodated a mixed military/naval force like the others and was designed to prevent raiders gaining access to the upper reaches of the Severn estuary and the wealth of rich villas and other sites in the surrounding landscape. There could well have been a naval station on the south shore of the Bristol Channel, perhaps at Sea Mills, near Bristol, in view of the military's long association with this harbour.[47] The fort at Cardiff cannot have existed in isolation and there is slight evidence for some form of reoccupation at the old forts at Neath and Loughor on the coast

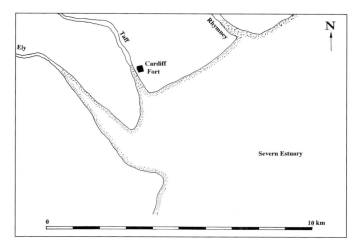

92 *Setting of Cardiff Shore Fort*

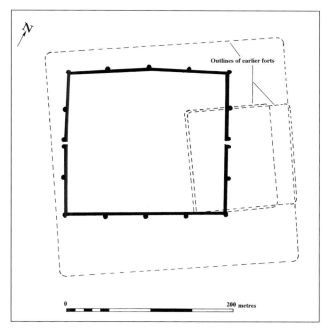

93 *Plan of Cardiff Shore Fort*

road to the west.[48] The walled town at Carmarthen (*Moridunum Demetarum*) with its harbour at the mouth of the Twyi would have afforded another secure anchorage while the existence of some form of late naval installation in the vicinity of Pembroke seems likely.

Moving around the Welsh coast, it is not until Carnarfon that the next site of interest is reached. The auxiliary fort here was one of the few in Wales to be occupied continuously throughout the Roman period.[49] Around 500ft (150m) west of the fort, situated at the edge of a precipitous slope down to the harbour at the mouth of the Seiont, stand the remains of a late Roman walled compound. Known as Hen Waliau, 'Old Walls', it measures approximately 230

94 *East wall of Cardiff Shore Fort*

by 165ft (70 x 50m).[50] It lacks projecting towers while excavation has shown it was never given a defensive ditch (**95**). Extensive post-Roman disturbance has removed traces of any internal structures. It seems best interpreted as a secure compound, perhaps for the temporary storage of taxes paid in kind or possibly for spare equipment (ropes, canvas, oars, etc.) required by the fleet. As to dating, it can only be said that it is later than *c.*AD 180 though it would fit best into a late third- or fourth-century context. The legionary fortress at Chester underwent extensive refurbishment at the beginning of the fourth century and was well-placed to be the principal fleet-base for much of the west coast.[51]

Command structure

The beginning of the fourth century saw the introduction of further administrative reforms as well as an overhaul of the organisation and command structure of the army. The civil and military branches of provincial administration were almost completely separated. Individual provinces were further sub-divided with groups of the new smaller provinces placed together in a new administrative unit known as a *diocese* headed by a *vicarius*. A number of *dioceses* were grouped together to form a prefecture, roughly corresponding to the areas allotted at one time or another to the two senior and two junior Augusti. Control of the armed forces was removed from provincial governors and placed instead in the hands of a new professional class of officers – with the rank of *dux* (basically 'leader' = modern Duke) or *comes* (literally 'companion' = modern Count) – whose authority could transcend provincial boundaries. There were the inevitable exceptions where the provincial governor or *praeses* commanded troops or the *dux* also took on civil functions. The size of the army and the number and type of units was increased, the second achieved partly by the sub-division of existing regiments into a number of new and smaller units.[52] Overall, the ambition was to endow the army with greater flexibility and mobility so as to respond more quickly to emergencies wherever they might occur. To that end, new and highly mobile reserve forces – the field armies of *comitatenses* – were formed which were superior in equipment, fighting skills and precedence to the static frontier garrison troops (*limitanei*). For Britain these changes meant a further subdivision into four provinces. *Superior* was split into *Maxima Caesariensis* and *Britannia Prima* while *Inferior* now became *Britannia Secunda* and *Flavia Caesariensis*; the four provincial capitals being London, Cirencester, York and Lincoln respectively. The four provinces collectively comprised the diocese of Britain, which in turn was an element of the Prefecture of the Gauls, with London doubling as the diocesan capital.

This new arrangement was already in place by 312, as the provinces are named in a document known as the Verona List which can be dated to that year. Also around this time two new military posts were established to command the

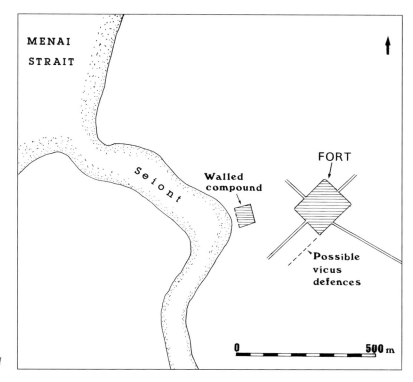

95 *Plan of Carnarvon showing position of fort and later walled compound*

armed forces throughout the island. One was the *Dux Britanniarum* – 'Duke of the Britains' – and the other the *Comes Maritimi Tractus* – 'Count of the Maritime Region'. The second of these, which very probably also began as a ducate command and later elevated to comital rank, is mentioned by the late fourth-century historian Ammianus Marcellinus in his account of the barbarian attacks on the province in the 360s, it is very probably the same post as the *Comes Litoris Saxonici per Britannias* ('Count of the Saxon Shore') mentioned in the *Notitia Dignitatum*[53]. The latter is thought to show the deployment of forces *c*.AD 395 in general but also incorporating subsequent changes owing to new postings. Whether an official document or one maintained privately, for example by an historian, is unclear. It is also possible that the document's principal purpose was a record of the chains of command and their insignia rather than a detailed list of regiments used for practical administration. The list of regiments and their bases listed under each command show that the *Dux Britanniarum* controlled all the forces across the north of England while the Count of the Saxon Shore had only nine units along the south-east coast. It is unusual for a higher-ranked *Comes* to have such a modest force under his command and most probably it depicts the situation after numerous withdrawals of troops for service on the Continent. The fact that two of the forts on the Gallic coast – *Marcae* and *Grannona* – are described in the *Notitia* as lying '*in Litore Saxonico*' has given rise to the suggestion that they too once belonged to the command of the *Comes Litoris Saxonici* which would thus have originally extended to both sides of the Channel (**87**). In essence this would have perpetuated the arrangements under the *Praefectus Classis Britannicae* with facilities and forces on both coasts and would, despite the risk of another Carausius emerging, have been the soundest strategic response to the problem of sea-raiders in the Channel. The restriction of the Count of the Saxon Shore's authority to the British side of the Channel probably occurred after the troubles of the 360s.[54] In the absence of evidence to the contrary it is assumed that the Twentieth Legion at Chester and the forces in Wales came under the command of the governor (*praeses*) of *Britannia Prima*.

10

WHOSE SAILS IN THE SUNSET?

Britain enjoyed something of a golden age for much of the first half of the fourth century, basking in the sun of its association with the great Emperor Constantine. His death in 337 brought the return of storm clouds to the horizon. With the division of the empire between his three sons, Britain, together with Gaul, Germany and Spain, came under the control of Constantine II. Relations with Constans, who held the central portion of the empire, deteriorated rapidly and in 340 Constantine launched an invasion of Italy. Very probably the British Navy once more transported thousands of men and hundreds of tons of equipment across the Channel. All to no avail as Constantine II was defeated and killed at Aquileia. The repercussions for Britain are unknown but something happened late in 342 to make Constans pay a surprise visit to the island in the middle of winter.[1] In all probability this was inspired by trouble on the northern frontier. Sea-raiding may have been a feature of the troubles in view of the strengthening of coastal defences now implemented (**96**).

In the west, the long-established fort at Lancaster, guarding the mouth of the River Lune, was demolished and a new Saxon Shore-style fort with projecting bastions erected partly over its remains (**97**).[2] The size of the fort is unknown but exceeded 5 acres (2ha). The garrison here in the third century was the 500-strong cavalry unit the *Ala Gallorum Sebosiana* along with a *numerus* of 'lightermen' or *Barcarii* like that at South Shields.[3] There is no evidence of any other units here and it seems likely that both continued in residence throughout the fourth century. The combination of cavalry with a naval unit using shallow-drafted *barcae* would have been well-suited to combating seaborne infiltrators and raiders amidst the creeks and shifting sands of Morecambe Bay. Further north, the important fort at Maryport was garrisoned throughout the fourth century as is indicated by both the coin evidence and by its listing in the *Notitia Dignitatum*.[4] Protection for the harbour may have been reinforced in some way at this time. Various writers from Camden onwards refer to the discovery of very substantial masonry structures near the mouth of the River Ellen south of the fort.[5] Although some of these features may in fact have been natural bedrock, as recently suggested, the possibility that a fortified compound was constructed beside the harbour cannot be discounted.[6]

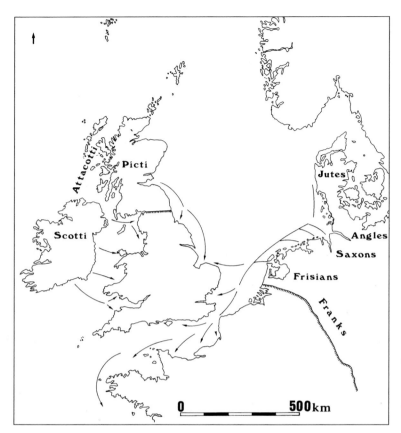

96 *Map showing origin and direction of seaborne attacks on late Roman Britain*

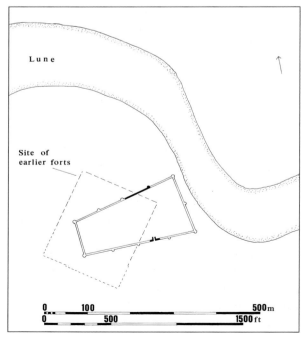

97 *Plan of Lancaster Shore Fort*

Constans was assassinated in 350 and Magnentius took over as Augustus in the western half of the Empire. He met Constantius II in battle near Mursa in Pannonia in 351 and suffered a heavy defeat. Two years later he was beaten again, this time in Gaul, and was driven to suicide. It is highly likely, given the modest proportion of the western field army under his control, that he had a considerable number of regiments shipped over from Britain to bolster his forces in preparation for the contest with Constantius. Few of these were to return and this may explain why the army in Britain had such a problem containing its enemies over the following 15 years. Having rooted out supporters of Magnentius in Britain, Constantius put his cousin Julian in charge of the western provinces in 355 with the rank of Caesar. A keen student of Roman history and an inspirational leader, Julian put new steel into the Roman forces in the West. He drove all barbarians out of Gaul, won a pitched battle at Strasbourg, and put the frontier defences into good order. Earlier in the fourth century it had become commonplace for the frontier garrisons in Germany to be supplied with grain shipped across the North Sea from Britain and then up the Rhine. By Julian's time attacks by barbarian ships had rendered this practice unsafe and, as Libanius puts it, 'the cargo vessels had long been hauled ashore and had rotted away. A few still plied, but since they discharged their cargo in coastal ports, it was necessary to transport the grain by wagon instead of by river, and this was a very expensive affair' (*Oratio* 18.82-3). It was vital to keep the troops along the Rhine supplied and Britain's agricultural production could make up for the deficiencies of ravaged Gaul. Julian built new granaries, took action against the sea-raiders at the mouth of the Rhine, and had more than 600 ships larger than galleys built to bring the grain across from Britain.[7] Presumably much of this shipping was setting out on its voyages from the British side from ports such as South Shields, Brough-on-Humber, and those in East Anglia although the vessels concerned may already have made their way around the British coast from the richest agricultural areas much farther south. It seems logical to assume that these vessels, presumably sailing in convoys, were escorted by British warships on their journey to the Rhine mouth.

In 360 the Picts of central Scotland and the Scotti of northern Ireland (who perhaps had already begun their colonisation of south-west Scotland) broke the treaty arrangements and 'laid waste the region near the frontier' (*Ammianus* 20.1). The nature of the attacks is unknown but sea-raiding was surely involved. Julian sent his *magister militum* Lupicinus to deal with the situation and he made a winter crossing from Boulogne to Richborough accompanied by four regiments of the Field Army. That Lupicinus was able to restore order quite easily is implied by his return to the Continent only a few months later. War between Constantius II and Julian was avoided by the former's death in 361. Two years later Julian too was dead. By 364 Valentinian I had become emperor in the West and his younger brother Valens emperor in the East. In that same year, or possibly that following, Ammianus tells us that Britain was again under attack from Picts, Scotti, Attacotti (from the Western Isles) and Saxons, suffering continual calamities at their hands.[8] Nothing substantial seems to have been done to counter these raids which must have affected both the west and the east coasts and, encouraged by the lack of a forceful response and either the incompetence or collusion of the frontier scouts, the raiders became more ambitious. In 367 they implemented a massive and carefully coordinated attack on Britain and Gaul. Ammianus describes this *barbarica conspiratio*:

> Valentinian had set out from Amiens and was hurrying towards Trier when he was overtaken by grave reports indicating that Britain had been plunged into the depths of distress by a conspiracy of the barbarians. Nectaridus, Count of the Coastal Region, had been killed, while Fullofaudes, Duke of the Britains, had been surrounded and captured in an enemy ambush. . . . The Picts, together with the warlike Attacotti and Scotti, were ranging over a wide area causing much devastation, while the Franks and their neighbours the Saxons ravaged the coast of Gaul with vicious acts of pillage, arson and the murder of all prisoners, wherever they could burst in by land or sea.
>
> (27.8)

The situation was desperate. The two senior military commanders in Britain had been lost, their forces leaderless, demoralised and dispersed, and the provinces of Britain left wide open to the whims of the merciless savages. Valentinian despatched a rapid succession of commanders before the right man for the job was found. This was Theodosius, whose son was to become the emperor Theodosius I and who accompanied his father to Britain. Theodosius made the Boulogne-Richborough crossing in the spring of 368 along with four regiments of the field army and thence made his way to London where he set up his operational headquarters. From here he:

> divided his troops into several detachments and attacked the marauding enemy bands who were roaming about laden with the weight of their booty and, quickly routing those who were driving along prisoners and cattle, he wrested from them the plunder that the wretched subjects of Rome had lost. All this he restored to its owners with the exception of a small part which was paid to his weary troops.

In this way Theodosius gradually cleared the countryside of the bands of pillagers. The fact that much of the action described took place in the southeast indicates that considerable numbers of raiders had sailed a long way down the east coast before making their final landfall. The same may have been true in the west with the Scotti concentrating their attacks along the English side of the Bristol Channel and the rich pickings to be had from the wealthy villa estates in the Cotswolds. We are told that Theodosius issued an amnesty to all those who had deserted (which illustrates the extent to which the defence forces had disintegrated) and their units were then reconstituted. Following clearance of the rest of the invaders from the country Theodosius carried out a punitive expedition beyond the Wall. This may well have included naval engagements in the far north judging from the words of Claudian:

> And so as to inflame you all the more with a love of battle, he would recount the deeds of your grandfather (the Elder Theodosius), before whom trembled the shores of sun-scorched Libya and Thule, beyond the reach of ships. He it was who vanquished the nimble Moors and apt-named Picts; he pursued the Scots with his far-ranging sword; he cleft Hyperborean waves with courageous oars . . . .

> *Panegyric on the Third Consulship of Honorius* 51-6

and

> He it was pitched camp amid the frosts of Caledonia, in armour bore the summer heat of Libya, a source of terror to the Moor, conqueror of the British shore, laying waste to North and South alike. What benefit to the Britons the eternal harshness and cold of their climate, or the uncharted seas? The Orkneys were drenched with slaughter of the Saxons; Thule was warm with Pictish blood, and icy Ireland wept for the heaps of Scottish dead.

> *Panegyric on the Fourth Consulship of Honorius* 24-33

also Pacatus

> Shall I relate how Britain was brought to her knees by battles on land? In that case the Saxon, exhausted by naval engagements, springs to mind. Shall I speak of the Scots driven back to their own marshes?

> *Panegyric on Theodosius* 5.2

That significant defeats were inflicted upon the invaders in their homelands is also suggested by the listing in the *Notitia* of four regiments of Attacotti who were presumably conscripted for service in the army as part of the treaty arrangements. These served in Gaul, Italy and *Illyricum*.[9]

The incursion of 367 had clearly by-passed or simply overwhelmed the coastal defence forces. As part of his restoration of the British provinces

Theodosius ordered the erection of additional installations along exposed stretches of the coast. The group of sites known as the Yorkshire Signal Stations also probably originated in the wake of the events of 367 as a counter-measure to the surprise outflanking of Hadrian's Wall by sea-raiders intent on attacking rural communities in its hinterland. The five recognised sites – Huntcliffe, Goldsborough, Ravenscar, Scarborough and Filey – are all located on high headlands facing out over the North Sea on the stretch of coast between Flamborough Head in the south and the mouth of the Tees in the north (**98**).[10] They all also overlook bays or coves suitable for beaching small shallow-draughted ships like those used by the Picts. Others stations are likely to have existed, not only between the known examples (at Whitby for example) but also continuing the system both southwards beyond Flamborough Head and northwards to the mouth of the Tyne, and either await discovery or have been lost through coastal erosion. All recognised examples have been subjected to formal excavation with the exception of Ravenscar, which is known from ruins seen in 1774 and an inscription recovered at the time which records the construction of 'a tower and fort from ground level (by men under the control of) Justinianus, regimental commander (*praepositus*), and Vindicianus, work-party commander (*magister*)'.[11]

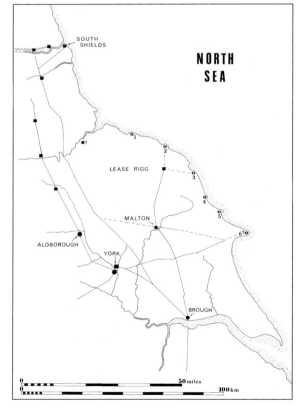

98 *Map of east coast between Humber and Tyne estuaries showing location of later fourth-century signal stations and main military centres inland. KEY: 1 - Huntcliffe, 2 - Goldsborough, 3 - Ravenscar, 4 - Scarborough, 5 - Filey, 6 - Flamborough Head*

The sites conform to a standard design indicating they were built contemporaneously as elements of a single planned system (**99-104**). The tower was a square structure 46 to 50ft (14-15m) in size with foundations 7 to 9ft (2.1-2.7m) wide standing at the centre of a small enclosure defined by a free-standing perimeter wall. The enclosure (the 'fort' of the Ravenscar inscription) was square in plan, with average sides of 115ft (35m), and at each of its rounded corners was a projecting bastion. There was a single gateway in the centre of one side which aligned with a causeway across the ditch which encircled the installation. The fort walls were probably around 18ft (5.5m) high while estimates of the overall height of the towers range from 58 to 100ft (17.2-30.4m). A median figure of around 75ft (22.8m) seems both reasonable and feasible. Large stone blocks with sockets in their tops to hold timbers are a regular feature of the towers. These obviously functioned as supports for the first floor and perhaps, by repetition of the system at higher levels, the upper floors as well. This substantial reinforcement indicates that the weight-loading on at least the first floor was expected to be considerable, either from goods stored or people accommodated, or both. While these towers were clearly designed to act as look-out and signal stations, alerting land and naval forces to the approach of raiders, they may also have functioned as refuges for the local population in times of peril. The late enclosure constructed on the Channel Island of Alderney is very similar in plan but apparently lacked the central tower (**105**).

On the west coast a new fortified landing-place was built at Holyhead at the north-west tip of Anglesey.[12] This was positioned at the edge of a low cliff beside the shoreline in what is now the Inner Harbour (**106**). Roughly trapezoidal in plan and measuring 250ft (75m) on its longest side it is enclosed by a freestanding wall about 13ft (4m) high. In places the rampart walk still survives along with a parapet nearly 4ft (1.2m) high. At the landward corners and at the points where the walls cross the low cliff there are round bastions (**107**). The side walls continue down to the low water-mark, thus forming a protected area where ships could have beached. No similar examples of a three-sided landing-place are known in Britain but there are a number along the Rhine frontier at places such as Engers and Zullestein in Germany and Dunafalva and Kodenica in Hungary where they are dated to the reign of Valentinian.[13] A signal/watch tower on the top of Holyhead Mountain, just over a mile to the west-north-west, was in use at the same time as the fortified landing-place as evidenced by a hoard of 15 coins datable to the 390s recovered from its interior (**106 & colour plate 18**).[14] Another tower is known at Carmel Head, lying at the north-western tip of the Anglesey mainland, while finds of late Roman material at other spots along the Anglesey coast and at a number of hilltop sites hint at the possibility of a chain of towers/lookout stations along the entire North Wales coast. These would have communicated with the forts at Caernarfon and Caerhun and ultimately with the fortress at Chester (**108**).[15]

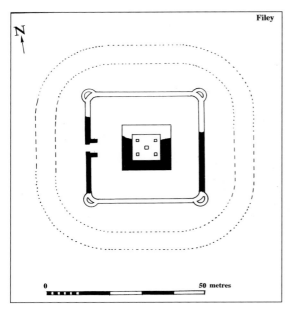

99 *Plan of Filey signal station*

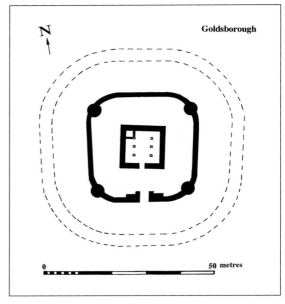

100 *Plan of Goldsborough signal station*

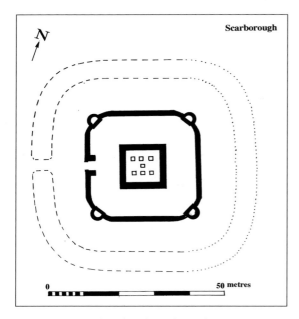

101 *Plan of Scarborough signal station*

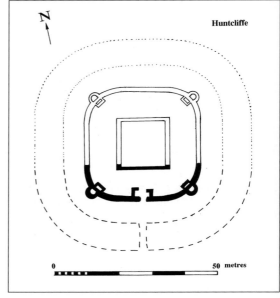

102 *Plan of Huntcliffe signal station*

103 *Reconstruction sketch of signal station looking out to sea.* After Chew

104 *Reconstruction sketch of signal station looking north along coast.* After Sorrell

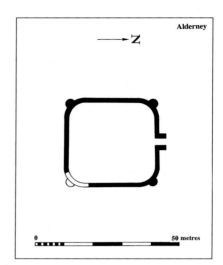

105 *Plan of lookout station on Alderney*

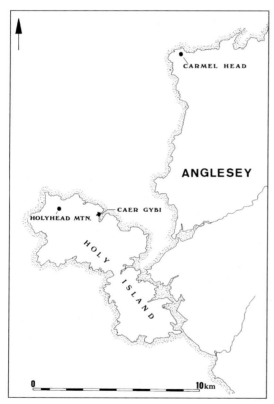

106 *Map showing location of fortified landing-place at Caer Gybi, Holyhead Island and neighbouring watch/signal towers*

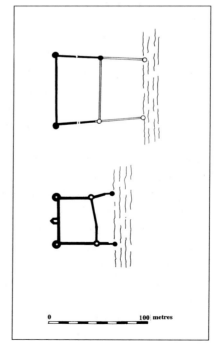

107 *Comparative plans of late Roman fortified landing-places at Caer Gybi and Kodenica on the Danube*

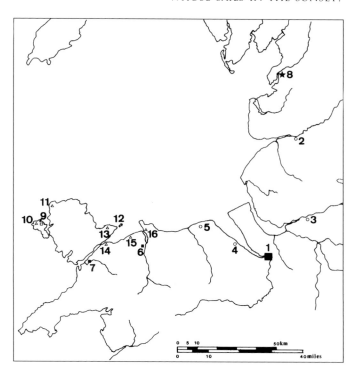

108 *Map showing putative late Roman coastal defence system in the North West. KEY:* Legionary fortress: *1 - Chester.* Existing civil ports: *2 - Walton le Dale, 3 - Wilderspool, 4 - Pentre, 5 - Prestatyn.* Existing military harbours: *6 - Caerhun, 7 - Carnarvon.* New 'Saxon Shore'-style fort: *8 - Lancaster.* New fortified landing-place: *9 - Caer Gybi.* New look-out posts/signal station: *10 - Holyhead Mountain, 11 - Pen Bryn yr Eglwys (Carmel Head), 12 - Ynys Seriol, 13 - Din Silwy, 14 - Bangor, 15 - Braich yr Ddinas, 16 - Deganwy Castle*

Evidence of a late Roman naval presence in the Bristol Channel comes from the temple complex dedicated to Mars Nodens at Lydney Park, situated on the north shore of the Severn estuary near Chepstow. A new temple along with a bath-house and guest-house were erected here at a date which reliable coin evidence shows lay after AD 367.[16] A mosaic in the temple itself was decorated with scenes of fish and other marine creatures suggesting the deity had associations with water and/or the sea.[17] This is also implied by fragments of bronze plaques bearing images of a sea deity with tritons and fishermen. Set in the border of the mosaic was an inscription recording its dedication to Mars Nodens by Titus Flavius Senilis, whose abbreviated title is given as *pr. rel.*, with the assistance of Victorinus, an *'interp(re)tiante'*. Senilis' title has usually been expanded as *praepositus reliquationis* meaning 'officer in charge of the supply-depot of the fleet' with Victorinus being a government interpreter.[18] Recently Wright and Hassall proffered an alternative which sees Senilis as a *praepositus religionis* – 'superintendent of the cult' – and Victorinus as an 'interpreter of dreams'.[19] Yet the site clearly had strong military connections. Another inscription records the dedication of a bronze plaque to Mars Nodens by Flavius Bandinus, an *armatura* or weapons instructor, while Fulford has drawn attention to the fact that the finds assemblage from Lydney has strong parallels with those from sites known to have been occupied by the military in the late fourth century.[20] Senilis then seems more likely to have been a senior naval officer attached to or even commanding the squadron guarding the Bristol Channel, most probably with its HQ at Cardiff. However, the title *praepositus reliquationis* may have had a slightly different meaning. The frequent absence of the bulk of the praetorian fleets, along with their Prefects, from their home bases in the late Roman period resulted in the appointment of acting commanders at Misenum and Ravenna known as *praepositi reliquationis*, literally 'officer in charge of the residue/remainder'.[21] If Senilis was this type of *praepositus* then it would imply he had been left in charge of a command which had recently been depleted by the secondment of one or more detachments to other postings. This is a very likely scenario in the aftermath of the catastrophe of 367 and it was perhaps at this juncture that the remaining core of *Legio II Augusta* was transferred to Richborough.

Apart from the high probability that the Twentieth Legion was still at Chester, albeit with a much reduced complement, practically nothing is known as to the identity of the garrisons of the coastal forts just mentioned, all of which lie within the province of *Britannia Prima*. Inscriptions are very rare by this period and the *Notitia* makes no reference to this area. This has led some to speculate that all the regular units were removed by Magnus Maximus for his attempt to win the purple in 383 with their function taken over either by local militia or by groups of allied barbarians – known variously as *foederati*, *gentiles* and *laeti* – transplanted from areas along or beyond the frontier. This is possible as the chapter of the *Notitia* which lists groups of such people in the western empire breaks off before reaching Britain. Yet the *Notitia* is a notoriously unreliable document; for example some forts known to have been garrisoned at the time it was compiled are omitted. It may simply be that the forces in *Britannia Prima* also came under the control of the *Dux Britanniarum* and that the relevant section of the list has been lost. Alternatively, they may have come under the authority of the governor or *praeses* of *Britannia Prima*. Then again there may have been another command heading up all the forces along the west coast between the remits of the *Dux Britanniarum* and the *Comes Maritimi Tractus* of which no record has survived.

Following the death of Valentinian in 375 the throne of the Western Empire passed to his sons Gratian and Valentinian II, the latter only four years old at the time. Gratian became less and less popular with the army for various reasons, and in 383 rebellion broke out in Britain led by Magnus Maximus. He was a senior commander – almost certainly holding the post or either *Dux Britanniarum* or *Comes Maritimi Tractus* – who had come to Britain with the elder Theodosius' expeditionary force 15 years or so earlier. Now he led an expeditionary force of his own in the opposite direction, landing in Gaul and soon winning over the forces in Germany to his cause. Maximus was seemingly very popular in Britain and the number of troops to be transported across the Channel was probably considerable. Gratian's army began to desert and Gratian himself was overtaken and killed by one of Maximus' generals at *Singidunum* (Belgrade). Maximus now controlled the entire prefecture of the Gauls. The

Picts and Scots took advantage of the situation and renewed their attacks on Britain necessitating Maximus' return in 384 when he secured a significant victory over them. By 387 Maximus had gathered a large army of 'Britons, neighbouring Gauls, Celts and the tribes thereabouts' which he employed to enter Italy and drive out Valentinian II who fled to the protection of Theodosius, Augustus of the Eastern Empire (Sozomenus *Ecclesiastical History* 7.13). The following year Andragathius, the general who had killed Gratian, was making preparations for a great naval expedition when Theodosius' forces broke through the Alpine passes, surrounded Maximus and eventually put him to death.

The mid-sixth-century British writer Gildas, the reliability and treatment of whose sources is admittedly uncertain, mentions a war with the Picts and Scots soon after the fall of Maximus:

> As a result of their attacks and terrible depredations Britain sent envoys to Rome with letters, making tearful appeals for an armed force to give them protection, and promising unwavering and whole-hearted submission to Roman rule, if only the enemy could be kept at a greater distance. Forgetting previous troubles, Rome soon prepared a legion, soundly equipped with arms. Crossing over Ocean to Britain in ships it engaged the fierce enemy, and killing a great number expelled them all from the place, freeing from imminent slavery a people that had been subjected to such dreadful mangling.

> *De excidio et conquestu Britanniae* 15

The 'legion' Gildas mentions is perhaps more likely to have been a detachment of the field army rather than one of the old style legions. It would have been commanded by a *Comes* who may in fact be the *Comes Britanniarum* in charge of nine units of *Comitatenses* listed in the *Notitia*. The menace of the sea-raiders to Britain increased in intensity during the final decade of the fourth century. By 398 some form of expedition was mounted on the orders of Stilicho, the Vandal general who was the real power behind Honorius, son of Theodosius and emperor of the Western Empire. Our only source of information is the comments of the eulogizing court-poet Claudian but a victory on land and sea was certainly achieved in 398.[22] Declaiming on the consulship of Stilicho early in 400 Claudian says:

> Next spoke Britannia, dressed in the skin of some Caledonian beast, her cheeks tattooed, her sea-blue mantle sweeping over her footsteps like the surge of Ocean: 'When I too was about to succumb to the attack of neighbouring tribes – for the Scots had raised all Ireland against me and the sea foamed under hostile oars – you Stilicho

protected me. His care ensured that I need no longer fear the missiles of the Scots, nor tremble at the Picts, nor watch on all my shores for the approaching Saxon on every shifting wind.'

De consulatu Stilichonis 2. 247-55

The wake of Stilicho's campaign is perhaps the most likely context for the reorganisation of the coastal command indicated by the arrangements recorded in the *Notitia*, with the Continental elements now being placed under the control of the *Dux Belgicae Secundae* and the *Dux Tractus Armoricani*.

In 401 Stilicho was withdrawing forces from Britain to counter a major Visigothic threat to Italy. These included 'the legion set to guard the furthest Britons, the legion that curbs the ferocious Scot and observes the tattoos on the bodies of dying Picts' (Claudian *de Bello Gothico* 416-18). The mention of Scots as well as Picts might suggest *Legio XX* at Chester rather than *Legio VI* at York. Alternatively this could be the 'legion' mentioned above sent over in 389 or 390. We also have to remember that a legion in this period could be a cohort-strength vexillation of one of the full-sized early imperial legions.[23] Other regiments were probably withdrawn on the same occasion. A unit called the *Seguntienses* mentioned in the *Notitia* as stationed in *Illyricum* may well be the former garrison of Carnarfon (*Segontium*).[24] Chester at least would have continued to be a centre of defence but its manpower was probably more a local militia than a regular army unit. Clearly, Roman naval forces were still perfectly capable of transporting large bodies of men across the Channel. No sooner had the 'legion' left however when, as Gildas tells it:

> . . . like predatory wolves driven mad by the extremes of hunger that leap dry-mouthed into the sheepfold when the shepherd is away, the old enemy burst over the frontiers, borne along by their oars like wings, by the arms of their oarsmen, by their sails swelling in the wind. Everything they slaughtered – whatever lay in their path they cut down like ripe corn, trampled underfoot, and passed on. So, once more plaintive envoys were sent, their clothes torn, so it is said, their heads covered in dust. Cowering like frightened chicks beneath the trusty wings of their parents, they beg the Romans for help lest their wretched homeland be utterly destroyed, and the Roman name, which echoed in their ears merely as a word, became a thing without worth and gnawed at by the insolent taunts of foreign tribes. The Romans, moved as much as is humanly possible by the tale of such tragedy, hastened the eagle-like flight of their cavalry on land and the passage of their sailors at sea, and into the necks of their enemies they plunged the talons of their swordpoints . . .

> Thus did our glorious allies quickly put to flight across the sea
> such enemy hordes as could escape; for year by year it was across
> the sea they piled up booty with no one to resist them.

De excidio et conquestu Britanniae 16-17

Irish sources mention attacks on the south coast of Britain by the 'high king'
of Ireland, Niall of the Nine Hostages, and these can perhaps be placed in the
years around 405. Abducting members of wealthy families for ransom, as
Niall's soubriquet implies, plunder, and the taking of prisoners to serve as slaves
– as the story of St Patrick illustrates – were all favoured pastimes of the sea-
raiders. The hoards of late Roman silver found at Balline, County Waterford,
and Ballinrees, County Derry, illustrate the scale of wealth that some raiders,
or more probably the leaders of raiding-parties, could amass.[25] In addition to
cut-up silver plates and vessels both hoards include ingots of a type used as
special payments to troops and others in the late Roman period while that
from Coleraine also contained 1,506 silver coins. Similarly impressive is the
hoard recovered from the environs of Traprain Law hillfort, the ancient capital
of the Votadini in southern Scotland.[26] Of course material like this could also
be used as payments, either to bribe raiders to cease their activities or to reward
barbarian mercenaries.[27]

Stilicho's preoccupation with the defence of Italy and the Balkans, coupled
with intelligence about barbarian forces massing on the far side of the Rhine
ready for a sweep across Gaul, led to a growing feeling in Britain that the West
would have to look after its own defence and so a usurper named Marcus was
chosen as leader in 406. The last day of that year saw a crossing of the frozen
Rhine by hordes of Alans, Sueves and Vandals. Roman forces were too
depleted to resist and the barbarians rapidly advanced through northern Gaul.
The military in Britain feared the enemy would take Boulogne and other
ports, thus isolating them from the rest of the Empire and perhaps opening up
the possibility of a barbarian invasion across the Channel. Marcus failed to act
and so was deposed and killed. The same fate befell his successor Gratian in
mid-407. He was replaced by Constantine III who quickly organised an expeditionary force and crossed the Channel, landing at Boulogne. From here he
sent officers ahead to take control of the surviving Roman units where possible
and restore order. By the end of the year, and having defeated opposition by
forces loyal to Honorius, Constantine controlled all Gaul and was in a position
to repair the Rhine defences. In 408, Spain too was won over following a
campaign by his son Constans and his British general Gerontius. The fact that
the army in Britain was capable of mounting an expedition across the Channel
with a strength sufficient both to defeat the invaders and take on any troops
who remained loyal to Honorius shows that the size of the armed forces in
Britain was still very considerable despite Stilicho's withdrawals. It also demon-

strates that the number of vessels required to transport a sizeable army across the Channel, whether naval transports and warships or requisitioned merchant galleys, could still be found.

Although successful for a brief period, Constantine III's regime, like that of Maximus before him, eventually came to grief. Already in 408 Britain suffered a serious attack by Saxons.[28] The following year Gerontius rebelled in Spain and

> . . . caused the barbarians in Gaul to make war on Constantine. Since Constantine failed to resist this attack, the barbarians from across the Rhine attacked everywhere with all their strength, and brought the people of Britain and some of the nations of Gaul to the point where they revolted from Roman rule and lived by themselves, no longer obeying Roman laws. The Britons took up arms and, fighting for themselves, freed the cities from the barbarian forces; and all of Armorica and other provinces of Gaul, in imitation of the Britons, freed themselves in the same manner, expelling Roman officials and setting up their own administration as best they could.
>
> Zosimus 6.5.2–3

With the accelerating disintegration of Constantine's grand ambitions and the renewal of barbarian attacks, the people of Britain clearly no longer felt any loyalty to his administration and deposed his officials in favour of their own. Zosimus refers to a letter sent by Honorius in 410 to the cities of Britain telling them he is unable to send help and that they should look to their own defence.[29] This must be a reply to a previous communication to the Emperor from the British leaders informing him what they had done and asking for assistance; a repeat of the situation after the fall of Maximus. Of course neither Honorius nor any of his immediate successors found themselves in a position to recover Britain, and the events of 409 effectively marked the end of Britain's membership of the Roman Empire.

The diocesan council, acting in collaboration with the *civitates* themselves, appear to have successfully organised the defences of the British provinces in the short term. The arrangements would obviously have varied from province to province, region to region, district to district, and town to town. There were still elements of the regular Roman army in Britain although now, with the severing of connections with the Empire and the administrative and logistical support systems it provided, the horizon of their loyalties will have narrowed sooner or later to the communities where they and their families were based, or to leaders who could provide them with accommodation, supplies, and a few luxuries in return for their fighting skills. The majority will soon have become local militias with others choosing the higher profile and riskier lifestyle of the hired sword. The ramifications of the break with Rome would probably have been felt more swiftly and more profoundly by the navy even than the army. To function effectively it was even more dependent on a well-organised infrastructure and the ability to mount an integrated military response over a wide geographical area. Neither of these is likely to have persisted very far into the fifth century. A lack of regular maintenance coupled with the increasing scarcity of the requisite specialist skills and materials will have soon reduced the number of seaworthy vessels and thus the operational capabilities of the fleet. At the same time, raids by Scots, Picts, and others are known to have continued unabated 'emerging from the vessels that had carried them across the gulf of the sea . . . like dark throngs of worms who wriggle out of narrow fissures in the rock when the sun is high and the weather grows warm' (Gildas *De excidio et conquestu Britanniae* 19).

Some of the signal-stations on the Yorkshire coast appear to have been casualties of the failing system. Those at Goldsborough and Huntcliff were destroyed by enemy attack, the remains of the men and their families who had formed the final garrisons being found amongst their fire-blackened ruins. At both, bodies had been thrown into wells but at Goldsborough there were two others which vividly illustrate the final moments of the catastrophe. Amidst the ruins of the tower the body of a short, thick-set man lay across the open hearth. Perhaps stabbed in the back, he lay face down, left hand behind his back, right hand touching the wall. At his feet lay a taller man, also face down, fallen across the body of a large and powerful dog, its head at the man's throat, paws on his shoulders. The dog had defended its home to the last, taking one of the attackers with it into the next world.[30]

Although not previously given the emphasis it perhaps deserves, it was very probably the inability or unwillingness of the new regime in Britain to maintain an effective naval force that was one of the prime reasons why Saxon federates were invited to settle in Kent and other areas, as recorded in Gildas, Bede and other early sources. It was the seafaring prowess of the Saxons that had first brought them into serious conflict with Rome and so it was a logical step − if an ultimately fatal one in view of their subsequent revolt − for the sub-Roman regime in Britain (in the person of Vortigern, '*superbus tyrannus*') to employ their skills against the Pictish and Scottish sea-raiders. The policy of 'setting a thief to catch a thief' by recruiting regiments from peoples of the frontier regions had long been employed by the Roman authorities. It was a great irony that the sea-wolves which the British Fleet had spent so many decades trying to destroy were now employed to defend Britain's shores. As so often happens in such cases, however, the hired protectors eventually turned against their employers. The Saxons rebelled and by the year 442, as the Gallic Chronicle records, a large part of Britain had succumbed to Saxon domination.

As Caesar had demonstrated nearly 500 years earlier, and as pivotal moments in later history were to show, he who controls the seas around Britain controls Britain herself. By giving up their fleet the sub-Roman regime allowed Britannia to be submerged beneath a rising barbarian tide. One day there would be another British Navy but this time it would be Britannia, not Roma, that ruled the waves.

NOTES

Chapter 1

1 Hopkins 1982, 84, 86 Table II.
2 Winbolt 1925, 118-32.
3 Winbolt 1925, 133-46.
4 Atkinson 1933.
5 Reculver-Philp 1969; Richborough-Cunliffe 1968; Portchester-Cunliffe 1975.
6 Cleere 1975; 1986.
7 Philp 1981.
8 Seillier & Gosselin 1969; Seillier *et al.* 1971; Seillier & Gosselin 1973; Seillier *et al.* 1976; Seillier 1977.
9 Brulet 1991, 158-63.
10 Saddington 1990; Casey 1994, 153-62.
11 Middleton 1971; 1981; 1989; Allen & Fulford 1999.
12 Dornier 1971; Livens 1974.
13 Ward 1901; Jones & Shotter 1988.
14 Bellhouse 1989; Jones 1982; Livens 1986.
15 E.g. Allen & Fulford 1986; 1992; Dark & Dark 1997; Mason 1987, 153-5; 2002, 64-72; Milne 1985; Toft 1992; Tooley & Switsur 1988; Waddelove & Waddelove 1990.
16 Pearson 2002, 99-124.
17 Brigham 1990; 1998.
18 Hibbert 1980; Brigham 1990, 146-9.

Chapter 2

1 1.20.13-14.
2 Polybius 1.20.7.
3 Morrison & Coates 1996, 205-7 with Pl. 12.
4 Detailed study see Wallinga 1956.
5 1.63.4.
6 Livy 29.25.3.
7 E.g. Polybius 8.34.3; Livy 26.39.19; 27.1-3; 32, 14.3; 44,7,10; Plutarch *Pompey* 11.2; Tacitus *Annals* 13.53; Dio Cassius 52.25.7; Appian *Hannibal* 6.34.
8 Evidence reviewed by Roth 1999, 252-56.
9 E.g. Livy 32.16.2-5.
10 Hopkins 1982, 82, 84 Table 2 estimates it at 50 to 1.
11 Plutarch *Pompey*, 11.2.
12 Plutarch *Sulla*, 27.1.
13 *Gallic War.* See chapter 5.
14 Plutarch *Pompey* 24; Cassius Dio, xxxvi, 20-23.
15 Appian *Mithridates* 116-7.
16 See Rodgers 1937, 432 - 539; Morrison & Coates 1996, 127-71.
17 Listed in Morrison & Coates 1996, 172-4.
18 Cassius Dio 54, 32.
19 *Res Gestae* 26, 4; also Pliny *Natural History* II, 67, 167; see Nicolet 1988, 258ff and Saddington 1990, 225.
20 Velleius Paterculus II, 106, 2; II, 121, 1.
21 See Schnurbein 2000, 29-30; Oberaden casks - Kuhlborn 1992, 100-21.
22 Tacitus *Annals* 1, 60-2.
23 Tarruntenus Paternus, *Digest* 50.6.7.
24 Tacitus *Annals* 2, 23-4.
25 Tacitus *Annals* 2. 26.
26 Tacitus *Annals* 2.26.
27 Cichorius scenes ii-iii.
28 *Ibid.*, iv-v.
29 *Ibid.*, Scene xxxiii.
30 Scene xxxiv-xxxv.
31 Scenes lxxix-lxxx.

32   Scene lxxxvii.
33   Starr 1960, 117–20.
34   *CIL* VIII 7030.

Chapter 3

1   Starr 1960 32n.10.
2   Starr 1960, 33n.13.
3   See Starr 1960, 37.
4   Livy 40.18.8; 41.1.2.
5   *CIL* XI 86; *CIL* X 3348, 3349, 3349.
6   *ILS* 2819–22, 2844, 2846, 2857, 2908, 2910–14.
7   *Digest* 37, 13.
8   *RIB* I 653.
9   *Letters* 56.
10   Tacitus *Histories* 2.17, 22; 3.55; Ritterling *s.v. æ legioÆ* col. 1267.
11   Philp 1981, 100–2; disputed by Breeze 1983.
12   Starr 1960 74–7 with Table I.
13   Easterners in *Classis Germanica* in the first century *CIL* XIII 12047; ILS 2827 & 2828.
14   Tacitus *Histories* 4.16.3.
15   *Ibid.*, 1.58.1.
16   Saddington 1990 227 on *AE* 1956 249.
17   *CIL* XIII 3543; 3544.
18   *CIL* XIII 3542.
19   *CIL* XIII 3546.
20   *CIL* XII 686.
21   *CIL* XIV 5341.
22   Pflaum 1960–1, No. 156bis.
23   *CIL* XI 5632.
24   *RIB* I 66.
25   *CIL* XVI 138.
26   Starr 1960,187.
27   Watson 1969, 101–2.
28   Watson 1969, n259 for refs.
29   Starr 1960, 92; Watson 1969, 138.
30   *CIL* X 3375; 238; and 3420.
31   Polybius 1.21.1–2; Dio Cassius 48.51.5.
32   Casson 1971, 278–9.
33   *P.Mich.*VIII 467. 20–21; 468 24–25.
34   *CIL* III 557, 6109, 7290, 7327.
35   Bollini 1969, 86–96.
36   *De Munitionibus Castrorum* 24.
37   *P.Mich.* VIII 467. 19–20.
38   *P.Mich.* VIII 468. 27–29.

Chapter 4

1   *Metamorphoses* 11.514–15.
2   Diogenes Laertius 1.103; Juvenal 12, 58–9.
3   Archaeological Museum, Ravenna.
4   See Casson 1971 ills 130, 132.
5   Discussed extensively in Morrison *et al.* 2000, 169–71, 196–9, 204–5, 220–1.
6   Appian *Hist.* 10.1.3.
7   Livy 37.23.5; 37.30.2.
8   *Gallic War* 5.1.1.
9   *CIL* XIII 3564; *Agricola* 28.
10   See now Morrison, Coates & Rankov 2000.
11   Conveniently assembled in Morrison & Coates 1996.
12   Blackman 1968; 1982; 1995.
13   *IG* 22 1604–32.
14   Casson 1971, 144–6.
15   Casson & Steffy 1991.
16   Morrison & Coates 1996 fig. 34.
17   Casson 1971 pl.125.
18   Lepper & Frere 1988, Plate XII Scene lxxxvi Cast 225.
19   Morrison, Coates & Rankov 2000, 210; 102–6.
20   Morrison & Coates 1996 fig. 56.
21   Casson 1971, 100–103; Morrison & Coates 1996, 267–71, 285–303.
22   Appian *Illyrian Wars*. 3.
23   Morrison & Coates 1996, 248–52.
24   Caesar *Gallic War* 3.14.
25   *Roman History* 10.1.3; *on the movement of animals* 10. 701 a 31.
26   *Mithidates* 92.
27   Casson 1971, 132.
28   *Gallic War* 4.26.4.
29   Rupprecht 1982; Hockmann 1993.
30   Hollstein 1982.
31   Casson figs 130 &132.
32   Wallinga 1956.
33   Appian *Civil Wars* 5.118.
34   *Gallic War* 3.14.5; Vegetius *Epitoma rei Militaris* 46.
35   *Gallic War* 2.6.3.
36   Used at Actium, Cassius Dio 50.32.8.
37   Livy 37.15; Appian *Syrian Wars*. 24.
38   *Gallic War* 4.25.1; and see pp infra.
39   Arrian, *Anabasis* 2.21.1.
40   Diodorus Siculus 20.47.1–2.

41 *Gallic War* 4.21.4.

42 *Gallic War* 5.1-2.

43 McGrail 1987; 1995; 2001; McGrail & Roberts 1999; Rule & Monaghan 1993; Marsden 1994; Gilmour 1994; Ellmers 1996.

44 Marsden 1994, 166-8; McGrail 1995, 139-40; Ellmers 1996, 68-71.

45 Gellius 10.25.5; Digest 49.15.2.

46 Lucian *Vera Hist.* 1.5; Althiburus mosaic.

47 25.30.10; 5.2.1.

48 *Alexandrian War* 44.3.

49 Polybius 3.42.2; 3.43.2, 3, 4 *et seq.*

50 Strabo 2.99; Livy 24.40.2.

51 For both see Casson 1971, 164-7.

52 Lucan 5.518; Catullus *Carmina* 4.

53 *Roman History* 3.8.

54 Strabo 16.780.

55 *Digest* 49.15.2.

56 Summarised in Parker 1992.

57 See Casson 1971 171-3, 183-90; Tchernia & Pomey 1978; Hopkins 1983; Parker 1992; Gibbins 1996.

58 Casson 145 vs 147.

59 Casson 1971, 171-3 & 183-90; Rouge 1975, 74-8; Houston 1988.

60 Casson 1971, ill. 147.

61 See Casson for details 239-44.

62 Plautus *Rudens* 1.2.74; Horace *Odes* 3.29.62; Petronius *Satyricon* 102.5.

63 Anderson 1984, 113; Walsh 2000, 57-8.

64 Fulford 1989b.

65 Marsden 1974; 1994 124-5.

66 Rule & Monaghan 1993, 128.

67 Casson 1971, 288; Sippel 1987, 41-2. Marsden 1994, 194-9; for useful summary see Grainge 2002, 26-44.

68 See Casson 1971, 297-9 and more generally 281-96.

69 Lamboglia 1961; Tchernia *et al.* 1978.

70 Now in the Landesmuseum, Trier. Illustrated in Gardiner (ed.) 1995, p. 120.

71 Casson 1971, 338 n52.

72 Marsden 1965a; 1974; 1994 124-5.

73 *Theodosian Code* 13.5.1; *CIL* XIV 252; Isidorus Hispalensis 19.1.19.

74 Marsden 1965b; 1994.

75 Marsden 1967; 1994.

76 Caesar *Gallic War* 3.13.

77 Casson 'Harbour Boats' 36-8 pls. 2.2, 2.3, 3.1, 4.2, 5.1.

78 Ammianus 17.2.3; 18.2.12; *Theodosian Code.* 7.17.1.

79 DeWeerd 1978; de Boe 1978.

80 Nayland *et al.* 1994.

81 *Epitoma rei Militaris* 4.39.

82 See now Grainge 2002, 62-74 & Appendices I and IX-XII.

83 Pliny *Natural History* 19.30; Livy 22.20.6; Caesar *Gallic* War 5.1.1.

84 Sails = Plutarch *Moralia* 664c.

85 Colours = Pliny Natural History 19.22; devices = Arrian *Parthica* fr. 67.

86 See Casson 1971, 229-45 273-8; for sails Morrison & Coates 1996, 333-340 with Morrison Coates *et al.* 2000, 259-67 for rowing performance.

87 Benoit 1961, fig. 95.

88 Desjardins 1876, 367.

89 Casson 1971, 350-8 with footnotes.

90 *Natural History* 35. 49.

91 4.37.

92 Casson 247 n88.

93 Pliny *Natural History* 19.22.

94 Vegetius 4.38.

95 Suetonius *Caligula* 37.

96 Arrian Parthica fr.67 = Casson 235 n49.

97 Xenophon *Hellenica* 2.1.17; Diodorus Siculus 20.51.1.

98 See now Woolliscroft 2001.

99 Meiggs 1973.

100 See Vitruvius *On Architecture* 10. 2. 8-10.

101 Vitruvius *On Architecture* 2. 6.1. Roweland & Howe 1999.

102 Morel 1986, 206-10.

103 London quays see Brigham 1998.

104 Bovini 1963.

105 Summary see H.G. Horn ed. 1987, 516-19.

106 Blackman 1968; 1982; 1987; 1995.

107 Coates 1993.

108 Appian 96; Diodorus 14. 42 45; Blackman 1968, 185-6; Blackman 1982, fig. 1 H.

109 Hockmann 1993.

110 Morel 1986, 205 & fig. 4.

111 Bartoccini 1958, 59 pl. 28; Meiggs 1973, 154, 158, 590.

112 Hutter & Hauschild 1991.
113 Woolliscroft 2001, 88-97.

Chapter 5

1 Gallic War 4.20.
2 *Geographica* 1, 5, 2.
3 Cunliffe 1987; Cunliffe & de Jersey 1997.
4 *Geographica* 4, 5, 2.
5 *Current Archaeology* 181, 7-11.
6 Caesar, *Gallic War* 3.8.
7 *Gallic War* 3.14.
8 *Gallic War* 4.22.
9 *Gallic War* 4.26.
10 *Gallic War* 4.29.
11 *Gallic War* 4.31.
12 *Gallic* War 5.8.
13 *Letters to Atticus* 4.18.5.
14 *Geographica* 4.5.2.
15 Cunliffe & de Jersey 1997.
16 Dio Cassius 49.38.2; 53.22.5; 53.25.2.
17 Tacitus, *Annals* 2.24.

Chapter 6

1 Suetonius, *Gaius*. 44-47; Cassius Dio 59.25.2.
2 Suetonius *Gaius*, 44.
3 Casson 1971, 93-4; Hyland 1990, 98-9.
4 Peddie 1987, 40; Fulford 2000, 42-3; Manley 2002, 84-6.
5 Peddie 1987, 40 Table II.
6 60. 21.
7 Grainge 2002, 7-8; Pearson 2002, 111-13.
8 Bushe Fox 1932, 10-13; 1949, 11-136; Cunliffe 1968, 231-7; Detsicas 1987, 11-13; Frere 1987, 48-50; Peddie 1987, 47-65; Todd 1997, 58-60; Webster 1997, 95-7.
9 E.g. Haverfield 1924, 101-3.
10 Down 1988, 7-16; Cunliffe 1998, 25-32. O'Neil & O'Neil 1952, 29-33; Cunliffe 1998, 21; Salway 1998, 82-3; Hind 1989; Bird 2000; Black 1998; 2000, 2001; Manley 2002.
11 Frere & Fulford 2001; Grainge 2002.
12 *ILS* 216 – see also Barrett 1991.

13 Dunnett 1975, 35 & 39; Crummy 1997, 71-2.
14 See now discussions by Hassall 2000 51-65; Manning 2000 69-81; Keppie 2000, 83-100.
15 Frere 1974; Dannell & Wild 1987.
16 Not the site of the later fortress but at Lower Common south of the Witham-Jones 1988, 145-7; 2002, 33-6; Darling 1984, 95-7. Leicester–Hassall 2000, 61.
17 Sauer 1999; 2000; Burnham, Keppie & Fitzpatrick 2001, 355.
18 Burnham & Wacher 1990, 138-40, fig. 38.
19 Fulford & Timby 2000.
20 Fishbourne-Cunliffe 1971, 72-3; Manley 2002; Chichester-Cunliffe in Down 1978, 178-83; Down 1988 7-14.
21 Cotton & Gathercole 1958.
22 Black 2000, 5 n.36; Burnham, Keppie & Fitzpatrick 2001, 374-6; Russell 2001.
23 For summary of Lake Farm fortress see Field 1992; Hamworthy-Dudley & Webster 1965, 104; Webster 1960, 57; Rigby 1979, 190; Rankov1981, 385-7.
24 Burnham, Keppie & Fitzpatrick 2001, 370.
25 Griffith 1995, 363.
26 Silvester 1984; Holbrook 1987.
27 Burnham & Wacher 1990, 62-5, fig. 12.
28 Thomas 1966, 85-6; Bidwell & Silvester 1988.
29 Cunliffe 1968, 232-41.
30 1999; *Geog.* 4.5.2.
31 2002, 91-5.
32 Fox & Ravenhill 1966.
33 Griffith 1995, 363.
34 *Trans. Devonshire Assoc.* 62, 1931, 119-20.
35 Todd 1976.
36 *Annals* 12.31.
37 Hurst 1985.
38 Manning 1981; Marvell 1991; White & Barker 1998, 32-50.
39 Webster P. 1991; Shoesmith 1991.
40 Jones 2002, 107-12.
41 Stead 1977.
42 Jones 1978.
43 E.g. Frere 1987, 70.

44 Mason 2001a, 8-12.

45 See Carrington 1986, 15.

46 Frere 1987, 285 & 293 n.5 discussing *RIB II.1* 2404.38.

47 Tacitus *Histories* 2. 66.

48 Tacitus *Histories* 4.79.

49 See Starr 1941, 180-6; Levick 1999, 56-63.

50 Shotter 1994; 2000a; 2000b; 2002.

51 Ottaway 1993.

52 Shotter 2002.

53 Mason 2001b, 32-3.

54 Caruana forthcoming.

55 Shotter 1993; 1994; 2000a; 2000b; 2002.

56 Hanson *et al.* 1979.

57 Burnham, Keppie & Esmonde Cleary 1998, 382; 1999, 334.

58 Mason 2000, 76-95; 2001, 89-100.

59 For detailed discussion of Agricola's campaigns see Hanson 1987; Jones & Mattingly 1990, 72-7.

60 Haverfield 1899; Gudeman 1900; Warner 1995; Robinson 2000.

61 Frere 1985, 267.

62 Robertson 1975, 394-6; Rivet & Smith 1979, 447 & 501-2.

63 *RIB* I 544.

64 Plutarch *de defectu Oraculorum*, 2.

65 RCHM *Roman York*, 133 No. 142, Pl. 65.

66 *Agricola* 28.5.

67 Hanson 1987, 127 & 167.

68 *Geographia*. 2.3.14.

69 Rivet & Smith 1979, 128, 372-3.

70 See Hanson 1987, 115-37; Jones & Mattingly 1990, 79-88 Maps 4.18-4.22.

71 *Agricola*. 38.

72 *Geographica*. 2, 3, 4; *Agricola*. 10.

73 Hind 1974; Rivet & Smith 1979, 478-80.

74 Pitts & St Joseph 1985.

75 Strong 1968.

Chapter 7

1 *CIL* XIII 3564.

2 Best drawing Desjardins 1876, i, 367. The other is the 'Ammilla Augusta' whose name appears on a bronze model, possibly votive, now in the British Museum RIB II.3 2432.1; see figure **46**.

3 Brulet 1991, 158-62.

4 Brulet 1989; 1991.

5 Suetonius *Gaius* 44; Wheeler 1929, 37.

6 *Geographica* 2.3.3.

7 Best still Rigold 1969.

8 Pearson 2002, 115.

9 Philp 1981, 82.

10 See Breeze's alternative in *Britannia* 14, 372-4.

11 Wheeler 1929.

12 Philp 1981, 7-9.

13 Hassall & Tomlin 1977, 426-7 No. 4.

14 *RIB* I 66; II 2481.7. ccxiii-ccxviii; 7A. lii-liii; 7B. xcvi; 8. cclxxxviii-ix; 10. vi-vii; 43. xxvii; 78; 92. lxi-lxiii.

15 Peacock 1977, 246.

16 *RIB* II.5 2481.7 ccxix & 2481.103. xi.

17 *RIB* II.5 2481.22.iv; *RIB* II.5 2481.7.ccxii also Crowley & Betts 1992, 218-22.

18 1925, 105; Cunliffe 1969, 260.

19 1977, 246.

20 1972.

21 Peacock 1977.

22 Cleere & Crossley 1985.

23 Brodribb & Cleere 1988.

24 Caesar *Gallic War* 3.13. Iron anchor with about 20ft of iron chain in Dorchester Museum – B.W. Cunliffe, 'Late Iron Age metalwork from Bulbury', *Antiquaries Journal* 52, 1972, 293-308.

25 1977.

26 Bidwell & Speak 1994; Bidwell ed. 1999, 74-5.

27 Wacher 1995, 394-8.

28 *RIB* I 544.

29 *RIB* I 445.

30 See Anderson 1992; Roth 1999, 270-8.

31 Peacock & Williams 1985.

32 Ellmers 1978, figures 9, 12, 15 and 16a.

33 Grenier 1937, 479-86.

34 *JRS* 11 1921, 101-7.

35 Hassall & Tomlin 1977, 430-1 No. 18.

36 *AE* 1975, 651.

37 *RIB* I 678.

38 H. Halbaek, *The New Phytologist* 63, 158-64.

39 For coastal supply to the North see Middleton 1979, 93; Fulford 1981, 203-4; 1989.

40 Mason 2002.

41 O'Leary, Blockley & Musson 1989.

42 *RIB* II.1 2404.31 & Shrubsole 1887; Mason 1987, 153.

43 *RIB* II.1 2404.33 and 2404.36.

44 Mason 1988, 183-4.

45 Arnold & Davies 2000, 104; copper ingots see *RIB* II 2403.

46 Allen & Fulford 1992.

47 See *RIB* II.4, 126 fig. 1.

48 50, 6, 7.

49 Sarnowski & Trynkowski 1986, 536-41.

50 Alteburg

51 *CIL* XIII 12348.5. Hockmann 1986.

52 *CIL* XIII 6712, 6714; *AE* 1911, 225.

53 Boon 1945; 1949; Todd 1976, 102-3.

54 1969, 3; 1974, 395-7; 1995, 394-8.

55 Boon 1978; also now Evans 2000, 488-9.

56 1992.

57 Mason 1987, 154-5; 2001, 114-7, 188-91; 2002, 64-72; Ward 1996.

58 Shrubsole 1887; Shone 101-6.

59 *RIB* II.1 2404.31.

60 Brock 1888, 62

61 Mason 1987, 154-5; 2001,188-91; 2002, 64-72.

62 RCHM York Mon. 52; Ottaway 1993, 68.

63 Reynolds 1930, 100-1.

64 Frere & St Joseph 1983, 106-7, pl. 60.

65 *Augustan History. Hadrian.* 5.2; Birley 1998.

66 Tomlin & Hassall 1998, 435-6 No. 7.

67 *ILS* 2726; 2735.

68 *RIB* II.3 2426.1.

69 Fulford 1981;1989.

70 *RIB* I 1319 & 1320.

71 *RIB* I 1944 & 1945;1340.

72 *CIL* XVI 93 = *RIB* II 2401.10.

73 See Rivet & Smith 1979, 360, 380-1; Shotter in Potter 1979, 315-21; Jones & Shotter 1988, 220-22; Holder 1997.

74 *AE* 1997 1001; Holder 1997; *RIB* II

75 1974, 287.

76 Woolliscroft 2001, 88-97.

77 *RIB* II.1 2401.8.

78 Atkinson 1942,193 n.1.

79 Bidwell & Griffiths 1999, 96; Burnham, Hunter & Fitzpatrick 2002, 291-3.

80 Bidwell 1999, 99.

81 *Itinerary* ed. T. Hearne 3rd edition 1768-9 vol. 7, 56; Bainbrigg BM MS Cotton, Julius VI. 319; 1726 It Sept, 97).

82 Philp 1981, 96.

83 Robertson 2001, 41.

84 Miller 1928, 31-2.

85 Cramond – Sibbald 1707, 33; Inveresk – Hanson 1980; Burnham, Keppie & Fitzpatrick 2001, 321; Carriden – Richmond & Steer 1959.

86 *JRS* 47, 229-30 No. 18.

87 Mason 1984, 1109-16 & 1132-40.

88 *RIB* I 2132 with *Britannia* 8, 433 no. 30.

89 Tatton Brown 1980.

90 *AE* 1960, 28.

91 *RIB* I 1322.

92 Cassius Dio 71.16.2.

93 72.8.

94 *RIB* I 946.

95 *CIL* 3 1919, 8513, 12813; *ILS* 2770.

Chapter 8

1 Hodgson 1999, 72-83; Burnham, Keppie & Fitzpatrick 2001, 323-6.

2 Cassius Dio 76.13.

3 Herodian 3.14.1.

4 *ILS* 9123.

5 Pflaum 1960. No. 259; Kienast 1966, 44.

6 Mattingly 1950, 352 No. 859, Pl. 52.6; 396.

7 Frere 1987, 159-62; Maxwell 1998, 24-6.

8 Wright 1974, 289-92.

9 *JRS* 55 223 and *Britannia* 2, 292 No. 15; *RIB* II.4 2460.71-4.

10 *JRS* 55, 223; Wright 1974, 289-92.

11 Bidwell 1999, 77-80.

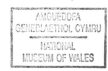

12 Cleere 1988, 243-4.

13 *CIL* 13.686.

14 For the most recent survey of the evidence relating to the foundation of these three forts see Pearson 2002, 11-16, 24-5, 54-5.

15 Richmond 1961; Mann 1977b; Birley 1981, 173-6.

16 E.g. Richmond 1963, 59-61; Philp 1981, 115-18.

17 *RIB* II.4 2466; 2468.

18 Peacock 1977.

19 Richmond 1963, 60.

20 Whitwell 1970, 52-3.

21 Dunnett 1975, 57.

22 Harrison & Flight 1969, 58 fig. 4, 61 fig. 6; see also Burnham & Wacher 1990, 76-8.

23 Wacher1975, 395 *contra* Ramm 1978, 60; Esmonde Cleary 1987, 17 & 128.

24 Birley 1937, 61 on *RIB* I 707.

25 Wacher 1969, 3; 1974, 395-7.

26 Most recent update see Hodgson 1999, 73-82; Burnham, Keppie & Cleary 2000, 385-9; Burnham, Keppie & Fitzpatrick 2001, 322-6.

27 *CIL* XIII 6780.

28 *RIC* 143.

Chapter 9

1 Butler 1959; Johnson 1983, Chapter 5.

2 Nemesianus, *Cynegetica* 65-75.

3 Mann 1989.

4 *Liber De Caesaribus*, 39. 20-21; *Breviarium* 9.13.

5 39. 20; 9. 21.

6 *Pan. Lat.* viii(v).6.

7 Bidwell ed.1999, 78-80.

8 Frere 1987, 332.

9 Casey 1994, 115-26; Pearson 2002, 57-66.

10 Johnson 1976; Maxfield 1989; Pearson 2002.

11 Wilson,1975, 283; Goodburn 1976, 376; Wilkinson 1997, 76-7; Cunliffe 1976.

12 Pearson 2002, 120.

13 Johnson 1976, 141-4; Fitzpatrick 2001, 374-6; Pearson 2002, 60-2.

14 Brulet 1991, 158-61.

15 Mertens 1978; Johnston 1977; Brulet 1991.

16 Langouet 1977; Sanquer 1977; Johnson 1976, 72-93.

17 Johnson 1976, 89-90.

18 Camden *Britannia* 1637; Richmond 1963 60-1; Johnson 1976, 114-31; Frere 1987, 329-30; Esmonde Cleary 1989, 43; Faulkner 2000, 90-1.

19 1961, 29-30.

20 Wood 1990; Milne 1990.

21 Mann 1989, 10-11.

22 1993, 228.

23 Nydam boats – Akerlund 1963, Greenhill 1976, 180-2, Rieck & Crumlin-Pedersen 1988, 103-18. Sutton Hoo – Bruce Mitford 1975, 350, 584-8, 678-82, 715-17.

24 Green 1963, 103-13; Crumlin-Pedersen 1990, 113.

25 Haywood 1991, 62-75.

26 Akerlund 1963, 63-73.

27 Thorvildsen1961, 22.

28 Fenwick 1978, 227, 251.

29 Todd 1975, 153.

30 Sidonius Apollinaris *Letters* 8.6.15; Ammianus Marcellinus 28.2.12.

31 McGrail 1987, 282.

32 McGrail 1987, 187.

33 Adomnan's Life of St Columba, Gildas, Voyage of St Brendan.

34 *Oratio* 18. 82-3.

35 Haywood 1991,174 fn. 86 commenting on Sidonius Apollinaris *Letters* 8.6.14.

36 Hassall 1976,111-12.

37 *Notitia Dignitatum, Occidens.* 37.

38 Hassall 1977, 9; Arnold & Davies 2000, 29-31.

39 *CIL* XIII 12560.

40 1976, 90-91.

41 *CIL* XII 686.

42 Hodgson 1996; 1999, 80-2.

43 Jones, G.D.B. 1993.

44 Daniels 1978, 264-5.

45 Breeze & Dobson 1987, 220.

46 Jarrett 1969, 70-3; Webster P 1981.

47 Todd, M. 1976, 102-4.

48 Marvell & Oetgen 1985; Marvell & Owen John 1997.

49 See now Casey & Davies 1993.
50 Wheeler 1923, 14 & 110; Boon 1969, 63; Goodburn 1978, 404-6.
51 Mason 2001, 196-204.
52 See generally Southern & Dixon 1996.
53 27.8.1
54 See Johnson 1976a, 142-8; 1976b; 1977; Mann 1977a; 1989; Hassall 1977.

Chapter 10

1 Julius Firmicus Maternus *De Errore Profanum Religionum* 28.6; Libanius *Oratio* 59. 139-141.
2 Jones & Shotter 1988, 21-3, 80-4, 216-18.
3 *RIB* I 601.
4 Shotter 1997, 138.
5 1600, 693-4; Bailey 1923, 146-7; Jarrett 1976, 6-8.
6 Turnbull 1996; Wilson 1997, 29.
7 Julian *Letter to the Athenians* 279-80; Zosimus 3.5.2.
8 26.4.5.
9 *Notitia Dignitatum. Occidens.* 5.197. 200; 5. 218; 7.24.74; 7.78. 200; *Oriens.* 9.29.
10 Cortis 1858; Hornsby & Stanton 1912; Hornsby & Laverick 1932; Wilson 1991; Ottaway 1997.
11 *RIB* I 721.
12 Griffiths 1954, Putnam1969.
13 Johnson 1976, 135-6.
14 Crew 1981; Casey 1989.
15 Livens 1986.
16 Wheeler & Wheeler 1932.
17 *RIB* II.4 2448.3.
18 Collingwood 1932.
19 Hassall 1980, 82; Wright 1985.
20 *RIB* I 305; Fulford 2002,100.
21 Rankov 1995, 84-5.
22 *In Eutropium* 1. 391-3.
23 For most recent discussion see Tomlin 2000.
24 *Notitia Dignitatum. Occidens.* 5.241; 7.84; 7.156.
25 O' Riordain 1947, 43-82; Bateson 1973, 42-3, 63-4, 73-4; 1976, 171-3; Mattingly & Pierce 1937.
26 Curle 1923.
27 Rance, 2002.
28 *Gallic Chronicle* No.281 n.17.
29 6.10.2.
30 Hornsby & Laverick 1932.

GLOSSARY OF NAUTICAL TERMS

aft: rear part of ship.

amidships: central part of a ship.

backstay: rope running from the mast aft.

ballast: heavy material carried deep in a ship's hold to improve stability.

beam: the breadth of a ship measured at the widest part.

belaying pin: wooden pin round which a rope is tied and secured.

bilge: the lowest part of the hull.

bollard: stout post to which mooring ropes are attached.

boom: spar along the foot of a sail.

bow: the front part of a ship.

boxing-in: enclosing the hull of an oared ship with a raised deck and side-screens to protect the oarsmen from missiles.

brace: rope attached to the end of a yard allowing the yard to be swung so that the sail catches the wind.

bracket: angular wooden support.

brail: rope attached to the bottom edge of a square sail, leading up its forward surface, over the yard and then to a point aft where it can be secured and manipulated. The brails enable the area of sail exposed to the wind to be varied and also allow the sail to be pulled up fully to the yard.

bulwark: raised timberwork running along sides of a ship above the level of the deck.

butt: a joint joining two timbers end to end.

capstan: winch with upright spindle used for moving heavy objects such as the anchor.

catch: the moment at the start of the pulling part of the stroke when the oar blades enter the water.

carvel-built: technique of shipbuilding in which planks are laid flush, edge to edge.

caulking: fibrous material rammed hard between the planks of a hull to make the shell watertight and to prevent the planks from sliding along one another when subjected to longitudinal stress.

clinker-built: ship built with hull formed of overlapping planks.

crutch: wooden prop on which the mast rests when lowered.

cutwater: the part of a ship's stem that cleaves the water when moving.

deck: horizontal level in a ship.

draft: the depth of water required by a ship; the vertical distance from the bottom of the keel to the waterline.

file: of oarsmen, fore to aft row of oarsmen.

flare: outward slope from the vertical of the sides of a ship.

forefoot: armoured projection forward of the stempost of a war galley.

forecastle: the space in the very forward part of the ship.

forestay: supporting line running forewards from mast.

frames: lateral timbers added to the keel forming the shape of the hull and giving it strength.

freeboard: distance from the waterline to the main deck.

galley: the kitchen.

gangplank: plank extended from ship to shore for embarking and disembarking.

garboards: the strakes on either side of the keel.

halyards: ropes for hoisting sail.

hatch: opening in the deck through which cargo is loaded/unloaded.

heel: of a ship, an angle of inclination from the upright.

helm: steering gear.

hog, **hogging**: distortion of a ship's hull under stress resulting in the prow and stern dropping relative to the midships section.

hogging truss: a rope tensioning device used to support ends of a vessel and prevent hogging.

hull: body of the ship.

keel: the 'backbone' of the ship, lowest part of the hull running from stem to stern.

inboard: within the ship.

lapstrake: same as clinker-built.

lee: away from the wind.

lifts: lines running from masthead to yard.

loom: of an oar, the inboard part between the tholepin and the handle.

louvre: of a ship, the open lattice-pattern timberwork providing a protected ventilation course in the side of a war galley.

luff: edge of a square sail that is toward the wind.

mast step: wooden fitting to hold base of mast secure.

moor: secure a ship when not in motion.

monoxylous: made from one piece of timber.

oarbox: the projection on each side of a multi-level galley required to accommodate the oarsystem.

oculus: eye-device painted on front of ship close to the waterline representing the all-seeing eye.

poop: rear part of the ship, a deck at the rear.

port: left-hand side facing forward.

port (noun): opening in hull for working the oar.

prow: forward part of the bow.

quarter: side of a ship near the stern.

quincunx: arrangement of units equidistant from one another in each of three parallel lines so that in depth each trio of neighbouring units, one in each line, forms a diagonal.

rigging: lines fitted to masts, yards and sails.

room: in an oared ship this is the space in the rowing area across the ship defined by the distance between one tholepin and another on each side. The area on one side only is a half-room; see *interscalmium*.

running rigging: lines that control movements of sails and spars.

scarf: butt joint in which the end of one timber is shaped to overlap and fit with the end of its partner to give added strength.

sheet: a rope holding down the aftermost bottom corner of a sail.

shrouds: supporting lines running from mast to the sides of the hull.

spinnaker: racing sail set so as to belly out before the wind.

sprit: spar supporting a spritsail, running from lower part of mast to upper after corner of sail.

square sail: sail that is set athwartships.

starboard: the right-hand side facing forward.

stay: rope attached to the mast to prevent fore and aft movement.

stem: foremost part of the ship rising from the forward tip of the keel.

stempost: in an oared warship the curved timber rising from the keel in the bow and terminating in a decorative figurehead.

stern: rear of a ship.

stockholm tar: softwood tar made from carbonised resinous root stumps.

stopping: a setting preparation applied to the seams of planks to make them watertight.

strake: a row of planks end-to-end.

stringer: longitudinal timber laid on and secured to transverse hull timbers.

stroke oarsman: oarsman nearest the stern.

tack (verb): to sail at an angle to the wind closer than 90 degrees.

tenon: rectangular block of wood fitted into opposing mortices to join together two timbers. Normally secured in place by being drilled through and pegged.

tholepin: pin against which the oar is worked.

thwarts: cross planks serving as seats for oarsmen.

topwale: timber running the length of a ship forming the upper edge of the hull; also 'gun'wale in recent times.

treenails: wooden pegs used as fastenings.

wale: a line of thick, broad planks along a ship's side. In a warship, these might support and reinforce the ram as well as providing protection for the shell of the hull.

wash strake: a strake fixed above the gunwale to increase the freeboard.

waterline: point on the hull that the water reaches when the ship is floating normally.

yard: the timber or spar supporting the top edge of a square sail.

GLOSSARY OF GREEK AND LATIN TERMS

Entries marked (L) are Latin, all others Greek.

actuaria (L): type of merchant galley.

adiutor (L): rating in navy with clerking duties.

akatos: type of merchant galley.

akroterion: sternpost.

ancorale (L): anchor cable.

aperta (navis) (L): ship that was aphract = undecked.

aphlaston: sternpost, ornament atop the sternpost.

aphract: open, undecked ship.

archinauphylax: ship's chief guard.

apogeion: mooring line.

arbor (L): mast.

armenon: sail.

artemon: bow-sail, foresail.

askoma: oarport cover.

beneficiarius (L): administrative officer in Roman Navy.

biremis (L): war-galley with two banks/levels of oars.

bucinator: bugler.

carina (L): keel.

caudicaria (L): type of coastal and river-craft.

caupulus (L): type of small vessel.

celeusta (L): officer acting as rowing master who controlled the oarcrew.

celox (L): type of fast merchant galley.

cheniscos = **cheniscus** (L): goose-headed sternpost ornament.

clavus (L): tiller.

corbita (L): type of merchant vessel.

cornu (L): yardarm.

coronarius (L): member of ship's crew charged with placing sacred wreaths on ship on special occasions.

corvus (L): the 'raven', a form of boarding-bridge.

costa (L): frame.

cuneus (L): tenon.

cybaea (L): type of merchant galley.

diaita = **diaeta** (L): cabin.

dolator (L): rating charged with using axe to cut enemy grapnels.

dromon: type of warship in Byzantine Navy.

duplicarius (L): rating on double pay because of specialist skills/extra responsibilities.

embolos: ram.

emporion: commercial harbour.

epibates: marine.

episeion: pennant.

episemon: name-device.

ergates: winch.

exceptor (L): naval rating acting as record-keeper.

faber navalis (L): shipwright, ship's carpenter.

forus (L): deck.

funis (L): rope.

gubernaculum (L): helm, steering-oar.

gubernator (L): helmsman, sailing master.

harpax: type of grapnel.

hemiolia: fast galley.

hepteres: a 'seven'.

herma: ballast.

hippagogos, hippegos: galley transport for horses.

histion: sail.

histos: mast.

hortator (L): time-beater on war galley.

hypozoma: undergird.

ikria: deck.

insigne (L): name-device.

karchesion: mast-top.

kataphractos: cataphract, oared warship with protective (non-structural) deck.

katastroma: deck.

keles: type of merchant galley.

keleuma: 'beat' for rowers in a galley.

keleustes: rowing master.

keras: yardarm.

kerkouros: type of merchant galley.

korax: type of grapnel.

kybaia: type of merchant galley.

kybernetes: captain, helmsman.

lembos = lembus (L): type of galley.

lenuncularius (L): operator of a lenunculus.

lenunculus (L): type of small craft.

levamentum (L): lighter.

librarius (L): keeper of records.

liburna (L): liburnian, type of bireme war-galley.

linter (L): type of small craft.

lusoria (L): type of galley used for commerce and war.

magister navis (L): ship's master.

medicus (L): doctor.

monores: galley with one bank of oars.

musculus (L): type of small boat.

myoparo (L): type of swift galley.

nauarchis (L = navarchus): commodore.

naumachia: mock naval battle.

naupegos: shipwright, ship's carpenter.

nauphylax: ship's guard.

nautes: oarsman.

navalia (L): naval base.

navicularius (L): shipowner or charterer.

navis constrata (L): enclosed (cataphract) warship with protective deck.

navis longa (L): literally 'long ship' = war galley.

navis oneraria (L): literally 'ship of burden' = merchant ship or transport.

navis oraria (L): coastal vessel.

navis praetoria (L): flagship.

navis speculatoria: reconnaissance craft.

navis tecta (L): cataphract.

optio (L): second in command to centurion.

ora (L): mooring line.

parados: gangway on each side of an oared ship, sometimes on the flat surface of the oarbox.

paraseion: pennant.

parasema: name-device.

pausarius (L): time-beater for rowing-crew.

penteres: a galley with 50 oars.

phaselos: type of merchant galley.

pitulus (L): time-beater.

ponto: type of Gallic merchantman.

portisculus (L): 'wielder of the mallet' = time-beater for rowing-crew.

proembolion: subsidiary ram.

prorates (L): bow officer on war galley.

quadrieres (L): a 'four'.

ratis (L): boat, raft.

remus (L): oar.

saburra (L): sand, ballast.

scala (L): ladder.

scapha (L): ship's boat.

scriba (L): warship's chief secretarial officer.

semion: flag, pennant.

siparum (L): topsail.

siphon: cannon for Greek fire.

skeuophylax: guard of ship's gear.

stlatta (L): type of small riverboat.

strategis: flagship.

stratiotis: galley for transporting troops.

stuppator (L): caulker.

stylis (L): identification device carried at the stern.

subscus (L): tenon.

subunctor (L): issuer of oil to crew.

symphoniacus (L): ship's flautist.

taballaria (L): despatch boat.

tabula (L): plank, strake.

tessararius (L): despatch galley.

tetreres = **tetreris** (L): a 'four'.

thalamia: oarport.

thalamios: thalamite = oarsman rowing at lowest level in a three-level ship.

thalamos: cabin.

thranitos: thranite, oarsman rowing in highest level in a three-level ship.

topeia: cordage.

transtrum (L): thwart, beam, hatch.

triemiolia: type of warship in which the highest of three levels of oars was confined to the mid-section, in other words it was a 'two and a half'.

trierarchos = **trierarchus** (L): captain of galley in Roman Navy.

trieres = **trieremis** (L): trireme, galley with three levels of oars.

trochileia: block and tackle.

tropis: keel.

tutela (L): image of ship's patron deity.

velarius (L): deckhand looking after sail/s and rigging.

velum (L): sail.

versus (L): file of rowers.

vexillum (L): flag or pennant.

zygios: zygite, oarsman in middle bank of rowers in three level ship.

ABBREVIATIONS

AE	*L'Année Épigraphique*. 1888-.
CIL	*Corpus Inscriptionum Latinarum*. 1863-
IG	*Inscriptiones Graecae*. 1890-
ILS	*Inscriptiones Latinae Selectae*. Ed. Dessau, H. 3 volumes in 5 parts 1895-1916.
JRS	*Journal of Roman Studies*. 1911-
Pflaum	Pflaum, H.-G., *Les carrières procuratoriennes equestres sous les Haut-Empire romain*, Paris 3 volumes, 1960-61.
P.Mich	*Michigan Papyri*, Youtie *et al.* Ann Arbor 1931-
RIB I	*Roman Inscriptions of Britain. I: Inscriptions on Stone*. Collingwood, R.G. & Wright, R.P. Oxford. Clarendon Press. 1965.
RIB II.1	*Roman Inscriptions of Britain. Vol. II. Instrumentum Domesticum. Fascicule 1*. Frere, S.S., Roxan, M. & Tomlin, R.S.O. eds Gloucester. Alan Sutton. 1990.
RIB II.3	*Fascicule 3*. Frere, S.S. & Tomlin, R.S.O. eds Stroud. Alan Sutton. 1991.
RIB II.4	*Fascicule 4*. Frere, S.S. & Tomlin, R.S.O. eds Stroud. Alan Sutton. 1992.
RIB II.5	*Fascicule 5*. Frere, S.S. & Tomlin, R.S.O. eds Stroud. Alan Sutton. 1993.
RIC	*Roman Imperial Coinage*. 1923-

BIBLIOGRAPHY

Åkerlund, H., 1963, *Nydamskeppen*, Gothenburg.

Allen, J.R.L. & Fulford, M.G., 1999, 'Fort building and military supply along Britain's Eastern Channel and North Sea coasts: the later second and third centuries', *Britannia* 30, 163-84.

Anderson, A.C. & A.S. (eds), 1981, *Roman Pottery Research in Britain and North-West Europe*, British Archaeological Reports International Series 123.

Anderson, A.C., 1984, *Interpreting Pottery*, London.

Anderson, J.D., 1992, *Roman Military Supply in North-East England*, British Archaeological Reports British Series 224, Oxford.

Arnold, C.J. & Davies, J.L., 2000, *Roman and Early Medieval Wales*, Sutton Publishing, Stroud.

Atkinson, D., 1933, '*Classis Britannica*', in *Historical Essays in Honour of James Tait*, Manchester, 1-11.

Atkinson, D., *Report on Excavations at Wroxeter 1923-27*, Birmingham.

Bailey, J.B., 1923, 'Maryport and the Tenth Iter', *Transactions of the Cumberland & Westmorland Archaeological Society* second series 23, 142-53.

Barrett, A.A., 'Claudius' British victory arch in Rome', *Britannia* 22, 1-21.

Bartoccini, R., 1958, *Il porto romano di Leptis Magna*, Rome.

Bateson, N., 1973, 'Roman material from Ireland: a reconsideration', *Proc. Royal Irish Academy* 73 Pt. C, 21-97.

Bellhouse, R.L., 1989, *Roman Sites on the Cumberland Coast*, Cumberland and Westmorland Archaeological & Antiquarian Society Research Series 3.

Benoit, F., 1961, *L'Épave du Grand Congloué à Marseille* (XIVe supplément à *Gallia*) Paris.

Bidwell, P.T. (ed.), 1999, *Hadrian's Wall 1989-99*, Kendal.

Bidwell, P.T. & Silvester, R.J., 1988 'The Roman pottery' in Cunliffe, B.W. (ed.), *Mount Batten, Plymouth: A Prehistoric and Roman Port*. Oxford Univ. Committee for Archaeology Monograph 26, 42-9.

Bidwell, P.T. & Speak, S.C., 1994, *Excavations at South Shields Roman Fort, Vol. I*, Society of Antiquaries of Newcastle-upon-Tyne Monograph Series No. 4, Newcastle-upon-Tyne.

Bidwell, P.T. & Griffiths, W., 1999, 'The Wall at Buddle Street', in Bidwell, P.T. (ed.), 95-7.

Bird, D.G., 1999, 'Early days at London and Richborough', *London Archaeologist* 8, 12, 331-4.

Bird, D.G., 2000, 'The Claudian invasion campaign reconsidered', *Oxford Journal of Archaeology* 19, 91-104.

Birley, A.R., 1981, *The Fasti of Roman Britain*, Oxford.

Birley, A.R., 1998, 'A new tombstone from Vindolanda', *Britannia* 29, 299-306.

Black, E.W., 2000, 'How many rivers to cross?' *Britannia* 29, 306-7.

Black, E.W., 2000, 'Sentius Saturninus and the Roman Invasion of Britain', *Britannia* 31, 1-10.

Blackman, D.J., 1968, 'The ship-sheds', in Morrison, J. & Williams, R.T., 181-6.

Blackman, D.J., 1982, 'Ancient harbours in the Mediterranean', *International Journal of Nautical Archaeology* 11/2, 79-104; 11/3, 185-221.

Blackman, D.J., 1987, 'Triremes and shipsheds', *Tropis* II, 35-52.

Blackman, D.J., 1995, 'Naval installations', in Gardiner, R. (ed.), *The Age of the Galley: Mediterranean Oared Vessels since Pre-Classical Times*, Conway Maritime Press, 224-33.

Bogaers, J.E., 1983, 'Foreign affairs', in Hartley, B. & Wacher, J.S. (eds), *Rome and Her Northern Provinces*, Alan Sutton, 13-32.

Bollini, M., 1969, *Antichita classiarie*, Ravenna.

Boon, G.C., 1945, 'The Roman site at Sea Mills 1945-6', *Transactions of the Bristol & Gloucestershire Archaeology Society* 66, 258-95.

Boon, G.C., 1949, 'A Claudian origin for Sea Mills', *Transactions of the Bristol & Gloucestershire Archaeology Society* 68, 184-88.

Boon, G.C., 1969, 'Caernarvon', in Nash Williams, V.E. (ed.), *The Roman Frontier in Wales*, second edition revised Jarrett, M.G., Cardiff, 59-64.

Boon, G.C., 1972, *ISCA: The Roman Legionary Fortress at Caerleon, Mon.*, National Museum of Wales, Cardiff.

Boon, G.C., 1978, 'Excavations on the site of a Roman quay at Caerleon, and its significance', in Boon, G.G. (ed.), *Roman Sites*, Cambrian Archaeological Association Monographs & Collections I, 1-24.

Bounegru, O. & Zahariade, M., 1996, *Les Forces Navales du Bas Danube et de la Mer Noire aux Ier-VIe Siècles.* Colloquia Pontica 2. Oxford, Oxbow Books.

Bovini, I., 1963, 'Il Problema della ricognizione archaeologica del "Portus Augusti" di Ravenna e del "Castrum Classis"', *Atti del I. Congresso Internazionale di Archaeologica dell'Italia Settentrionale*, Turin.

Breeze, D.J., 1983, Review of Philp's *Excavations of the Classis Britannica Forts at Dover*, *Britannia* 14, 372-5.

Breeze, D.J. & Dobson, B., 1987, *Hadrian's Wall*, third edition, London.

Brewer, R. (ed.), 2000, *Roman Fortresses and their Legions*, Society of Antiquaries of London Occasional Papers 20.

Brigham, T., 1990, 'The late Roman waterfront in London', *Britannia* 21, 99-184.

Brigham, T., 1998, ' The port of Roman London', in Watson, B. (ed.), *Roman London: Recent Archaeological Work.* Journal of Roman Archaeology Supplementary Series 24, 23-34.

Brock, E.P.L., 1888, 'The age of the walls of Chester', *Journal of Chester Archaeology Society* New Series 2, 40-66.

Brodribb, G. & Cleere, H.F., 1988, 'The *Classis Britannica* bath-house at Beauport Park, east Sussex', *Britannia* 19, 217-74.

Bruce-Mitford, R.L.S., 1975, *The Sutton Hoo Ship Burial. Vol. I, Excavation, Background, the Ship, Dating and Inventory*, London.

Brulet, R., 1989, 'The continental *Litus Saxonicum*', in Maxfield, V.A. (ed.), *The Saxon Shore: A Handbook*, Exeter.

Brulet, R., 1991, 'Le Litus Saxonicum continental', in Maxfield, V.A. & Dobson, M.J. (eds) *Roman Frontier Studies 1989*, 'Proceedings of the XVth International Congress of Roman Frontier Studies', Exeter, 155-69.

Burnham, B.C., Keppie, L.J.F. & Esmonde Cleary, A.S., 1998, 'Roman Britain in 1997: Sites explored', *Britannia* 29, 365-432.

Burnham, B.C., Keppie, L.J.F. & Esmonde Cleary, A.S., 1999, 'Roman Britain in 1998: Sites explored', *Britannia* 30, 319-74.

Burnham, B.C., Keppie, L.J.F. & Esmonde Cleary, A.S., 2000, 'Roman Britain in 1999: Sites explored', *Britannia* 31, 372-432.

Burnham, B.C., Keppie, L.J.F. & Fitzpatrick, A.P., 2001, 'Roman Britain in 2000: Sites explored', *Britannia* 32, 311-86.

Burnham, B.C., Hunter, F. & Fitzpatrick, A.P., 2002, 'Roman Britain in 2001: Sites explored', *Britannia* 33, 275-354.

Burnham, B.C. & Wacher, J.S., 1990, *The Small Towns of Roman Britain*, London, Batsford.

Bushe-Fox, J.P., 1932, *Third Report on the Excavations of the Roman Fort at Richborough, Kent*, Society of Antiquaries Research Report 10.

Bushe-Fox, J.P., 1949, *Fourth Report on the Excavations of the Roman Fort at Richborough, Kent*, Society of Antiquaries Research Report 16.

Carrington, P., 1986, 'The Roman advance into the North-Western Midlands before AD 71', *Journal of Chester Archaeological Society*, New Series 68, 5-22.

Caruana, I.D., 1997, 'Maryport and the Flavian Conquest of North Britain', in Wilson (ed.), 40-51.

Casey, P.J., 1989, 'Coin evidence and the end of Roman Wales', *The Archaeological Journal* 146, 320-9.

Casey, P.J., 1994, *Carausius and Allectus: The British Usurpers*, Batsford, London.

Casey, P.J. & Davies, J.L., 1993, *Excavations at Segontium (Caernarvon) Roman Fort 1975-1979*, CBA Research Report 90.

Casson, L., 1971, *Ships and Seamanship in the Ancient World*, Princeton.

Casson, L., 1994, *Ships and Seafaring in Ancient Times*, London.

Casson, L. & Steffy, J.R., 1991, *The Athlit Ram*, Texas.

Cleary, S.E., 1987, *The Extra-Mural Areas of Romano-British Towns*, British Archaeological Reports British Series 169.

Cleere, H.F., 1975, 'The Roman iron industry of the Weald and its connections with the *Classis Britannica*', *The Archaeological Journal* 131, 171-99.

Cleere, H.F., 1977, 'The *Classis Britannica*', in Johnston, D.E. (ed.), *The Saxon Shore*, CBA Research Report No. 18, 16-19.

Cleere, H.F. & Crossley, D., 1985, *The Iron Industry of the Weald*, Leicester.

Coates, J.F., 1993, 'Hauling a trireme up a slipway and up a beach', in Shaw, J.T. (ed.), *HN Ship Olympias: A Reconstructed Trireme*, Oxford.

Collingwood, R.G., 1932, 'Inscriptions', in Wheeler & Wheeler, 1932, 100-4.

Cortis, W.S., 1858, 'Roman and British remains at Filey', *Transactions of the Scarborough Philosophical Society* 18-26.

Cotterill, J., 1993, 'Saxon raiding and the role of the late Roman coastal forts of Britain', *Britannia* 24, 227-40.

Cotton, M. & Gathercole, P., 1958, *Excavations at Clausentum, Southampton, 1951-54*.

Crew, P., 1981, 'Holyhead Mountain', *Archaeology in Wales* 1981, 35-6.

Crowley, N. & Betts, I.M., 1992, 'Three *Classis Britannica* stamps from London', *Britannia* 23, 218-22.

Crummy, P., 1997, *City of Victory. The Story of Colchester – Britain's First Roman Town*, Colchester Archaeological Trust.

Cunliffe, B.W., 1968, *Fifth Report on the Excavations of the Roman Fort at Richborough, Kent*, Society of Antiquaries of London Research Report 23.

Cunliffe, B.W., 1971, *Excavations at Fishbourne 1961-69*. Society of Antiquaries of London Research Report 26.

Cunliffe, B.W., 1976, *Excavations at Portchester Castle I: Roman*. Society of Antiquaries Research Report 32.

Cunliffe, B.W., 1987, *Hengistbury Head, Dorset, I: the Prehistoric and Roman Settlement 3500 BC-AD 500*, Oxford University Committee for Archaeology Monograph 13.

Cunliffe, B.W., 1998, *Fishbourne Roman Palace*, Tempus, Stroud.

Cunliffe, B.W., Down, A. & Rudkin, D., 1996, *Chichester Excavations, 9*. Chichester District Council.

Cunliffe, B.W. & de Jersey, P., 1997, *Armorica and Britain: Cross-Channel Relationships in the First Millennium BC*, Oxford University Committee for Archaeology Monograph 45.

Curle, A.O., 1923, *The Treasure of Traprain*. Glasgow.

Daniels, C.M., 1978, *Handbook to the Roman Wall*, thirteenth edition, Newcastle-upon-Tyne.

Dannell, G.B. & Wild, J.P., 1987, *Longthorpe II: The Military Works-Depot*, *Britannia* Monograph series 8.

Darling, M.J., 1984, 'Roman pottery from the upper defences' *The Archaeology of Lincoln* 16.2, 43-100.

Davies, J.L., 1997, 'Native producers and Roman consumers: the mechanisms of military supply in Wales from Claudius to Theodosius', in van Waateringe, W.G., van Beek, B.L., Willems, W.J.H. & Wynia, S.L. (eds), *Roman Frontier Studies 1995*. Proceedings of the XVIth International Congress of Roman Frontier Studies, Oxbow Monograph 91, 267-72.

Desjardins, E., 1876, *Géographie historique et administrative de la Gaule ancienne*.

Detsicas, A., 1987, *The Cantiaci*, Gloucester.

De Weerd, M.D., 1990, 'Barges of the Zwammerdam type and their building procedures', in McGrail, S. (ed.), *Maritime Celts, Frisians and Saxons*, CBA Research Report 71, 75-6.

Dore, J. & Greene, K. (eds), 1977, *Roman Pottery Studies in Britain and Beyond*, Oxford, British Archaeological Reports International Series 30.

Dornier, A., 1971, 'Was there a coastal *limes* in western Britain in the fourth century?' in Applebaum, S. (ed.), *Roman Frontier Studies 1967*, Tel Aviv, 14-20.

Dove, C.E., 1971, 'The first British navy', *Antiquity* 45, 15-20.

Down, A., 1978, *Chichester Excavations 3*, Chichester, Phillimore.

Down, A., 1988, *Chichester Excavations 5*, Chichester, Phillimore.

Dudley, D.R. & Webster, G., 1967, *The Roman Conquest of Britain*, Batsford, London.

Dunnett, R., 1975, *The Trinovantes*, Duckworth, London.

Ellmers, D., 1978, 'Shipping on the Rhine during the Roman period: the pictorial evidence' in Taylor, J. du P. & Cleere, H.F. (eds), *Roman Shipping and Trade: Britain and the Rhine Provinces*, CBA Res. Rep. 24, 1-14.

Ellmers, D., 1996, 'Celtic plank-boats and ships, 500 BC-AD 1000', in Christiansen, A.E. (ed.), *The Earliest Ships: The Evolution of Boats into Ships*, Conway Maritime Press, London, 52-71.

Evans, E., 2000, *The Caerleon Canabae: Excavations in the Civil Settlement 1984-90*, Britannia Monograph Series 16.

Fenwick, V., 1978, *The Graveney Boat*, British Archaeological Reports, Oxford, British Series 53.

Field, N.H., 1992, *Dorset and the Second Legion, New Light on a Roman Campaign*, Tiverton.

Fox, E. & Ravenhill, W., 1959, 'The Stoke Hill Roman signal station', *Transactions of the Devon Association* 91, 71-82.

Fox, E. & Ravenhill, W., 1966, 'Early Roman outposts on the North Devon coast, Old Burrow and Martinho', *Proceedings of the Devon Archaeological Exploration Society* 24, 3-39.

Frere, S.S., 1985, 'Roman Britain in 1984. Sites Explored', *Britannia* 16, 252-316.

Frere, S.S., 1991, 'Roman Britain in 1990: Sites Explored', *Britannia* 22.

Frere, S.S. & St Joseph, J.K., 1974, 'The Roman fortress at Longthorpe', *Britannia* 5, 1-129.

Frere, S.S. & St Joseph, J.K., 1983, *Roman Britain from the Air*, Cambridge Univ. Press.

Frere, S.S. & Fulford, M.G., 2001, 'The Roman invasion of AD 43', *Britannia* 32, 35-45.

Fulford, M.G., 1989a, 'The economy of Roman Britain', in Todd, M. (ed.) *Research on Roman Britain 1960-89*. *Britannia* Monograph Series No. 11, 175-202.

Fulford, M.G., 1989b, 'A Roman shipwreck off Nonour, Isles of Scilly?' *Britannia* 20, 245-8.

Fulford, M.G., 2000, 'The organisation of legionary supply: the Claudian invasion of Britain', in Brewer, R. (ed.), 41-50.

Fulford, M.G., 2002, 'The Second Augustan Legion in the west of Britain', in Brewer, R.J. (ed.), *The Second Augustan Legion and the Roman Military Machine*, National Museum Wales, Cardiff, 83-102.

Fulford, M.G. & Timby, J., 2000, *Late Iron Age and Roman Silchester: Excavations on the Site of the Forum-Basilica 1977, 1980-6*, Britannia Monograph Series 18.

Gardiner, R. (ed.), 1995, *The Age of the Galley. Mediterranean Oared Vessels Since Pre-Classical Times*, Conway Maritime Press, London.

Gibbins, D., 1996, 'Roman shipping and trade – a view from the Mediterranean', in Carrington, P. (ed.), *'Where Deva Spreads Her Wizard Stream': Trade and the Port of Chester*, Chester City Council.

Gilmour, B., 1994, 'Metallographic analysis of nails from Blackfriars Ship I', in Marsden, P., 1994, 181-7.

Goodburn, R., 1976, 'Roman Britain in 1975: Sites explored', *Britannia* 7, 291-377.

Goodburn, R., 1978, 'Roman Britain in 1977: Sites explored', *Britannia* 9, 403-72.

Grainge, G., 2002, *The Roman Channel Crossing of AD 43: The constraints on Claudius' naval strategy*, British Archaeological Reports British Series 332, Oxford.

Green, C., 1963, *Sutton Hoo*, London.

Greene, K.T., 1986, *The Archaeology of the Roman Economy*, Batsford, London.

Greenhill, B., 1979, *Archaeology of the Boat*, A & C Black, London.

Grenier, A., 1937, 'La Gaule romaine', in Frank, T. (ed.), *An Economic Survey of Ancient Rome 3: Britain, Spain, Sicily, Gaul*. Baltimore, 379-644.

Griffith, F.M., 1995, 'Developments in the study of Roman military sites in south-west England', in Waateringe *et al.* (eds), 361-7.

Griffiths, W.E., 1954, 'Excavations at Caer Gybi, Holyhead, 1952', *Archaeologia Cambrensis* 103, 113-16.

Gudeman, A., 1900, 'Agricola's invasion of Ireland once more', *Classical Review* 14, 51-3 & 96.

Hanson, W.S., 1987, *Agricola and the Conquest of the North*, London.

Hanson, W.S., Daniels, C.M., Dore, J.N. & Gillam, J.P., 1979, 'The Agricolan supply-base at Red House, Corbridge', *Archaeologia Aeliana* Fifth Series 7, 1-98.

Harrison, A.C. & Flight, C., 1969, 'The Roman and Medieval defences at Rochester in the light of recent excavations', *Archaeologia Cantiana* 83, 55-104.

Hassall, M.W.C., 1976, 'Britain in the *Notitia*', in Goodburn, R. & Bartholomew, P. (eds) *Aspects of the Notitia Dignitatum*, British Archaeological Reports International Series 15, 103-18, Oxford.

Hassall, M.W.C., 1977, 'The historical background and military units of the Saxon Shore', in Johnston, D.E. (ed.), *The Saxon Shore*, CBA Research Report No.18, 7-10.

Hassall, M.W.C., 1978, 'Britain and the Rhine provinces: epigraphic evidence for Roman trade', in Taylor, J du P. & Cleere, H.F. (eds), *Roman Shipping and Trade: Britain and the Rhine Provinces*. CBA Res. Rep 24, 41-8.

Hassall, M.W.C., 1980, 'Altars, curses, and other epigraphic evidence', in Rodwell, W.J. (ed.), *Temples, Churches and Religion in Roman Britain*, British Archaeological Reports British Series 77, 79-89, Oxford.

Hassall, M.W.C., 2000, 'Pre-Hadrianic legionary dispositions in Britain', in Brewer, R. (ed.) 51-68.

Hassall, M.W.C. & Tomlin, R.S.O., 1977, 'Roman Britain in 1976: Inscriptions', *Britannia* 8, 426-49.

Haverfield, F.J., 1899, 'Did Agricola invade Ireland?' *Classical Review* 13, 302-3.

Haverfield, F., 1924, *The Roman Occupation of Britain*, revised by Macdonald, G. Oxford.

Haywood, J., 1991, *Dark Age Naval Power: A Re-assessment of Frankish and Anglo-Saxon Seafaring Activity*, Routledge, London.

Henig, M. & Ross, A., 1998, 'A Roman intaglio depicting a warship from the foreshore at King' Reach, Winchester Wharf, Southwark', *Britannia* 29, 325-7.

Hind, J.G.F., 1974, 'Agricola's fleet and the Portus Trucculensis', *Britannia* 5, 285-8.

Hind, J.G.F., 1989, 'The invasion of Britain in AD 43 – an alternative strategy for Aulus Plautius', *Britannia* 20, 1-21.

Höckmann, O., 1986, 'Romische Schiffsverbände auf dem Ober- und Mittelrhein und die Verteidigung der Rheingrenze in der Spätantike', *Jarbuch des Römisch-Germanischen Zentralmuseums, Mainz,* 33, 369-416.

Höckmann, O., 1993, 'Late Roman Rhine vessels from Mainz, Germany', *International Journal of Nautical Archaeology* 22, 125-35.

Hodgson, N. 1999, 'South Shields', in Biddle, P.T. (ed.), *Hadrian's Wall 1989-99*, Kendal, 73-82.

Holbrook, N., 1987, 'Trial excavations at Honeyditches and the nature of the Roman occupation at Seaton', *Proceedings of the Devon Archaeological Society* 45, 59-74.

Hollstein, E., 1982, 'Dendrochronologie der römerzeitlichen Schiffe von Mainz', in Rupprecht, G., 114-23.

Hopkins, K., 1982, 'The transport of staples in the Roman Empire', in Garnsey, P. & Whittaker, C.R. (eds) *Trade and Staples in Antiquity (Greece and Rome)*, Budapest, 80-7.

Hopkins, K., 1983, 'Models, ships and staples', in Garnsey, P. & Whittaker, C.R. (eds) *Trade and Famine in Classical Antiquity*, Cambridge Philological Society Supplementary Vol. 8, 84-109.

Horn, H.G. (ed.), 1987, *Die Römer in Nordrhein-Westfalen*, Theiss, Stuttgart.

Hornsby, W. & Laverick, J.D., 1932, 'The Roman signal station at Goldsborough, near Whitby, Yorks.', *The Archaeological Journal* 89, 203-19.

Hornsby, W. & Stanton, R., 1912, 'The Roman fort at Huntcliffe near Saltburn', *Journ. Roman Studies* 2, 215-32.

Hurst, H.R., 1985, *Kingsholm*, Gloucester Archaeological Reports 1.

Hurst, H.R., 1986, *Gloucester: the Roman and Later Defences*, Gloucester Archaeological Reports 2.

Hutter, S. & Hauschild, T., 1991, *El faro romano de La Coruna*. La Coruna.

Jarrett, M.G., 1969, 'Cardiff', in Nash Williams, V.E. (ed.), *The Roman Frontier in Wales*, second edition revised Jarrett, M.G., Cardiff, 70-3.

Jarrett, M.G., 1976, *Maryport, Cumbria: A Roman Fort and its Garrison*, Cumberland & Westmorland Archaeological Society Extra Series 22.

Johnson, S., 1976a, *The Roman Forts of the Saxon Shore*, Elek, London.

Johnson, S., 1976b, 'Channel commands in the *Notitia*', in Goodburn, R. & Bartholomew, P. (eds), *Aspects of the Notitia Dignitatum*, British Archaeological Reports International Series 15, 81-102, Oxford.

Johnson, S., 1977, 'Late Roman defences and the *limes*', in Johnston, D.E. (ed.), *The Saxon Shore*. CBA Research Report No. 18, 63-9.

Johnson, S., 1983, *Late Roman Fortifications*, Batsford, London.

Jones, G.D.B., 1978, *Rhyn Park Roman Fortress*, Manchester.

Jones, G.D.B., 1983, 'The Solway frontier: an interim report 1976-81', *Britannia* 13, 283-97.

Jones, G.D.B., 1993, 'Excavations on a coastal tower, Hadrian's Wall: Campfield Tower 2B, Bowness-on-Solway', *Manchester Archaeological Bulletin* 8, 31-9.

Jones, G.D.B. & Mattingly, D., 1990, *An Atlas of Roman Britain*, London.

Jones, G.D.B. & Shotter, D.C.A., 1988, *Roman Lancaster: Rescue Archaeology in an Historic City 1970-75*, Brigantia Monograph Series 1.

Jones, M.J., 1988, 'Lincoln (*Lindum*)' in Webster, G. (ed.) *Fortress into City: The Consolidation of Roman Britain, First Century AD*, Batsford, London, 145-66.

Jones, M.J., 2002, *Roman Lincoln: Conquest, Colony and Capital*, Tempus, Stroud.

Keppie, L.J.F., 2000, '*Legio VIIII* in Britain: the beginning and the end', in Brewer, R. (ed.), 83-100.

Kienast, D., 1966, *Untersuchungen zu den Kriegsflotten der römischen Kaiserzeit*, Bonn.

Kuhlborn, J.S., 1992, *Das Römerlager Oberaden III*, Münster.

Lamboglia, N., 1961, 'Il rilevamento totale della nave romana di Albenga', *Rivista di studi liguri*, 213-20

Landels, J.G., 1978, *Engineering in the Ancient World*, Berkeley.

Langoët, L., 1977, The fourth-century Gallo-Roman site at Alet (St Malo), in Johnston, D.E. (ed.), 38-45.

Lemmon, C.H. & Hill, J.D., 1966, 'The Romano-British site at Bodiam', *Archaeologia Cantiana* 104, 86-102.

Lepper, F. & Frere, S.S., 1988, *Trajan's Column: A New Edition of the Cichorius Plates*, Alan Sutton, Gloucester.

Livens, R., 1986, 'Roman coastal defences in North Wales, Holyhead Mountain and Caer Gybi', in Unz, C. (ed.), *Studien zu den Militärgrenzen Roms III*, Vorträge des 13, Internationalen Limeskongresses. Aalen, 58-9.

McGrail, S. 1987, *Ancient Boats in N.W. Europe: The Archaeology of Water Transport to AD 1500*, Longman, London.

McGrail, S., 1995, 'Romano-Celtic boats and ships: characteristic features', *International Journal of Nautical Archaeology* 24, 139-45.

McGrail, S. (ed.), 1990, *Maritime Celts, Frisians and Saxons*, CBA Research Report No. 71.

McGrail, S., 2001, 'The Barland's Farm Boat within the Romano-Celtic Tradition', *Archaeologisches Korrespondenzblatt* Vol. I, 31, 117-32.

McGrail, S. & Roberts, O., 1999, 'A Romano-British boat from the shores of the Severn Estuary', *Mariner's Mirror* 85, 133-46.

Manley, J., 2002, *AD 43 The Roman Invasion of Britain: A Reassessment*, Tempus, Stroud.

Mann, J.C., 1976, 'What was the *Notitia* for?', in Goodburn, R. & Bartholomew, P. (eds), *Aspects of the Notitia Dignitatum*, British Archaeological Reports International Series 15, 1-10, Oxford.

Mann, J.C., 1977a, '*Duces* and *Comites* in the fourth century', in Johnston, D.E. (ed.), *The Saxon Shore*, CBA Research Report No. 18, 11-14.

Mann, J.C., 1977b, 'The Reculver inscription – a note', in Johnston, D.E. (ed.), *The Saxon Shore*, CBA Research Report No. 18, 15.

Mann, J.C., 1989, 'The historical development of the Saxon Shore', in Maxfield, V.A. (ed.), *The Saxon Shore: a handbook*, Exeter.

Manning, W.H., 1981, *Report on the Excavations at Usk, 1965-76: the Fortress Excavations 1968-71*, National Museum of Wales, Cardiff.

Manning, W.H., 2000, 'The fortresses of *legio XX*', in Brewer, R. (ed.), 69-82.

Marsden, E.W., 1969, *Greek and Roman Artillery: Historical Development*, Oxford.

Marsden, P., 1965a, 'The County Hall Ship', *Transactions of the London & Middlesex Archaeological Society* 21, 109-17.

Marsden, P., 1965b, 'A boat of the Roman period discovered on the site of New Guys House, Bermondsey, 1958', *Transactions of the London & Middlesex Archaeological Society* 21, 118-31.

Marsden, P., 1967, *A Ship of the Roman Period from Blackfriars, in the City of London*, Guildhall Museum, London.

Marsden, P., 1980, *Roman London*, Thames & Hudson, London.

Marsden, P., 1994, *Ships of the Port of London: First to Eleventh Centuries AD*, English Heritage, London.

Marvell, A.G., 1991, 'Recent work on the Neronian fortress at Usk', in Burnham, B.C. & Davies, J.L. (eds), *Conquest, Co-existence and Change: Recent Work in Roman Wales*, Trivium 25. Lampeter, 19-26.

Marvell, A.G. & Oetgen, J., 1985, '*Nidum*: an interim report', *Glamorgan Gwent Archaeological Trust Annual Report*, Part 2, 1983-4, 116-25.

Marvell, A.G. & Owen-John, H., 1997, *Leucarum. Excavations at the Roman Auxiliary Fort at Loughor, West Glamorgan 1982-4 and 1987-8*, London.

Mason, D.J.P., 1984, *The Canabae and Vici of Roman Britain*. Unpublished PhD thesis University of Liverpool.

Mason, D.J.P., 1987, 'Chester: the *canabae legionis*', *Britannia* 18, 143-68.

Mason, D.J.P., 1988, '*Prata Legionis* in Britain', *Britannia* 19, 163-90.

Mason, D.J.P., 2000, *Excavations at Chester. The Elliptical Building: An Image of the Roman World?* Chester City Council.

Mason, D.J.P., 2001, *Roman Chester: City of the Eagles*, Tempus, Stroud.

Mason, D.J.P., 2002, 'The town and port of Roman Chester', in Carrington, P. (ed.), *Deva Victrix: Roman Chester Re-assessed*, Chester Archaeological Society, 53-74.

Mattingly, H., 1950, *Coins of the Roman Empire in the British Museum Vol. 5*, London.

Mattingly, H. & Pierce, J.W.E., 1937, 'The Coleraine hoard', *Antiquity* 11, 39-45.

Maxwell, G., 1998, *A Gathering of Eagles: Scenes from Roman Scotland*, Edinburgh.

Meiggs, R., 1973, *Roman Ostia*, second edition, Oxford.

Meiggs, R., 1983, *Trees and Timber in the Ancient World*, Oxford.

Mertens, J., 1978, 'Het Laat-Romeins *castellum* te Oudenburg', *Archaeologica Belgica* 206, 73-6.

Middleton, P., 1979, 'Army supply in Roman Gaul: an hypothesis for Roman Britain', in Burnham, B. & Johnson. H. (eds), *Invasion and Response: The Case of Roman Britain*, British Archaeological Reports 77, 81-97, Oxford.

Middleton, P., 1983, 'The Roman army and long distance trade', in Garnsey, P. & Whittaker, C.R. (eds), *Trade and Famine in Classical Antiquity*, Cambridge Philological Society Supplementary Volume 8, 75-83.

Miller, S.N., 1928, *The Roman Fort at Old Kilpatrick*, Glasgow, 1928.

Milne, G., 1985, *The Port of Roman London*, Batsford, London.

Milne, G., 1995, *Roman London*, Batsford, London.

Morel, J-M.A.W., 1986, 'The early Roman defended harbours at Velsen, North Holland', in Unz, C. (ed.), *Studien zu den Militärgrenzen Roms III*. Vorträge des 13. Internationalen Limeskongresses. Aalen, 200-12.

Morrison, J.S., 1980, *Long Ships and Round Ships*, London.

Morrison, J.S., 1996, *Greek and Roman Oared Warships 399-30 BC*, Oxbow Monograph No. 62.

Morrison, J.S., Coates, J.F. & Rankov, N.B., 2000, *The Athenian Trireme*, second edition, Cambridge University Press.

Morrison, J. & Williams, R.T., 1968, *Greek Oared Ships 900-322 BC*, Cambridge.

Nayling, N., Maynard, D. & McGrail, S., 1994, 'Barland's Farm, Magor, Gwent: A Romano-Celtic boat', *Antiquity* 68, 596-603.

Nicolet, C., 1988, *L'Inventaire du Monde*, Paris.

O'Neil, B.H. St & O'Neil, H.E., 1952, 'The Roman conquest of the Cotswolds', *The Archaeological Journal* 109, 23-38.

O'Riordain, O, 1947, 'Roman material in Ireland', *Proceedings of the Royal Irish Academy* 51, 35-82.

Ottaway, P., 1993, *Roman York*, English Heritage.

Ottaway, P., 1997, 'Recent excavations of the late Roman signal station at Filey, North Yorkshire', in van Waateringe, W.G., van Beek, B.L., Willems, W.J.H. & Wynia, S.L. (eds), *Roman Frontier Studies 1995*, Proccedings of the XVIth International Congress of Roman Frontier Studies, Oxbow Monograph 91, 135-42.

Parker, A.J., 1992, *Ancient Shipwrecks of the Mediterranean and the Roman Provinces*, British Archaeological Reports International Series 580, Oxford.

Peacock, D.P.S., 1977, 'Bricks and tiles of the "*Classis Britannica*": petrology and origin', *Britannia* 8, 235-48.

Peacock, D.P.S. & Williams, D.F., 1985, *Amphorae in the Roman Economy*.

Pearson, A., 2002, *The Roman Shore Forts: Coastal Defences of Southern Britain*. Tempus, Stroud.

Peddie, J., 1987, *Invasion: The Roman Conquest of Britain*, Gloucester.

Philp, B.J., 1969, 'The Roman fort at Reculver', *The Archaeological Journal* 126, 223-5.

Philp, B.J., 1981, *The Excavation of the Roman Forts of the Classis Britannica at Dover 1970-77*, Kent Monograph Series No. 3.

Philp, B.J., 1989, *The Roman House with Bacchic Murals at Dover*. Kent Monograph Series No. 5.

Pitts, L.F. & St Joseph, J.K., 1985, *Inchtuthil: The Roman Legionary Fortress. Britannia* Monograph Series 6.

Potter, T.W., 1979, *Romans in North-West England: Excavations at the Roman Forts of Ravenglass, Watercrook and Bowness-on-Solway*, Cumberland & Westmorland Antiquarian and Archaeological Society Research Series 1.

Putnam, W.G., 1967, 'Caer Gybi', in Nash Williams, V.E. (ed.), *The Roman Frontier in Wales*, second edition revised by M.G. Jarrett, National Museum of Wales, 135-7, Cardiff.

Ramm, H., 1978, *The Parisi*, Duckworth, London.

Rance, P., 2001, 'Attacotti, Deisi and Magnus Maximus: the case for Irish federates in late Roman Britain', *Britannia* 32, 243-70.

Rankov, N.B., 1982, 'Roman Britain in 1981: Sites explored', *Britannia* 13, 328-95.

Rankov, N.B., 1995, 'Fleets of the early Roman Empire', in Gardiner, R. (ed.), 78-85.

Reynolds, P.K.B., 1930, 'Excavations on the site of the Roman fort at Caerhun: fourth interim report', *Archaeologia Cambrensis* 85, 74-102.

Richmond, I.A., 1963, *Roman Britain*, second edition, Penguin.

Richmond, I.A. & Steer, K.A., 1959, '*Castellum Veluniate* and civilians on a Roman frontier', *Proceedings of the Society of Antiquities of Scotland* 90, 1-6.

Rieck, F. & Crumlin-Pedersen, O., 1988, *Bade fra Danmarks oldtid*, Roskilde.

Rigby, V., 1979, 'The Gallo-Belgic imports from Exeter – a summary', in Bidwell, P.T. *The Legionary Bath-House and Basilica and Forum at Exeter*, Exeter City Council Archaeological Reports 1.

Rigold, S.E., 1969, 'The Roman haven of Dover', *The Archaeological Journal* 126, 78-100.

Rivet, A.L.F. & Smith, C., 1979, *The Place-Names of Roman Britain*, Cambridge.

Roache Smith, C., 1850, *The Antiquities of Richborough, Reculver and Lympne in Kent*, London.

Roache Smith, C., *Report on Excavations made on the site of the Roman Castrum at Lympne in Kent in 1850*, Lympne Castle, Kent.

Robertson, A.S., 1975, 'The Romans in north Britain: the coin evidence', in Temporini, H. (ed.), *Aufstieg und Niedergang der romischen Welt* II.3., Berlin, 364-428.

Robertson, A.S., 2001, *The Antonine Wall*, Revised edition Keppie, L.J.F., Glasgow Archaeological Society

Robinson, D.J., 2000, 'The Romans and Ireland again: Some thoughts on Tacitus' Agricola Chapter 24', *Journal of Chester Archaeological Society* New Series 75, 19-32.

Rogers, W.L., 1937, *Greek and Roman Naval Warfare* (reprinted 1964), Annapolis.

Roth, J.P., 1999, *The Logistics of the Roman Army at War (264 BC - AD 235)*, Boston.

Rougé, J., 1975, *La marine dans l'antiquite*, Paris.

Rougé, J., 1981, *Ships and Fleets of the Ancient Mediterranean*, Middletown.

Rule, M. & Monaghan, J., 1993, *A Gallo-Roman Trading Vessel from Guernsey: The Excavation and Recovery of a Third Century Shipwreck*. St Peter Port: Guernsey Museum Monograph 5.

Rupprecht, G., 1982, *Die Mainzer Römerschiffe: Berichte uber Endeckung, Ausgrabung und Bergung*. Mainz.

Russel, J.I., 2001, *Archaeological report on the Watching-Brief and Excavation for the New Parts Centre at Hawkeswood Road, Bitterne Manor, Southampton*, Southampton City Council Archaeology Unit Report 409.

Sanquer, R., 1977, 'The *castellum* at Brest', in Johnston, D.E. (ed.), 45-50.

Sauer, E., 1999, 'The military origins of the Roman town of Alchester, Oxfordshire', *Britannia* 30, 289-96.

Sauer, E., 2000, 'Alchester: a Claudian 'vexillation fortress' near the western boundary of the Catuvellauni: new light on the Roman invasion of Britain', *The Archaeological Journal* 157, 1-78.

Schnurbein, S. von, 2000, 'The organisation of the fortresses in Augustan Germany', in Brewer, R. (ed.) 29-40.

Seillier, C., 1977, 'The Gallic evidence. Boulogne and coastal defences in the fourth and fifth centuries' in Johnston, D.E. (ed.), *The Saxon Shore*, CBA Research Report No. 18, 35-8.

Seillier, C. & Gosselin, J.-Y., 1969, 'Nouvelles estampiles de la Flotte de Bretagne en provenance de Boulogne-sur-Mer (*Bononia*)', *Revue du Nord* 202, 363-72.

Seillier, C. & Gosselin, J.-Y., 1973, 'La flotte de Bretagne à Boulogne-sur-Mer', *Septentrion* 3, 55-6.

Seillier, C., Gosselin, J.-Y., Leclerq, P. & Piton, D., 1971, 'Fouilles de Boulogne-sur-Mer (*Bononia*). Rapport préliminaire', *Revue du Nord* 211, 669-79.

Shoesmith, R., 1991, *Excavations at Chepstow 1973-4*, Leeds.

Shone, W., 1911, *Prehistoric Man in Cheshire*, Chester.

Shotter, D. C.A., 1993, 'Coin loss and the Roman occupation of North-West England', *British Numisimatic Journal* 63, 1-19.

Shotter, D.C.A., 1994, 'Rome and the Brigantes: early hostilities', *Transactions of the Cumberland & Westmorland Antiquarian & Archaeological* Society series 2 94, 21-34.

Shotter, D.C.A., 2000a, 'The Roman conquest of the North-West', *Transactions of the Cumberland & Westmorland Antiquarian & Archaeological* Society series 2 100, 33-53.

Shotter, D.C.A., 2000b, 'Petilius Cerialis in northern Britain', *Northern History* 36, 189-98.

Shotter, D.C.A., 2002, 'Chester: early Roman occupation', in Carrington, P. (ed.), *Deva Victrix: Roman Chester Re-assessed*, Chester Archaeological Society.

Shrubsole, G.W.,1886, 'The traffic between Deva and North Wales in Roman times', *Journal Chester Archaeological Society* New Series 1, 76-90.

Sibbald, R. Sir, 1707, *Historical Enquiries Concerning the Roman Roman Monuments in the North Part of Britain Called Scotland*, London.

Sippel, D.V., 1987, 'Some observations on the means and cost of the transport of bulk commodities in the late Republic and early Empire', *Ancient World* 16, 35-45.

Silvester, R.J., 1984, 'Roman Seaton and the Axe', *Devon Archaeology* 2, 25-8.

Southern, P. & Dixon, K.R., 1996, *The Late Roman Army*, London.

Starr, C.G., 1960, *The Roman Imperial Navy 31 BC-AD 324* (second edition), Cambridge.

Stead, I.M., 1977, *Winterton Roman Villa and Other Roman Sites in North Lincolnshire*, DoE Research Report 9.

Strong, D., 1968, 'The Monument', in Cunliffe 1968, 40-73.

Tatton-Brown, T.W.T., 1980, 'Camelon, Arthur's Oon and the main supply-base for the Antonine Wall', *Britannia* 11, 340-3.

Tchernia, A. & Pomey, P., 1978, 'Le tonnage maximum des navires de commerce romains', *Archaeonautica* 2, 233-51.

Thomas, C., 1966, 'The character and origins of Roman Dumnonia', in Thomas, C. (ed.), *Rural Settlement in Roman Britain*, London.

Thorvildsen, K., 1961, *The Viking Ship of Ladby*, Copenhagen.

Todd, M., 1973, *The Coritani*, Duckworth, London.

Todd, M., 1975, *The Northern Barbarians 100 BC-AD 300*, London.

Todd, M., 1976, 'The *vici* of Western England', in Branigan, K. & Fowler, P.J. (eds), *The Roman West Country*, London, 99-119.

Todd, M., 1997, *Roman Britain*, London.

Toft, L.A., 1992, 'Roman quays and tide levels', *Britannia* 23, 249-53.

Tomlin, R.S.O., 2000, 'The legions in the late Empire', in Brewer, R.J. (ed.), 159-82.

Tomlin, R.S.O. & Hassall. M.W.C., 1998, 'Roman Britain in 1997: Inscriptions', *Britannia* 29, 433-47.

Tooley, M. & Switsur, R., 1988, 'Water level changes and sedimentation during the Flandrian Age in the Romney Marsh area', in Eddison, J. & Green, C. (eds), *Romney Marsh: Evolution, Occupation, Reclamation*. Oxford Univ. Committee for Archaeology Monograph 24, 53-71.

Turnbull, P., 1996, 'The supposed Roman harbour at Maryport', *Transactions of the Cumberland & Westmorland Archaeological Society*, second series 96, 33-5.

Viereck, H.D., 1975, *Die römische Flotte: Classis Romana*, Hereford.

Waateringe, W.G. van, Beek, B.L. van, Willems, W.J.H. & Wynia, S.L. (eds), 1995, *Roman Frontier Studies 1995*, Proceedings of the XVIth International Congress of Roman Frontier Studies, Oxbow Monograph 91, Oxford.

Wacher, J.S., 1969, *Excavations at Brough-on-Humber 1958-61*. Report of the Research Committee of the Society of Antiquaries of London XXV.

Wacher, J.S., 1975, *The Towns of Roman Britain*, Batsford, London.

Wacher, J.S., 1995, *The Towns of Roman Britain*, (second revised edition), London: Batsford.

Wallinga, H.T., 1956, *The Boarding-Bridge of the Romans.* Groningen.

Walsh, M., 2000, 'Roman maritime activities around Britain: what is the evidence and how might it be enhanced?' in Fincham, G. *et al.* (eds), *TRAC 99: Proceedings of the Ninth Annual Theoretical Roman Archaeology Conference Durham 1999*, Oxbow, 53-63, Oxford.

Ward, J., 1901, 'Cardiff Castle: its Roman origin', *Archaeologia* 57, 335-52.

Warner, R.B., 1995, 'Tuathal Techtmar: a myth or ancient literary evidence for a Roman invasion?' *EMANIA* (Bulletin of the Navian Research Group) 13, 23-32.

Watson, G.R., 1969, *The Roman Soldier*, London.

Webster, G., 1981, *Rome Against Caratacus*, Batsford, London.

Webster, G., 1993, *The Roman Invasion of Britain*, London.

Webster, P.V., 1981, 'Cardiff Castle excavations, 1974-81', *Morgannwg* 25, 201-11.

Webster, P.V., 1991, 'The first Roman fort at Cardiff', in Burnham, B.C. & Davies, J.L. (eds), *Conquest, Co-existence and Change: Recent Work in Roman Wales*, *Trivium* 25, 35-9.

Wheeler, R.E.M., 1923, *Segontium and the Roman Occupation of Wales*, London.

Wheeler, R.E.M. & Wheeler, T.V., 1932, *Report on the Excavation of the Prehistoric, Roman and Post-Roman Site in Lydney Park, Gloucestershire*, Report of the Research Committee of the Society of Antiquaries of London IX.

White, D.A., 1961, *Litus Saxonicum:the British Saxon Shore in scholarship and history*, Wisconsin.

White, R. & Barker, P., 1998, *Wroxeter: Life & Death of a Roman City*, Tempus, Stroud.

Whitwell, J.B., 1970, *Roman Lincolnshire*, Lincoln.

Wilkinson, D.R.P., 1994, 'Excavations on the White Cliffs Experience site, Dover 1998-91', *Archaeologia Cantiana* 114, 51-148.

Wilson, D.R., 1975, 'Roman Britain in 1974: Sites explored', *Britannia* 6, 221-83.

Wilson, P., 1991, 'Aspects of the Yorkshire signal stations', in Maxfield, V.A. & Dobson, M.J. (eds), *Roman Frontier Studies 1989*, Proceedings of the XVth International Congress of Roman Frontier Studies, Exeter University Press, 142-7.

Wilson, R.J.A., 1997, 'Maryport from the first to the fourth centuries: some current problems', in Wilson, R.J.A. (ed.), *Roman Maryport and its Setting: Essays in Memory of Michael G. Jarrett*, Cumberland & Westmorland Antiquarian & Archaeological Society Extra Series 28, 1-39.

Woolliscroft, D.I., 2001, *Roman Military Signalling*, Tempus, Stroud.

Wood, I., 1990, 'The Channel from the fourth to the seventh centuries AD', in McGrail, S. (ed.), 93-8.

Wright, R.P., 1985, 'A revised restoration of the inscription on the mosaic pavement found in the temple at Lydney Park, Gloucestershire', *Britannia* 16, 248-9.

INDEX

Entries in **bold** refer to figure numbers